Deep Magic

Advanced Strategies
for Experienced Players of
Magic: The Gathering™

by
Charles Wolfe
and
George H. Baxter

Wordware Publishing, Inc.

Library of Congress Cataloging-in-Publication Data

Wolfe, Charles, 1974-
   Deep Magic : advanced strategies for experienced players of Magic,
the gathering / by Charles Wolfe and George H. Baxter.
      p.   cm.
   Includes index.
   ISBN 1-55622-461-3 (pbk.)
   1. Magic: The Gathering (Game)   I. Baxter, George, 1972-
   II. Title.
   GV1469.62.M34W65   1995
   793.93'2—dc20   95-31591
                                            CIP

ISBN 1-55622-461-3
10 9 8 7 6 5 4 3 2 1
9508

All inquiries for volume purchases of this book should be addressed to Wordware
Publishing, Inc., at the above address. Telephone inquiries may be made by calling:

(214) 423-0090

This book is dedicated to our families and the Palace of Pleasure Crew.

The illustrations in this book were created
by Christopher Pickrell of Heath, Ohio.

Table of Contents

Table of Contents

Acknowledgments

Thanks to Regan Reece for his help with the list.

We would also like to recognize all who contributed from the net and our friends from the Palace for their guidance.

Thanks to Sally Spratlen for allowing us to use her apartment as a base of operations...and for providing sustenance to fuel our thoughts.

Thanks to the Game Chest and its staff for providing guidance and a place for Dallas gamers to gather.

Foreword

by Zak Dolan

Magic: The Gathering™ is a fascinating game, combining the collectibility of baseball cards, the strategy of bridge, the bluffing of poker, the trading of Monopoly®, the ranking system of chess, and the fantasy setting of Dungeons & Dragons® into a single game that only takes a few minutes to play.

From the time you start playing, you continue to discover new cards that you've never seen before, adding to the excitement of the game. No wonder it's such a huge success.

With the recent card changes from Revised to Fourth Edition in preparation for the mass market, it looks like Magic will soon become a household name, just like Monopoly®.

Currently available in four languages—English, Italian, French, and German, with more coming out soon—it's just a matter of time until the game completely spans the globe.

Wizards of the Coast is making it easy for new players to start playing the game with the introduction of the Type II tournament. It's now possible to compete with only a Fourth Edition Starter Deck, a Booster or two, and some trading. This could be one of the best things to happen to new Magic players in a long time.

I do hope that Wizards of the Coast continues to support the Type I tournaments, however. The wide variety of decks and strategies that you encounter, combined with the nearly unlimited selection of cards for your own deck, make these tournaments a lot of fun. I realize that not everyone can get all the cards they would like for their deck, but the challenge of trading for the cards you want or making do with what you've got is part of the appeal of the game.

Ever since I found out that the next World Championships will be Type II, I've had some concerns. Even though I like the prospect of being the all-time Type I Tournament World Champion, I'm concerned that people who have just started playing the game will be favored at the expense of people who have been playing for over a year, which could result in people quitting the game.

Once Revised is no longer allowed, most players will own cards that they won't be able to play in Type II tournaments. I'm a little worried that people won't play the game as much if they aren't allowed to use their favorite cards in tournament play. Worse still, they might stop introducing new people to the game. I think that Magic will continue to be popular and it won't become just another fad, but a lot depends on what Wizards of the Coast does to support the needs of their existing customers.

I believe that the introduction of the new chess-style rating system by the Duelist's Convocation for sanctioned tournaments will help the game significantly. This will make it possible to change tournaments from single elimination to a Swiss system, so that everyone gets to play more games. It will also make player rankings more realistic, since people's ratings will be determined by their win record against other ranked players, instead of by how many tournaments they've entered (like in the previous system). People will be able to compete against other people at their own skill level. The result will be even more sanctioned tournaments, giving everyone more chances to try and win a few games.

However, in order to have a chance of winning, you need to know what to trade for, how to set up a deck, and how to play your deck, which is where this book should help. By reading it, you will gain a working knowledge of the fundamental skills that top players use to consistently dominate tournaments.

It is my hope that you will obtain new insights into the game that will help you enjoy playing it even more by learning how the authors look at the game. You'll have the opportunity to try out the decks in the book against your own deck. You will also be better able to analyze and tune your deck. But don't get too caught up in winning—remember, the point is to have fun playing. After all, it's just a game. Isn't it?

Zak Dolan

Introduction

Deep Magic takes an in-depth look at such concepts as action vs. reaction, sequential card use, draw value, and bridge combinational theory. There is an emphasis on guiding the reader in analyzing deck construction and the actual cards they employ. We hope to illustrate a method for finding flaws in decks and identifying their strengths and weaknesses. The goal is to allow those players who have already achieved strong playing abilities to further perfect their skills and compete in tournaments with greater proficiency.

This book has been written for the advanced player. A good understanding of advanced deck construction and playing techniques is necessary to get the most from this book.

Considerable information regarding the most recent trends in tournament play is included, as well as a helpful guide for dealing with them. We also provide some tips for preparing for tournaments and ways to feel out the competition.

Deep Magic also includes twenty-five tournament or concept decks. Some of the decks displayed contain combinations of cards valued at over $400, while some are as cheap as $25. We are sensitive to the fact that many readers may not have the resources to build some of the more expensive decks, and we hope to emphasize that you do not have to possess an expensive collection to construct powerful tournament decks. The more expensive cards simply broaden the variety of strong tournament decks that can be constructed—they are not completely necessary for high quality. Also the listing of the more expensive decks will help prepare the thrifty player by assisting him in identifying possible threats.

Once again we throw ourselves into the great search for the ultimate deck. After you have read this book you should be one step closer to perfecting your game play and your ability to cut a powerful tournament deck.

Chapter 1

Recapping the Basics

This book contains advanced Magic strategies that build on basic concepts of the game. Those fundamental concepts need to be understood in order to progress; for those who need a reminder, this chapter is a short review of key concepts. Many more advanced players will already be aware of most if not all of these concepts; however, certain terminology may be unfamiliar and thus it is a good idea to read this chapter regardless of how advanced you are. If you feel that you are already aware of these basic concepts, then feel free to skip this chapter.

Deck Evaluation: The Basic Rules of Deck Construction

A firm grasp of the basics of deck construction is essential to understanding the concepts presented in this book. Deck construction is the fundamental skill in Magic. Following are the most important basic principles of deck construction.

The first rule you should observe is that of playing with the minimum number of required cards in a deck. For convocation tournaments you should typically play with sixty cards. This allows the deck builder to have greater control over the randomness involved in drawing from the deck, and since only four of each card are allowed it increases the deck's ability to generate any needed

1

card or specific combinations. There is also a higher chance of drawing the more powerful "spoiler cards," which are restricted to one per deck. Whenever a deck contains more than sixty cards it should generally be cut down to the minimum required size.

You should also observe the importance of fast mana, such as Moxes, the Black Lotus, Sol Ring, Dark Ritual, Wild Growth, and others. Most decks rely upon speed to establish dominance early in the game. Regardless of the philosophy of the deck, invariably players seek to develop mana as quickly as possible. Though some decks do not require a large amount of fast mana to achieve a desired environment or overcome an opponent, many do. The difference in being able to influence the game in the first two turns is typically a telling factor, since the ramifications of the actions taken in early turns will have great impact later in the game. Additionally, almost any deck can benefit from the inclusion of fast mana even if it is not necessary, and only a very few are actually harmed by its inclusion.

Another important concept is that of card economy. Although we will elaborate on this later on in this book, a basic understanding is necessary. Card economy essentially describes the expenditures and advantages gained by the use of each card in a deck. In other words, good card economy is achieved when you glean numerous benefits out of few cards. This is a very broad but very important consideration in deck design.

Finally, there is the draw rule. Typically if you draw and can play more cards than your opponent, you will have a large advantage. The differential in drawing creates a differential in options, which is a great boon for most decks, and very few decks are not helped by an increased ability to draw cards. Though there is more to each of these rules, it is expected that the reader already has some prior knowledge of them.

Challenging the Five Basic Decks

When a deck is constructed you should keep in mind all of the most common obstacles that deck might face. There are five basic types of decks that are the most common in tournament play and whose elements appear in almost any deck. One can expect to have to meet these decks because many players will often try to create these in the most efficient manner possible to overcome their opponents. Elements of these decks appear in almost every deck in some form or another, and thus a firm understanding of what comprises each, and their strengths and weaknesses, is essential for advanced deck design and gameplay.

The first of these decks and perhaps the most common is the **fast creature deck**. There are two basic types of fast creature decks: the large fast creature deck and the small fast creature deck. The large fast creature deck is typically constructed around generating a large creature through the employment of a good deal of fast mana. Typically these decks are rarer than their small fast creature deck counterparts because they tend to rely on a good deal of expensive and hard-to-find cards. Small creature decks typically produce a horde of small creatures that work together to deal a large amount of damage. The difference in these two decks is that one invests many different cards into one powerful and durable creature while the other spreads its investment out into several small and fragile creatures. Each of these are solid tournament decks and typically will be present in any tournament.

The second deck you should be prepared to face is a **burn deck**. These are perhaps the weakest of all of the five basic decks because they are probably the easiest to prepare to play. They tend to rely upon direct damage spells to remove opposing creatures and reduce an opponent's life to zero. They generally are straightforward and sequential and suffer from a lack of versatility. If properly constructed, these decks can be inconsistently dangerous. Oftentimes they will have combinations which can unleash a torrent of damage in a small amount of time. Thus although they are generally weak overall, it is still necessary to be prepared to counter them.

The third basic deck type is the **hand destruction deck**. These decks are made to remove cards from an opponent's hand, reducing his or her options and ability to generate opposition. This type of deck has grown in popularity and strength since the introduction of the Fallen Empires set and the Hymn to Tourach. These decks are some of the most powerful; however, they suffer to the Psychic Purge—a devastating counter. Unfortunately the Psychic Purge is not available in Type II play, and thus these decks are very prevalent in this type of play. The hand destruction deck can be an effective weapon, as it can leave an opponent without options and can destroy important members of relationships in a deck. Thus it is also imperative to be ready to deal with the threat of hand destruction.

The last two basic deck types, **land destruction** and **counter-spell decks**, are often considered to be the most effective; however, the land destruction decks can be quite expensive to build. Land destruction's ability to prevent opponents from developing their deck tends to allow its controller the time to front an unopposed offense. The difficulty of these decks is that they tend to be sequential in play. The removal of mixed lands and of the Sink Hole and Ice Storm have made Type II land destruction decks less common, but the Icequake and Thermokarst have restored their value as a deck type. In Type II tournaments you will typically find land destruction as a supplement to another major theme.

The last type of basic deck is the counterspell deck. These decks rely upon stopping you from casting spells basically on a one-for-one card basis. Although these are extremely powerful decks, they are typically limited in removal once a card has been cast and uncountered.

When you construct an advanced tournament deck it should have some method of circumventing each of these decks to a point where it can win at least fifty percent of the time against the finest version of each of them. These basic decks are effective but pure forms of them are somewhat uncommon in tournament play because they are expected and their actions tend to be no surprise to tournament players.

Chapter 2

Deck Construction

The process of deck construction is the fundamental skill in playing Magic. In order to be an effective Magic player you must be able to design and develop effective decks. The following outline is a good reference guide for designing decks. It provides a logical, structured procedure to follow to achieve effective deck designs and clarifies what the process of deck design entails. Although most

Deck Design Procedure

I. Devise a driving idea for your deck
II. Specify other cards that work well with this idea
III. Record the deck
IV. Perform analysis
   A. Calculate mana distribution
   B. Calculate removal capability and importance of removal
   C. Calculate effectiveness versus the five basic decks
V. Identify weaknesses
VI. Assemble deck
VII. Play against the five basic decks
VIII. Remove unnecessary cards and make appropriate modifications and enhancements
IX. Assemble sideboard
X. Record changes
XI. Return to step IV

players generally follow some process similar to this, many may omit some steps or fail to think about some aspects. As such this chapter provides a well-defined method to follow each time a deck is constructed in order to make the process more streamlined and efficient.

Following these steps each time you create a deck will allow you to have a methodology by which you can assemble effective decks and will allow you to feel confident that you have developed a versatile deck which will be able to perform competently in high-level play. Each step in the process is important and should not be omitted if at all possible.

I. Devise a driving idea for your deck

The idea or concept of the deck is the cornerstone of the development of your deck. This concept has a great deal to do with what philosophy of deck construction you wish to employ, but essentially it boils down to the driving idea behind your deck. These usually fall into one of three categories.

The first category is offensive and action-oriented. The idea is to make your deck generate a great deal of damage quickly and kill your opponent before he or she has time to react. As with all strategies, you will attempt to achieve the development of your deck as quickly as possible, but speed is generally even more important in action-oriented decks. For example, white small creature decks are typically dependent on eliminating an opponent within the first four to ten rounds. They are able to maintain this average by deploying multiple creatures with a minimal casting cost and later enhancing them with cards like Jihad, Crusade, Call to Arms, and Army of Allah. These decks are not designed to react to an opponent's actions but to force the opposing player to react to its quick and powerful offenses. These decks usually fail if they do not generate enough action to keep an opponent reacting for the duration of the game. Each time your opponent is able to counter your offenses and move forward with his own, when you are playing an action-oriented deck, you have lost a great deal of ground. Keeping your opponent on the defensive is of paramount importance with these decks. Fast creature decks and burn decks are examples of offensive and action-oriented decks.

A second type of strategy is based on the idea of versatility. This philosophy is much less action-oriented and more reactive. The cornerstone concept of reaction deck philosophy is that a deck should be capable of overcoming all of an opponent's offensives. These types of decks generally will rely heavily on removal capability, counter magic, or a mixture of the two. Thus the reactionary decks should be able to deal with creatures, sorcery, enchantments, instants and interrupts, and possibly even land. Reactionary decks are not made for pure reaction, or else they will only win if their opponent runs out of cards. They are dependent on a secondary theme to achieve victory. These themes are generally not the focus of the deck design but should fit well into the original theme or the deck will lack effective interconnections between the cards. Counterspell decks are an example of this kind of deck.

The third type of design philosophy is resource denial. This philosophy's strength stems from denying an opponent the availability of game resources like mana generators and cards. Denial decks grind away at an opponent's resources while building their own in order to achieve a superior position from which to launch an assault. This philosophy, like the reaction philosophy, is typically reliant upon a secondary theme to achieve victory, since sooner or later you must stop denying your opponent's plans and begin moving forward with your own offense. Land destruction and hand destruction are examples of this kind of deck.

It is not uncommon for these philosophies to be intermingled. Most decks function with a mixture of two of the three. Usually when they are intermingled, one of the methods is dominant over the other. For example the House of Pain deck in Appendix A uses its Juzam Djinns as action-based strategy but reduces an opponent's ability to react by using land destruction as a form of resource denial. Generally decks are referred to by the dominant philosophy in the deck. For example, a deck which focuses on reactive strategies would be a reactive deck even if it includes direct damage cards in an active role. Thus most decks involve at least two if not all three of these philosophies.

II. Specify other cards that work well with this idea

After the basic idea of the deck has been achieved, there is still a considerable amount of work left to do before you even have a deck. Once you have an idea, you must now seek to find other cards and combinations that fit in well with your original scheme. To do this, you think about what will strengthen the original idea for the deck and simultaneously add new dimensions. You also analyze what will be some obvious difficulties and how to overcome them. For example, if you were designing the white turbo deck and had the basic idea that you would use small creatures and Crusades, you would then look for cards that would strengthen this concept and allow you to overcome difficulties. One immediate problem you might recognize is the deck's weakness if the quick kill is not achieved. In order to compensate you must now look for a card that fits in with this scheme. It must be white, since speed is of the essence in this type of deck. A good solution would be Eye for an Eye. It is inexpensive to cast, like the rest of the cards in the deck, and would be a great boon in dealing with late game damage. Typically your opponent cannot afford the damage dealt from the Eye for an Eye because of the early damage inflicted by the white horde. Thus during this phase of deck construction you seek to simultaneously strengthen the current dimensions and add new ones to the concept.

III. Record the deck

After you have the preliminary deck constructed, it is a good idea to record it on paper or a worksheet. Although this is not strictly necessary, it can be of great help when calculating mana requirements, looking for weaknesses, and revising the deck. It is much easier to proceed with the deck analysis when the deck is all right there in front of you on paper. Although many people like to lay the cards out in front of them, it is less cumbersome to work with a paper blueprint of the deck and can be easier to analyze. Also decks can oftentimes accidentally find themselves mingled together or somehow returned to your collection. A written copy provides a permanent record just in case of such occurrences, or if you want to make a new deck with the same cards.

IV. Perform Analysis

A. Calculate mana distribution Next it is time to assess the mana requirements of the deck. Although sometimes the mana distribution of the deck is part of the preliminary deck design, usually its inclusion comes afterward. Mana distribution is a key concept in advanced deck design and should not be taken lightly. In order to calculate how many of each type of mana producing cards to put in your deck, you must weigh many factors. First of all, you must look at how many cards there are that require each type of mana; that is, how many blue, red, white, green, and black cards you have in your deck. Then you must look at how much colored mana each of these cards costs to cast. You must also factor in the importance of the cards of each color. You should find where the power lies in your deck and balance your mana accordingly. For example, if you only have two black cards in your deck, you might be tempted to include very little black mana. This can be dangerous in many ways. First of all, if you have little black mana in your deck and you draw your two black cards early but draw no swamps or other black mana, these cards will sit idly in your hand. Also, what if these cards are Lords of the Pit? Then you will need a great deal more mana to cast them, and if these are the only damage-dealing cards in your deck their importance also merits considerable more mana allocation. Thus the inclusion of mana in your deck is not strictly a matter of direct proportion to the number of cards of each color you have. A good way to determine how much of each to use is to make a proportion of card colors, and then alter it for the other factors. That is, if there is one color that requires more colored mana than the other colors, shift mana from the other colors to that one. If your main power cards lie in one color, then shift some mana to that color. Then you should do some test draws to see how this distribution works. Mixed lands can make this process easier, but the Blood Moon card makes them dangerous to use and thus it is generally not a good idea to rely solely on mixed lands. You will generally have to work with your deck for some time before you will achieve the best mana distribution. Successfully distributing your mana is a key to success in designing effective decks.

B. Calculate removal capability and importance of removal
The ability to remove an opponent's cards is of varying importance
in different decks. For example, in most decks it is important to be
able to rid your opponent of creatures; on the other hand other decks
diffuse creatures' effectiveness and thus have no need to remove
them. Many times a deck is vulnerable to certain enchantments,
and thus it is important that you be able to rid your opponent of
them. For example, if you are playing with a high proportion of
mixed or expansion lands in your deck it may be necessary to rid
yourself of your opponent's Blood Moons. On the other hand, many
action-oriented decks are concerned mainly with speed, and thus
removal is not a high priority and may simply slow the deck down.
In analyzing the removal capability of your deck, the first thing you
must look at is whether or not your deck needs removal. To do this
you should look at what type of problem cards might arise against
you. If there are many of them it is a good idea to include some type
of removal for those types of cards. Now you must assess how
capable your deck is of removing potential obstacles. This is simply
a matter of analyzing how many cards you have which are capable
of removing these obstacles. You must also weigh exactly how
important the destruction of each of these problem cards is, and
include removal for each obstacle in proportion to its danger. Removal capacity should be a function of necessity and susceptibility.

C. Calculate effectiveness versus the five basic decks The
next step in creating an effective deck is to look over the deck and
conceptualize how it will work against the five basic decks.
Although very few players play strictly one of the five basic decks,
elements of them will be in almost any deck you face, and thus if
you can deal with these five elements you should be fairly capable
against many decks. Essentially, this is a rating of your deck's
versatility. To calculate this type of effectiveness you must look at
each of the five basic decks individually. To assess your ability
against burn decks you should look at several things. How quickly
does you deck develop? Will your opponent have time to amass a
great deal of mana while your deck is developing? Does your deck
have the ability to counter or reverse large damage spells? Against
counterspell decks you must ask yourself: Do I have important
combinations that can be disrupted by countering one spell? Are

there specific cards which are necessary for me to win? Do I have any way to counter or nullify my opponent's Counterspells? For hand destruction: Do I generally have many cards in my hand? Will the loss of these cards disrupt important combinations or the deck environment? Can I replace an empty hand quickly? For land destruction: How much land do I have in my deck? How much mana is necessary to cast most of my spells? Do I have any way to replace land quickly? Against fast creature decks: How quickly does my deck develop? Can I destroy creatures quickly? These questions must not all strictly come out in your benefit, but if the answers are all bad for one kind of deck it is generally a good idea to analyze your deck more closely.

V. Identify Weaknesses

This effectiveness rating should lead you to some conclusions regarding the weaknesses of your deck. Almost all decks contain at least one of the five elements that are reflected in the five basic decks, and thus you should be able to assess where your deck is weak by this point. Additionally, there are other things to consider. You should look at whether you need to be able to draw more cards, deal more damage, develop more quickly, and make other action-oriented evaluations. You should essentially look at your deck and decide what the worst thing is that could happen to it, and then look for a way to deal with this deficiency. For example, the White Blitzing Wind in Appendix B was originally very susceptible to decks with Gloom in them. It was very difficult to achieve victory if an opponent's Gloom came into play. In order to attempt to deal with this, red damage spells were added to finish off a Glooming opponent. Thus you must weigh the weaknesses of your deck and find methods to rectify them.

VI. Assemble deck and play against the five basic decks

Now you should assemble the deck and play it against the five basic decks. This is a matter of assessing whether or not your deck performs as expected. Very often it will be the case that your deck will behave in ways you did not expect. Sometimes this can lead you to new ideas concerning the strengths of your deck, and sometimes this will cause you to realize fundamental and possibly inescapable weaknesses of your deck. More often, however, it will simply lead you to find more problems which must be rectified in your design. You may, for example, find yourself wishing for certain cards repeatedly; this is generally a good indication that more of this type card, or a similar one, would be a good addition to your deck. The testing process is also an excellent time to discover the best ways to use your deck. It is an opportunity to discover if there is a certain order in which you should cast spells or use effects and whether there are card combinations which should be played in a particular sequence. This step in the design process is important for obtaining new ideas and for discovering whether your deck is weak in certain areas. Additionally there are certain aspects of your deck which you will only be able to understand by playing, so experimenting against the five basic decks will help you both in the design process and in the playing process.

VII. Remove unnecessary cards and make appropriate modifications and enhancements

One important revision to note during this process is the extraneous card. That is, are there cards in your deck that should be removed or replaced? The most common sign that a card is not effective is that it sits in your hand frequently. If a card is not being played then it is taking up space that could be used by a more effective card. Cards sitting in your hand are also a sign that you have too many cards that perform the same function in your deck. Another possibility is that there is a card that could perform this same function, only more effectively. In this case, you may find yourself wishing you had more cards of this type. For example, if you find yourself constantly wishing that you had more Disenchants even after adding all four to your deck, then you should identify why you are using them and add other cards that can perform the same function. For example, if you find that your four Disenchants are not sufficient because you are forced to split them between artifacts and enchantments, it may be a good idea to include some Divine Offerings or other artifact removal so that you can save some Disenchants for enchantments.

VIII. Assemble sideboard

This step is perhaps one of the most complex in the deck design process. It is in this step that a deck architect compensates for the weaknesses that he or she has discovered in the early stages of design. This topic is explored in greater depth in Chapter 10.

IX. Record changes

Finally, you should record your deck with its new modifications and then go back to the fourth step, starting by recalculating the mana distribution. This process is circular because many of the steps are repeated over and over again to cause the deck to come closer and closer to perfection. In many ways a deck is never complete. Every time you play it against another deck you may very likely discover another weakness that needs to be rectified, or you may be spurred to a new idea regarding a beneficial modification to your deck. Additionally, each new set of cards offers you possibilities for your deck that could lead to new changes. Thus the process of deck construction essentially continues throughout the duration of the time in which you actively use the deck.

X. Return to step IV

Chapter 3

Deck Theory
and Design Philosophies

The methods of deck construction among the best Magic players can be divided up into a number of **deck theories** and **design philosophies**. These are simply the driving ideas and basic concepts into which deck design methods can be divided. Many of these are known by different names by different individuals, but the ideas behind them are generally consistent. This chapter is intended to display the majority of the more popular and effective philosophies and tactics which are widely used by Magic players.

Deck Theory

Deck theory is the background behind all decks. Every deck has methods by which it progresses toward victory. Deck theory is concerned with the speed at which victory is achieved. In other words, does the deck seek to destroy its opponent with the utmost speed, or does it seek a slower, possibly more reliable victory? Of course it is impossible to say for certain that one method is better than the other, but each method has various advantages and disadvantages intrinsic to it. There are two broad categories into which deck theories can be divided: fast and slow.

15

Fast Deck Theory

The first deck theory that beginning players usually develop is fast deck theory. Fast deck theory is based on trying to defeat an opponent as quickly as possible. Fast decks are designed to defeat an opponent before a hostile environment or powerful defense can be established. These decks tend to achieve victory or are near it within the first ten rounds. Generally if victory is not achieved by this point, the fast deck theory has failed and the deck will probably not win. The beauty of the fast deck theory is its simplicity. These decks are usually very straightforward and there are rarely difficult decisions to make. Speed is an important factor in any deck and a difficult weapon to beat, since any defense that will be thrown up against a fast deck must also be created quickly. Thus although generally simple to design and use, decks utilizing fast deck theory can often be very effective.

Slow Deck Theory

Slow deck theory is usually based around narrowing an opponent's options down until they are rendered incapable of defending themselves. These decks tend to achieve victory slowly but this does not mean that they are slow to develop. If these decks develop slowly they will fail continuously against decks under the fast deck theory. Instead, these decks are usually designed under a principle of having a short-term defense that slowly develops over the course of the game. Generally these decks work under the principle of slowing down an opponent until an environment can be established and maintained where the opponent is rendered helpless. Generally if these decks can hold out and weather the assault of fast decks, they should be able to defeat them in the end since they are usually more versatile and will usually have more options in the late game. Most of the time decks that operate under the slow deck theory function best after the first five turns. This means that the deck must include some way to survive these first five turns or it is doomed to failure. Thus slow decks are usually more difficult to play but can glean considerable versatility and often some degree of reliability.

Design Philosophies

Design philosophies are basic ideas that a deck designer comes up with before or during the deck designing process. There are two different types of design philosophies. There are the all-encompassing **theme philosophies** and the narrow **minor philosophies**. Whenever a deck is developed its designer must make decisions about which philosophy to follow under each of these categories. These philosophies are typically guides for designers that lead them to the character of the deck, and many players and designers make these kinds of design decisions subconsciously without ever really analyzing what they are doing.

Theme Philosophies

Theme philosophies are the fundamental concepts that a deck is designed around and describe how the deck is intended to behave. There are three different theme philosophies: **action**, **reaction**, and **denial**. Each is concerned with the manner in which a deck functions and works toward victory. Most decks incorporate some mixture of these three themes, but most have one dominant theme philosophy that generally takes up about forty percent of the deck space. Other decks are very heavily weighted toward one philosophy and have little or no elements of the others. These decisions are usually made keeping the deck concept in mind. Each of these specific types will be described in more detail in Chapter 6, Action and Reaction.

Action Philosophy The best way to describe action philosophy is that an action-based deck is typically cut to eliminate an opponent before he has an opportunity to eliminate you. Action philosophy typically falls under fast deck theory, but the two should not be confused. Action philosophy is not centered around speed but around forcing an opponent to react without trying to compensate for the actions of an opponent. Action philosophy can be looked at as a kind of all-out assault on an opponent. Defense is not given a heavy weight under this kind of philosophy.

Reaction Philosophy Reaction is, as you would probably guess, just the opposite of action philosophy. Reaction decks are designed to eliminate threats until enough security is established to initiate action. Reaction decks maintain dominance through control of the environment and by effective removal of obstacles. These decks are usually more versatile than action decks but suffer from lack of speed. They tend to fall under slow deck theory. These decks basically seek to thwart all of an opponent's assaults and then counterattack once an opponent is disarmed.

Denial Philosophy Denial is a philosophy based on denying an opponent the availability of resources. These decks are usually based on eliminating opponents' mana production or forcing them to discard cards from their hands. Denial decks are similar to reaction decks because they usually do not mount an assault until an opponent's resources have been depleted to a point where the denial deck maintains control of the environment. There are exceptions, but this is generally the cornerstone of a denial-based deck. These decks also tend to fall under the slow deck theory, as they must work over a long period of time in order to achieve a state in which the opponent does not possess the resources to defend against its weaponry.

Minor Philosophies

Roads to victory When constructing a deck it is wise to understand just how the deck will achieve victory in a duel. The methods for winning a duel are called roads to victory. Roads to victory tend to vary from one deck to another. Action decks tend to have multiple roads to victory, where reaction decks usually operate with only a few. In an action deck there are usually so many roads to victory that an opponent can not cut them all off since such a high percentage of the deck is devoted to attack. In reaction and denial decks there are a limited number of roads to victory but they are well protected by the deck's primary themes. That is, by the time these slower decks begin to attack, their opponent should be in no condition to oppose them. Generally speaking one should always work to maintain many roads to victory; since many will probably be cut off, the more that exist, the more likely the deck is to succeed.

Sometimes the roads to victory can be very hard to realize. In some cases the cards in your deck might possess a subtle road to victory. For instance, Braingeyser becomes a formidable weapon in the late game. You can capture victory by forcing an opponent to draw this deck. The Fork is another example of these subtle roads, as they work as independent roads to victory because you can turn an opponent's spells against him and capture victory.

Some decks spread their roads to victory out with many different weak sources; others concentrate them in a few very powerful sources. For example, the White Blitzing Winds spreads its roads to victory out amongst several different creatures and instants. The FBD counterspell deck concentrates its roads to victory into its large creatures. The White Blitzing Winds is not greatly affected if some of its roads to victory are cut because it simply lays more roads. Each creature in the deck is one road to victory, and it is difficult for an opponent to deal with each one. The FBD counterspell deck relies on its limited sources of victory but has the capability to protect them with counter magic. This deck seeks to use one road which is more powerful and better protected; however, if an opponent can circumvent this protection then the deck has lost a significant amount of its killing power.

You should always be aware of how many roads to victory your deck possesses and how fragile each of those roads is. Once you have estimated your roads to victory it will assist you in deck play. You will have a better sense of when to start laying your roads and how to maintain them. For instance, the White Blitzing Winds will lay its roads immediately and the FBD counterspell deck will wait until it has the mana to support its creatures with counter magic. If the roads are laid too quickly they can be cut, and since this deck has so few sources of damage it is imperative that this not happen. Thus proper management and maintenance of the roads to victory in a deck is absolutely necessary to succeed in a duel.

Surprise Value Many players tend to load down their decks with four of each card they employ in order to pad the statistics of getting each card or combinations of the cards. Generally this is done to ensure deck consistency and to make the deck as predictable as possible. There is a flaw to this strategy, simply because an opponent will begin to know what to expect from the deck and as such will be able to play against it better in each successive duel, and moreover, in each successive turn.

If instead you add one or two of a certain type of card, your opponent will make decisions based around what he has seen your deck do. This can be very advantageous. He may tap out to cast a Fireball and you could react with an unexpected Power Sink. He may attack with a Blood Lusted, Giant Growthed, Berserking, Kird Ape only to find that it is unexpectedly Unsummoned. Also, if these cards are used early in the game he may think that you have four of each of them in your deck. For instance, if your opponent casts a Juzam Djinn on the first turn and you cast your only Force Spike to counter it, he may always leave an extra mana untapped when casting for fear of another Force Spike. You can make this worse by acting discouraged because he will not tap out.

Additionally, surprise value manifests itself in the way the deck differs from the common incarnations of decks. Many decks have been played into the ground, and often by round one or two an experienced opponent will understand exactly what these decks are doing. As such it is always a good idea to try to improve on your deck ideas and create new ones. If you continually play the same deck in tournaments you will begin to be beaten more and more often. Many tournaments have been lost and won because of the little surprises contained in many decks.

Chapter 4

Card Relationships

Beginning Magic players often make the mistake of constructing decks by taking all of what they consider to be their best cards and putting them in a stack. The essential flaw with this is the fact that although the cards may be good by themselves, they do not interact in any way. Two very powerful cards with no connection between them are not nearly as powerful as two mediocre cards which have some connection. Having cards with relationships separates a deck from a simple collection of cards. The interaction of cards increases the effectiveness of each card in the relationship, and thus relationships make each card in a deck worth considerably more than its standalone value. When cards interact, each card in the deck increases the other's play value. Thus relationships are necessary in order to make a deck truly effective.

The concept of a relationship is very simple. If any two cards in your deck are designed to work in conjunction, then they have a relationship between them. This is not the same as a combination, which is two cards that are used in sequential conjunction. Combinations are a very specific form of relationship in which the cards are used at the same time, whereas a basic relationship does not set any kind of time constraint on the use of the cards involved. For example, using a Fireball and then Forking it to double its damage is a combination between the Fork and the Fireball. On the other hand, using a Mind Twist early in the game and then a Rack a turn or two later to deal damage because of your opponent's lack of cards is a relationship. The Rack could have been played first and it would have made no difference; it is simply the fact that the cards work together that creates the relationship between them. Thus generally speaking, in a well-constructed deck many of the cards will have relationships between them, but it is not strictly necessary that a deck have any combinations. The stronger the relationships in your deck and the higher the percentage of cards that are members of these relationships, the more powerful the deck becomes.

Relationships can be further broken down into two categories: **dependent relationships** and **independent relationships**. In an independent relationship, each of the cards in the relationship is useful on its own; however, in conjunction the two cards are particularly formidable. Thus the cards are independently powerful and simply benefit from the inclusion of each other. A dependent relationship means that the cards lose something from the lack of the others. That is, one or both of the cards in the relationship is not particularly useful on its own. The fact that the relationships can be broken down into these sub-categories should also make it clear that these categories are also applicable to combinations. Since combinations are strictly a narrow form of relationship it is apparent that these groupings apply to them as well.

Generally, most decks include some form of independent relationship. These relationships create much of the strength in most decks and are usually fairly easy to see. One example of an independent combination is the Rukh Egg and the Earthquake. Each of these cards is very powerful. Rukh Eggs make excellent blockers, and if it can be arranged that they should find their way to the graveyard they become 4/4 flying creatures. Thus they are powerful in their own right. Simultaneously, the Earthquake is a very useful card as well. When facing an opponent who is utilizing a small creature deck they can be devastating, and they can also be used as a form of direct damage. Both of the cards have their own individual uses, but when included together they boost each other's power. If a Rukh Egg is in play and a three-point or more Earthquake is cast, then not only do all of your opponent's creatures take damage, and hopefully die, but your Rukh Egg goes to the graveyard and you are soon to be the proud recipient of a 4/4 flying creature. Thus independent relationships can be a good source of power in a well-constructed deck.

Card Relationships:

Black Vice, Ankh of Mishra, Howling Mine, and Winter Orb

Sylvan Library and Sinbad

Land Tax, Zuran Orb, and Winds of Change

Mind Twist, Hymn to Tourach, and Rack

White Knight, Circles of Protection, and Slight of Mind

Card Combinations:

Fireball and Fork

Ancestral Recall and Black Vice

Righteousness, Swords to Plowshares, and any creature

The power of the independent relationships should not lead one to believe that dependent relationships should be avoided in deck construction. Although the individual cards in dependent relationships are not as powerful as in independent relationships, often when used in conjunction the cards are even more powerful than the independent relationships together. For example, an Ankh of Mishra on its own is not an incredibly potent card. For the most part it will hurt you just as much as it will your opponent, so unless you are leading in life total it will not create a sizeable advantage for you. Additionally there is no reason for your opponent to seek to lay land any faster than you, since you will both suffer equally from the Ankh. However, when these cards are combined with a Black Vise, the results can be deadly. The Black Vise forces your opponent to remove cards from his hand or suffer severe damage; at the same time in order to play cards from his hand, your opponent must have good sources of mana. Thus he will either be forced to lay land and take damage in order to play his cards or he will be forced to hold his cards and take damage from the Vise. At the same time you are not under the same stress and can afford to take your time in playing your hand, avoiding taking as much damage from the Ankhs. Thus although one card in a dependent relationship may not be intrinsically powerful, the two cards working together may net a more powerful relationship than two cards which are useful in their own right.

Independent combinations are generally the rarer of the two types of combinations. In independent combinations, like independent relationships, the cards involved must be individually useful as well as useful in conjunction. This is often difficult to achieve. Many cards are intrinsically useful, such as the Ancestral Recall or Fireball, but it is difficult to find ways in which to make them work together. At the same time, there are many combinations which work well together but are not particularly effective on their own. Finding combinations in which both of these are satisfied is often difficult. At the same time the results can be very rewarding. In an independent combination the cards are much more versatile and options are often a key to winning the game. Take for example Righteousness and Swords to Plowshares. Righteousness is a very intrinsically powerful card. A Grizzly Bear with Righteousness cast on it will kill a Force of Nature and survive itself. Additionally there is a great deal of **surprise value**, since Righteousness creates a great deal of difference between a 1/1 creature and an 8/8 creature. Swords to Plowshares is also an excellent card, since it allows you to not only destroy any creature but simultaneously remove it from the game. Both of the cards are strong on their own, but they can also work well together. For instance, in the Grizzly Bear example, after the Bear had killed the Force of Nature you could then cast Swords to Plowshares on it and gain 9 life points. The use of these cards together thus creates an even more powerful combination. Unfortunately it is often difficult to find cards that will work well independently and in conjunction when there is a stipulation that they must be cast within a short time of each other.

Far more common are **dependent combinations** in which the cards must be used in conjunction in order to be particularly effective. Once again, the hope is that at the expense of dependence, the combination will be even more powerful. Dependent combinations are dangerous however, because oftentimes if only one card of the combination is available, it will simply sit in your hand and do nothing. Wasted card draws will significantly weaken your options and thus give your opponent an advantage. Hopefully, this advantage will be temporary, only lasting until the other member of the combination appears. This is a very dangerous risk, however, and can be particularly problematic if, for example, you are taking Vise damage. Thus the power involved in the combination must make this danger worthwhile. For example, a Chaos Lace and a Blue Elemental Blast could be used as a dependent combination. Chaos Lace is essentially useless on its own, but when combined with a Blue Blast it can collectively remove any permanent in the game or counter any spell as it is cast. The only question is whether it was worth it. In this case, probably not. Although a card can be removed from the table at the cost of one blue and one red mana, the **card economy** of this combination is inefficient, and if you only have a Chaos Lace in your hand, you have wasted a draw. On the other hand, a Fork and Fireball may well be worth the danger in order to inflict double the damage of the Fireball on the opponent. Although there is a danger of getting a Fork without anything to use it on, the card economy of a Forked Fireball is good and there are many targets for a Fork in the game.

In order to make dependent combinations and relationships less risky, it is better to try to achieve combinations in which each card is a member of several dependent combinations. In this case it is much more likely that two members of some combination or relationship will come into your hand simultaneously. This is called **bridge theory**: the combinations or relationships are linked to one another. For example, use a Winter Orb with Paralyzes, Relic Barriers, Power Sinks, and Black Vises. The Winter Orb makes the Paralyzes almost eliminate a creature from the game. The Power Sinks become particularly annoying with Winter Orb in play or after paying to untap a Paralyzed creature. The Black Vises tend to force an opponent to cast things, which can be difficult for a player only able to untap one land a turn with a Winter Orb out. Thus dependent combinations must be analyzed on several criteria to assess whether they are worth the risk and expenditure.

In order to truly maximize the usefulness of the cards in the deck, it is a good idea to seek a kind of **synergy** among the cards.

Synergy occurs when two cards in the deck form a powerful relationship, then the addition of another makes the relationship even more powerful. The more cards that can be included in this type of relationship, the more powerful the deck will be as a whole. In order to achieve synergy, there should be no real necessity as to which members of the synergistic relationship come out first. All of the cards of the relationship should work well together. For example, as was previously mentioned, an Ankh and a Black Vise work well together. They form a strong relationship when used in conjunction. Simultaneously, a Howling Mine works well with both of these cards. When used with an Ankh it can force your opponent to discard cards he or she would have liked to have kept because they are unwilling to lay land at a rate to keep up with the extra cards the Mine is providing. Simultaneously, it works well with the Vise since it will provide more and more cards, hopefully at a rate which will be too fast for your opponent to keep up with. Thereby they will take more damage from the Vise. More importantly when all three of these cards are in play they are particularly deadly. To add to the deck's synergy one might add Lightning Bolts, Incinerates, and Chain Lightnings to increase the speed at which damage is dealt. These relationships build on each other, and your opponent will be forced to take damage in one way or another. Because the relationships between these cards are so strong and because they are strengthened by each other, they have a synergy which will be hard for an opponent to overcome. Synergy is a good quality to seek when constructing a deck, since the results can oftentimes provide a game-winning advantage.

Relationships are a necessary element of any deck. If the cards in a deck have no relationships then the deck will not be competitive. This does not mean that a deck necessarily has to have combinations in which the cards must be used in succession. Instead, relationships simply add power to each card that they would not possess on their own. This is very consistent with the philosophy of card economy in which we seek each of our cards to generate as many positive effects as possible. Thus by including relationships in our decks and trying to make them as synergistic as possible we can make each card worth more than it seems to be at face value.

Chapter 5

Card Economy

One of the most important concepts to master for effective deck construction, as well as effective game play, is **card economy**. Card economy is a measurement for determining the effectiveness of decks, combination relationships, and even individual cards. It is essentially a rating of how much value you are getting from a specific card or group of cards versus the negative aspects of utilizing them, including the draw involved in getting the card or cards themselves. There are three different types of card economy ratings: **card count**, **utility**, and **turn economy**. Each of these is closely related to the others; however, they have variations in the way in which they are judged and are oftentimes in direct opposition to each other. Designing effective decks is often a matter of negotiating tradeoffs between each of these kinds of card economy.

Card Count Economy

The first type of card economy is **card count economy**—the rating of how many of your cards you are utilizing compared to how many of your opponent's cards are being affected in some way. In this rating you simply count the number of cards you employed to remove or disable an opponent's card or put a card into play. For instance, when a player casts Dust to Dust and destroys an opponent's Mox and Juggernaut, that player nets one card over an

27

opponent. The concept here is that you are able to remove two of your opponent's cards at the cost of one of your own. Thus to achieve good card economy under this rating you seek cards which remove as many as possible of your opponent's cards. Some cards like Balance, Wrath of God, and Shatterstorm have a high potential for card economy.

Card economy is very important to assess in hand destruction decks because you seek to force your opponent to lose as many cards from his or her hand as possible at the least cost to yourself. This is why the Mind Twist is such a powerful card, and thus limited under convocation rules. At a cost of one card to yourself you can remove your opponent's entire hand. Hymn to Tourach presents a more reasonable trade but still maintains a 2:1 card count economy ratio, since your opponent must discard two cards for each Hymn you play.

Another element of count economy involves the concept of **draw strength**. If you draw more cards relative to your opponent then your count ratio is higher and thus you can expend more cards vs. your opponent for an equal effect. Cards like Braingeyser, Ancestral Recall, and the Jayemdae Tome may all be used to increase a deck's draw strength. An increased draw strength in a deck allows you to use more cards for the same effect, meaning that you may possibly be able to work with a less efficient card count economy.

Utility

The second form of card economy is measured by **utility**. Utility is the measure of effectiveness that a card has on the game. Some cards have a very high utility at certain points in the game and low at others. For instance, if you cast a Dust to Dust late in the game when both players have accumulated a relatively high number of effective mana producers and eliminate two Moxes, you experience a low level of utility for your employment of that card. However if you are able to utilize it early to negate an advantage gained by your opponent through artifact mana or creatures, then you have achieved a much higher card utility.

Most cards exhibit varying levels of utility at different points in the game. For example, a Dark Ritual has a very high level of

utility early in the game. However, after the first three turns the Dark Ritual becomes less and less powerful. Of course, this too is subject to change if your opponent is, for example, playing land destruction. Conversely, some cards with large casting costs such as the Lord of the Pit tend to have a greater value later in the game when more mana is available for casting them. If you get these cards early they can be wasted draws since you may not be able to cast them.

What this all boils down to is that you should try to construct a deck that allows you to employ the cards you draw when you draw them. It is for this reason that cards like Howling Mines provide a greater benefit to certain decks. A small creature deck will experience a greater benefit from a Howling Mine than a burn deck that relies heavily on red X damage spells. The player with the small creature deck will typically be able to cast each card drawn, while the player with a red X burn deck will be caught with multiple cards in hand which will not be able to be used effectively on the same turn.

The idea of card utility is also closely related to the concept of inter-card relationships. When the cards in your deck are related and strengthen each other, you gain more utility from each card in your deck. This means that from drawing the same number of cards you glean more utility and thus achieve more potency than if the cards were utilized individually. For example if you use Ashnod's Altar and Living Plane together, by tapping and then sacrificing lands as creatures you gain three mana for each one. If you already have the Living Plane in play and cast the Altar, your Altar has a higher utility than it would on its own, and you glean more from your one card than the card's intrinsic value. Thus the act of simply utilizing better card count economy will not suffice if your opponent is able to create significantly better card utility from his or her fewer cards.

Turn Economy

Turn economy is an estimation of how effectively you use each turn. When two equally matched players and decks meet, usually the deciding factor is who goes first. Going first is almost equivalent to taking an extra Time Walk (UL-r). This is important because turns are another method to judge the economy of a deck. If you must take an entire turn to perform one action and your opponent can effectively react to the action you took on your turn and simultaneously perform some other action during his turn, then he enjoys greater turn economy than you do. In other words he has undone your turn and proceeded with his own.

For example, on your first turn you play a Swamp and a Mox Jet and tap them both to cast a Dark Ritual and a Juzam Djinn. Your opponent follows up by playing a Swamp, casting a Mox Emerald, a Paralyze on the Djinn, and a Crumble on the Mox Jet. In doing this your opponent enjoys both turn and card count economy: turn economy because he was able to perform two functions during the turn (Paralyze Djinn, Crumble Mox) as opposed to your one (cast Djinn); card count economy because he effectively eliminated two cards you cast (Djinn, Dark Ritual) with one (Paralyze). In essence your opponent has undone your turn and furthered his own deck by coming out a Mox ahead.

There are a few cards that can increase your turn economy in a very straightforward fashion. One that is obvious is the Time Walk (UL-r) but there are some that can increase your turn economy by simply denying your opponent the ability to perform actions during his turn. These cards are environmental cards like Stasis and Winter Orb, which will decrease your opponent's ability to act and should not hurt your deck if it is constructed under the premise that they will be used. Thus you can gain turns on your opponent by creating an environment hostile to their development and simultaneously ambivalent to your own development.

Oftentimes these factors are closely associated. For example, if your opponent is using a two-card combination and you counter the second spell, making the first spell useless, you have won on two counts. You have won on card count and utility, since you have rendered several cards useless simultaneously.

All of these factors work in conjunction with one another and often in opposition. Card economy will be a constant theme throughout this book in order to rate the effectiveness of certain cards and combinations. There are many different ways to view card economy. Oftentimes a play that is beneficial in one form of economy is detrimental in another. For example, if you use a Dark Ritual with a Celestial Prism to get one blue mana and one black to cast a Time Walk, you have gained a turn advantage but a card disadvantage. Thus it is necessary to weigh the benefits in any category against the detriments in another. Cards which allow you benefits in all the categories are oftentimes the strongest additions to a deck.

Chapter 6

Action and Reaction

Almost any deck will employ the philosophies of action or reaction or a combination of the two. These deck philosophies deal with how the deck is intended to achieve superiority. Action-based decks work around the premise of forcing an opponent to react to your moves and keeping him too occupied to create an effective offense. Reaction decks are based more on the idea of being prepared for any eventuality and being capable of dealing with it. Additionally, there is a third type of philosophy which is common and combines the two. This philosophy is known as **denial**. In a denial deck the player seeks to refuse his opponent the resources necessary to move forward with his plans. The refused resources are usually mana-producing cards or cards in hand. These philosophies are related to the concepts of fast and slow deck theory, but they should not be confused with them. Fast and slow deck theories deal with how quickly the deck develops and not the philosophy of whether it is you or your opponent who is creating the action.

Action decks seek to keep an opponent in a state of reaction until he is incapable of keeping up and eventually succumbs to the overwhelming forces. These decks generally subscribe to fast deck theory; for example, small fast creature decks, which seek to overwhelm an opponent with a great many small creatures before an opponent can create sufficient defense. However, quickness and action are not necessarily one and the same. For example, a burn deck may be based on the concept of slowly building up enough mana to do a large amount of damage in one turn. These decks are action-oriented, since they seek to keep an opponent reacting to direct damage spells; however, they do not strictly require speed.

Action decks glean several advantages from their philosophy. Their association with speed can often make them overwhelmingly fast. This can be an advantage, since speed can often be a decisive factor. Additionally, regardless of how fast they are, if at any time an opponent is unable to react to an action-based deck's actions, he will suffer damage or some other negative ramification. Action decks are more capable of doing damage early in the game, and oftentimes this, too, can be a decisive advantage. One of the strongest advantages of action-oriented decks is that they generally keep an opponent on the defensive. If an action-based deck is well-designed it should create enough offense that an opponent must be solely concerned with survival, not success. An opponent cannot win from a strictly defensive strategy, and at the same time cannot reduce his defense in order to attack or he will succumb to the already initiated action. For example, if you are playing a white turbo deck against a burn deck, if your opponent is forced to utilize his direct damage spells to neutralize your creatures, he will be unable to cast any of them against you. Thus you are keeping him in a strictly defensive position from which he cannot win. It will be necessary for him to somehow free up his spells to launch his own attack or he will certainly lose. Thus there are certain advantages inherent in action-oriented decks.

There are disadvantages to action decks as well. In general, strictly action-based decks tend to be less versatile than reaction decks. For example, if you are playing an action-based deck and your opponent is also, if your opponent can create more action and offense than you, you may well find yourself incapable of dealing with your opponent's advantage. This means that if a deck relies on action as its main philosophy, it had better be able to be more aggressive than its opposition. Action is often weak when it is the sole philosophy manifested in a deck design.

Reaction decks do not seek to force an opponent into a reactionary state as action decks do. Instead players of reaction decks try to prepare for any eventuality in order to react strongly enough that not all the resources of the deck will be forced into reaction. These players hope to be well enough prepared for any type of action so that it will not cost them as much to defeat the action as it will for their opponents to generate the action. As such, these decks generally utilize slow deck theory. It usually takes several cards in a relationship to make each card sufficient to minimize several threats at once, and thus it takes the deck a few turns to create an environment that will lead to economic reaction. Therefore the reaction-based player seeks to instill each card in the deck with a higher utility than those of an opponent's. For example, the epitome of the reaction deck is the counterspell deck. These decks are heavily laden with counter magic and seek to keep an opponent from getting offensive cards into play. This may at first seem to be a one-to-one relationship between counter magic cards and an opponent's cards; however, this does not necessarily mean that the counterspells are getting bad utility. Since there will be relationships between the cards in an opponent's deck, by countering some of the spells you have not only achieved one-to-one card count economy but you have also come out ahead as far as utility value is concerned. Thus reaction decks seek to minimize the threat of the action elements in an opponent's deck design.

The main advantage of reaction philosophy is its versatility. Since the deck is designed around the premise of being able to deal with contingencies, it is usually ready to deal with most occurrences. This makes it unlikely that your opponent will be able to take some course of action that will render the reaction deck incapable of doing anything. For example, a burn deck built around red damage spells, an action-based deck, could be almost completely halted by a Circle of Protection—Red. On the other hand, most reaction decks will have some way to circumvent occurrences such as this. Reaction decks are by their very nature more versatile than action-based decks and thus more capable of dealing with problems. It is for this reason that most decks contain at least some reactionary element.

There are also several disadvantages that arise from playing reaction-based decks. One of these is a speed deficit. By reacting to your opponent's plays, you are intrinsically going to be burdened with a slower development. Reaction decks cannot hope for quick victory and can often be overwhelmed by particularly fast decks. Another problem with reaction-based decks is that they tend to suffer from a decreased card utility. In an action deck, generally all your cards work toward the goal of destroying your opponent, and thus they will all be useful when they are played. Reaction decks rely on removal capacity so much that often a card will be included in the deck which has no effect on an opponent's deck. For example, if you have Shatter in your deck and your opponent is playing with few or no artifacts, then you have suffered a horrendous utility deficit which will also lead to a turn and count economy deficit due to the wasted draw. Another consideration is the fact that reaction decks have a tendency to hold cards. Since you must wait for your opponent to do something in order to react to it, it is likely that while you are waiting you will have a tendency to build up a large number of cards. This can be a large deficit against a hand destruction deck or one that utilizes the Black Vise. Finally, reaction decks generally suffer from few roads to victory. Reaction decks often have few cards with the goal of defeating an opponent, since the focus of the deck is on removing or countering an opponent's threats. Thus there is only room for a few cards which are intended to lead to victory. This means that if these cards are dealt with by your opponent you will be at a serious disadvantage. One should take all of these things into consideration whenever designing a reaction-based deck.

Denial decks contain elements of both action and reaction, as well as some unique elements. Denial decks work on a principle of refusing an opponent the resources necessary for deck development. These usually consist of mana producers or cards themselves. In each case the goal is to prevent an opponent's deck from developing by refusing to allow them these resources. The desired result is that a modest offensive on the denial deck's part should net a victory for the player. These decks are often very powerful, and this is an important deck philosophy to understand.

The first few turns of the game are the most important and generally have a great impact on the outcome of the game. If the growth potential of a deck is stunted during these turns, it is difficult to ever regain an advantage. It is from this importance that denial decks gain their main advantage. By denying an opponent cards or mana during the first few turns, a denial deck is able to stunt an opponent's growth and, ideally, maintain an advantage throughout the game. Additionally, these type of decks generally enjoy a high card economy. The utility of each card in the deck is generally very high due to the fact that every deck has a target for them. Almost every deck employs land, and every deck certainly employs cards; this means that the denial cards in the deck will seldom want for a target. Additionally, by destroying the resources of an opponent these decks slowly gain a high degree of turn utility. Each time an opponent has to hold a card he would have been able to play had he had the land you just destroyed, you are slowly amassing turn economy. Because your opponent had to wait an extra turn to play that card, you slowed him down while still developing your own plans. Thus high card economy is the major advantage to be gleaned by utilizing a denial philosophy.

Denial decks can suffer from some of the same disadvantages as reaction-based decks. As with reaction decks, denial decks suffer from limited roads to victory. Because it is important that they be able to effectively counter an opponent's resources, they will have little room left for damage dealing or other roads to victory. At the same time, your opponent will often suffer from having to hold cards. If at some point you have destroyed all of an opponent's resources and are unable to destroy any more, you will begin to amass the denial cards, which are now useless. This can once again make you vulnerable to Vise damage. For example, if you have two Hymn to Tourachs in your hand but your opponent's hand is empty and he keeps playing his cards every turn, you will never receive an opportunity to play them and will be forced to hold them indefinitely. As with reaction decks, this can oftentimes become very problematic.

These three deck philosophies encompass the schemes involved in most types of decks. Generally decks consist of a mixture of two or all three elements. For example, Corey's Void/Disk deck contains elements of all three philosophies. It contains Sedge Trolls and Rukh Eggs to provide the action element to its scheme. These are effective for dealing damage to an opponent. At the same time it contains Mana Drains which give it a reactive element and allow it some versatility, since everything but land can be countered. At the same time Strip Mines and other land destruction cards provide a denial element to the deck. The goal of this deck is to blend the three philosophies smoothly, maximizing the advantages of each while trying to decrease the deficits. In designing a deck it is generally a good idea to seek to combine philosophies in such a way as to maximize the positive side and minimize the negative. At the same time only those philosophies that apply to the general deck concept should be considered. Thus the act of deck designing is once again a matter of weighing the pros and cons of each decision.

Chapter 7

Characteristics of Card Types

In order to design effective decks, an understanding of the strengths and weaknesses of each of the different card types is integral to success. A competent analysis of the attributes of each of the various types can help you to develop new deck ideas and to compensate for weaknesses in current deck designs. There are essentially seven different card types: land, summons, instants, interrupts, sorceries, artifacts, and enchantments. All of these various card types have subgroupings, and each card should be examined on an individual basis. There are many different variations to each type of card, and this chapter mainly seeks to show the overall characteristics of each group and general trends involving the card types. This type of analysis can be useful in helping to understand the concentration of each card type in a deck and the ramifications of these various concentrations. For example, there are many players who fervently support the use of creatureless decks. This may initially seem to be a good idea, but there are also certain negative ramifications to this strategy. Although each card is different, there are trends and common characteristics that tend to be present in most of the cards of a certain type. This chapter draws out these similarities and analyzes them. It is important to keep in mind that each card type is powerful in its own right and all have their drawbacks. In other words there is no best type of card and no best card, just good uses for each.

Land

Land is an essential and common element of all but the most experimental decks. There have been only ninety different land cards up through the Ice Age set. This makes land second only to interrupts in its infrequency as a card type. Land has many unique and intriguing characteristics and has certain attributes which no other cards possess. When exploring the strengths and weaknesses of land it is important to realize that not all lands are the same. Land can be broken up into two major categories: basic and special. Basic lands are further divided into their five distinct types: swamp, mountain, plain, forest, and island. Special lands can be broken up into two other categories: double lands and expansion lands.

Strengths

The first distinguishing advantage of land is that it is not cast. When land is brought into play it cannot be countered. Land is the exception in this case because all other card types can be countered*. This is considerably more of an advantage than it might seem at first. Counterspell decks are considered by many to be the most powerful of the five basic decks, and there is very little that they can do about land. For example, many decks evade the countering ability of counterspell decks by using Strip Mines to destroy available blue mana so that important spells can be cast without fear of a counter. Although the basic lands offer little weaponry, many of the expansion lands do offer options based on the fact that lands cannot be countered since they aren't cast.

Tied to the concept of lands not being cast is the fact that lands are brought into play with no expenditure of mana. This advantage makes certain cards immensely powerful, such as Strip Mine, Mishra's Factory, Maze of Ith, Library of Alexandria, and others.

---

*   One exception to this is the Psychic Purge.

These cards can be brought into play on the first turn and have significant effects on the play of the game. They can bring a great deal of speed and effectiveness to almost any deck. For example, the Factory presents the option to have a 2/2 creature in play very quickly and is also versatile in the respect that it can provide mana. Thus the speed and versatility of lands, especially of expansion lands, should not be overlooked when designing a deck.

Weaknesses

The most intrinsic difficulty with lands is the fact that only one may be put into play per turn. This makes decks that concentrate much of their power in lands very slow and unwieldy. There are some cards that help to overcome this weakness, such as Fastbond. There are other cards that allow land to be brought into play at a rate greater than one per turn, but they require the drawing and playing of these cards, and thus many difficulties can arise from using many lands.

Basic lands are simply what their name implies, basic. They are used almost solely for the casting of spells. In some cases they can be turned into creatures with the aid of permanents such as Living Land, Living Plane, or the Kormus Bell, but for the most part they act only as generators to provide power for mages. This is perhaps the greatest disadvantage of basic lands—that they are not versatile and serve only as a resource to accomplish other things.

Obviously one of the difficulties of land is that it is susceptible to land destruction. Though land destruction is less prevalent because of the difficulty in acquiring out-of-print cards like Sinkholes and Ice Storms, it is still perhaps one of the most popular deck themes around. Some of the basic lands are more susceptible to land destruction than others. Islands, forests, and plains can all be destroyed en masse by single cards (Flashfires, Tsunami, Acid Rain). This does not mean that the controllers of swamps or mountains have escaped such grand difficulties. Karma may not destroy all swamps in play but it will certainly make a black player wish it had. Conversion will typically ruin the day of any red player. Its permanence is actually often more daunting than the one-shot mass land destruction cards.

Special lands have their own disadvantages. In the case of double lands they are more apt to be hurt by mass land destruction and Karma than basic lands, because any spell or effect that affects half of a mixed land affects the entire land. In the case of Conversion or Gaea's Leige, only half of the double lands will be affected. This can often cause these lands to be affected by several effects and can lead to some problems for their controller.

Another major disadvantage of the special lands is that they are victimized by Blood Moon. Blood Moon is a particularly powerful

sideboard card because it damages so many tournament decks. One should always consider the effects of Blood Moon when preparing a tournament deck. That is, your deck should not simply roll over and die when your opponent plays a Blood Moon. Thus lands, although special in many ways, have intrinsic advantages and disadvantages just like any other card type.

Summons

In many ways, creatures are simultaneously the most simple and most complicated of the card types. Summons are the most common card type. There are 532 different creatures in Magic through Ice Age. Beginners tend to load their decks with them because many are relatively simple to master, then as they progress they begin to see creatures as fragile and susceptible to too many effects. It is strange to see the cycle that many players go through regarding creatures. Generally they waffle back and forth between employing and avoiding their use. This is because of the rather elaborate dynamics of creatures. The basic use of creatures is to attack an opponent or to block an opponent's attacking creatures, but there are some creatures that really don't even function as creatures, like the Time Elementals or Ali from Cairo. These cards are very powerful and tend to act more like artifacts or enchantments, but they have the added fragility associated with creatures. Thus there are many aspects of creatures which should be considered before including or excluding them from decks.

Strengths

The greatest advantage of creatures is their damage-dealing efficiency. Creatures are the most efficient mediums from which to deal damage in the game. If you look at a card like the Juggernaut you will observe that for a four colorless casting cost you can deal five points of damage a turn. If this is compared to the direct damage spells like Fireballs or Disintegrates, the Juggernaut actually possesses more card economy, especially if it is able to attack and deal damage more than one time before it is destroyed. One reason creatures are such a strong medium for damage dealing is because they have permanence. Once they are cast they may be used over and over again turn after turn and thus can amass a huge damage to cost ratio if they are able to remain in play for any length of time.

Another advantage that creatures have is that they are the card type most capable of being enhanced. To some degree most permanents can be enchanted or enhanced in some way; however, creatures have far and away the most enhancements available to them. Although this can often be a source of bad card economy it can also lead to some devastating effects. For example, casting an Instill Energy on a Colossus can lead to a very powerful creature, but you have now invested two cards in a creature which is very susceptible to many different types of effects. Thus if balanced with card economy, the ability to be enhanced can be an excellent boon for creatures.

Weaknesses

The primary difficulty with creatures is quite simply that they are extremely fragile. There are more cards that remove or disable creatures than there are for any other card type. If your opponent employs creatures, he can block your creatures, thus reducing their effectiveness. If he does not have creatures, then he will surely have a means by which to destroy them. Creatures are employed in many decks, and any deck you face will have some method of dealing with your creatures. Thus creatures are subject to the difficulty of being easy to destroy and highly predictable. You will not take an opponent by surprise by using creatures.

Another serious difficulty of creatures is that they suffer from summoning sickness. This facet of creatures is problematic in many ways. First of all, creatures provide a higher damage-to-cost ratio than most cards, but you must wait to employ them. Many times creatures with summoning sickness will not get an opportunity to be used before they are destroyed. This is particularly problematic because it is so easy to remove creatures. Thus although creatures are often the vessels for some of the most powerful abilities in the game, they are also subject to many weaknesses to compensate.

Instants

Instants are some of the most versatile and fast acting cards in the game. They are typically found in almost every deck and their proper use is important for successful game play and deck design. There have been 121 different instants printed in the card pool through the Ice Age set.

Strengths

Instants are extremely versatile and have a great many uses, since they can be played at almost any point in the game. This is a powerful attribute for several reasons. The first of these reasons is that you can play an instant during your opponent's turn. This can be advantageous because it allows you to use the mana expended on the instant during your next turn. For example, if you cast an Ancestral Recall during your opponent's turn, you will have the blue mana available for your turn. Additionally, this ability adds some versatility to your mana. For example, if you are holding both a Counterspell and an Ancestral Recall, you can wait to see if your opponent casts anything you should counter, and if he does not you can then cast Ancestral Recall at the end of his turn. The ability to cast instants during your opponent's turn also makes the instant more resistant to counterspells than summons, enchantments, sorcery, or artifacts, because your opponent must tap his mana during his turn to counter an instant you cast during that turn and will be denied that mana during your turn. Thus you may be able to cast an important enchantment or sorcery during your turn since your opponent was forced to cast a Counterspell during his turn.

An additional advantage of the instant is that it may be played during the attack phase. This is an important ability because of the support that the instants provide for creatures. They allow a player to strengthen the position of his or her creatures in an attack or in defense. Cards like Lightning Bolt, Disenchant, Dwarven Catapult, and Giant Growth are all powerful aids in combat and can provide synergy with all the creatures in a deck.

There is also the **surprise value** that instants provide as another advantage. Your opponent very seldomly sees your hand. This means that your opponent will make decisions based upon what he sees in play. If you play an instant in response to an opponent's actions he may make decisions based upon the fact that you can repeat that response throughout the game. This is a particularly powerful aspect because it can cause an opponent to second guess himself and make poor decisions. Additionally because instants can be played at nearly any point in the game, your opponent can never be sure that he will not be forced to counter an instant. As such he may need to keep mana for such purposes. Overall the main advantage of the instant is the versatility which allows it to glean the benefits of several advantages.

Weaknesses

Instants are relatively free of most weaknesses inherent in the other cards. Perhaps the only major weakness is that they are one-shots—they are played and then discarded. There are not that many ways to stop instants except with counter magic and other instants, but they are weakened by having a very specific base of reaction. That is, the use of instants to stop other spells is difficult to manifest due to the fact that there are only a very few types of spells that they will be effective against. For example, a Giant Growth could be used to counter the effects of a Lightning Bolt on a creature, but it would be ineffective against a Lightning Bolt cast against you. Instants are perhaps just a little more susceptible to counter magic than sorcery because of Flash Counters (LG-c).

Interrupts

Interrupts are the fastest cards in Magic. They are also the most uncommon of the seven card types. There are only thirty interrupts in Magic up through the Ice Age set. Five are red, three are green, fifteen are blue, six are black, and one is white. Though black and red have some powerful interrupts like the Fork and Dark Ritual, blue obviously dominates them in number.

Most interrupts are cast in response to other spells. There are a few exceptions, like Sacrifice, Dark Ritual, and Reset, but for the most part they are cast in a spell sequence*. Interrupts like Sleight of Mind, Magical Hack, and Red and Blue Elemental Blast can be cast responding to spells in a casting sequence or targeted at cards in play.

Strengths

Interrupts, like instants, can be played during either player's turn. Interrupts are perhaps the most difficult of spells for an opponent to deal with. This is because of their speed in resolution of their effects. For example, an instant can be countered by another instant (Lightning Bolt/Unsummon), but an interrupt cannot because its effect is resolved before any instants. For example if you attempted to Blue Elemental Blast a Kird Ape, your opponent could not Unsummon in order to save it. The interrupt is very powerful because when it is played it actually takes effect before the last unresolved action in a sequence of spells. Most of the blue counter interrupts tend to be devastatingly powerful because of this quality. Some of them, like Mana Drain and Counterspell, can prevent any spell from being cast. This ability makes them some of the most powerful and versatile cards in the game, giving them a very broad base of reaction. In other words, although these cards are only useable in reactionary effects, they are able to react to any kind of spell. Thus, presuming your opponent is not playing with strictly land, they have a great deal of usefulness in almost any deck. Although interrupts are the least common group of cards, many are extremely powerful cards in the game.

Weaknesses

One of the principle weaknesses of the interrupts is their inability to deal with permanents, which are already in play. The only major exceptions to this rule are Red and Blue Elemental Blasts,

---

* All of the spells mentioned in this sentence could be cast in response to a Power Sink or in conjunction with another responding counter.

and they are color-specific. Another major difficulty of interrupts is that they tend to be dependent on target spells. For instance, a Counterspell cannot be cast without a target spell to counter. This means that interrupts are likely to sit in a caster's hand if they have nothing to react to. There is a good chance that decks that are loaded with interrupts are very vulnerable to Vise damage. The reaction-based nature of the interrupt can be dangerous if an opponent is aware of it and capitalizes upon it.

Sorcery

Sorcery spells tend to be variable in their power. Sorcery has a wide range of effects and thus has fewer common traits than the rest of the spell groupings. Up to the Ice Age set there have been 101 sorceries. Some sorcery is very directed, taking only one target, while others are very broad with **blanket effects**. Some sorceries like Balance and Wrath of God can even establish deck **environment** despite the fact that they are one-shots; thus, it is very difficult to come up with many consistencies in sorceries, although many are very powerful indeed.

Strengths

Like instants and interrupts, sorcery is difficult to nullify. It is perhaps the second most difficult type of spell to nullify, inferior only to interrupts. This point is somewhat debatable depending on the concentration of an opponent's counter magic or mana destruction capability. The lower an opponent's concentration of these two, the less susceptible sorcery is relative to instants. This margin exists only because sorcery is not able to be countered by Flash Counters (LG-c).

There tends to be a great deal of card economy with most sorcery spells. Cards like Dust to Dust, Hymn to Tourach, Balance, Mind Twist, Fireball, and Wrath of God possess a high potential for denying an opponent cards with at least a two-for-one ratio in favor of their caster. For example, a Mind Twist can often force an opponent to discard his or her entire hand at the cost of only one expended card. This can sometimes be as high as seven-to-one card economy, a devastating effect.

Additionally, many sorceries tend to be very powerful. This is due to the fact that most are one-shots and do not have the versatility of the instant or the interrupt. Thus some of the particularly powerful cards in Magic tend to be sorceries: for example, Time Walk, Wheel of Fortune, Demonic Tutor, and Timetwister.

Weaknesses

Sorcery is the slowest of the three one-shots, making it susceptible to both instants and interrupts. An opponent can react to your cast sorcery, and both instants and interrupts will occur before the sorcery is resolved. This allows an opponent to do several things in response to a sorcery, which can often allow him to nullify or decrease the effect of the sorcery. The slowness of sorcery is difficult to manage.

The second limiting factor of sorcery is that it must be played during the main phase. This means that it is more predictable than the other one-shots and that it requires leaving mana tapped during an opponent's turn. Because you cannot play sorcery during an opponent's turn, you cannot force him to react during that turn. This is a difficult problem because of the sequencing involved. If you are playing against a heavy counter deck and are able to cast spells during your opponent's turn then he or she is forced to react to the spells during that turn. When your opponent reacts during his turn he is forced to tap mana, denying him power to counter spells during your turn. Because sorcery does not share the ability to be cast during an opponent's turn, its versatility is narrowed as a card type. Additionally, because sorcery must be played in the main phase, problems can occur even if it is your turn. For example, if your opponent has played a Black Vise, you cannot play a sorcery during your upkeep before the effects of the Vise occur.

Finally, the last weakness that sorcery shares with instants and interrupts is that it is a one-shot; once it is cast and its effects are resolved, it goes to the graveyard. However, this is not as large of a deficit for sorceries because their effects tend to have more card economy than their instant or interrupt counterparts. Overall, sorceries tend to be somewhat more powerful than the other one-shots but simultaneously less versatile and easier to cast.

Artifacts

There are several different artifacts in Magic and they are as variable in their uses as sorcery is. This card type is capable of functions ranging from **mana production** to **hand destruction**. Artifacts are the third most frequent card type. Up through the Ice Age set there have been 209 artifacts. Artifacts should be analyzed in separate groups, divided into those that have activation costs and those that possess continuous effects. Artifacts, like sorcery, can be very directional (these are typically artifacts with activation costs) or can employ **blanket effects** (these usually have continuous effects). Artifacts are perhaps second only to enchantments in providing deck environments, since they have such a wide range of effects.

Strengths

The are several strengths to artifacts, and none of them tend to have great superiority over others. The first of such strengths is their ability to be cast with colorless mana, allowing them to fit in any deck regardless of the mix of colors. This makes them versatile and forces opponents to be prepared for them regardless of what type of deck you are playing.

Another strong ability possessed by artifacts is that they can be activated or their effects begin to work on the turn they come out. Thus if an artifact has the same effect as a creature, it is often a better idea to utilize the artifact, since it will not suffer from the summoning sickness which will affect its creature counterpart.

Most artifacts have the power of permanence, allowing their effects to carry over into many turns. This is something which makes them very powerful. Like creatures, this can give them good card economy since their effects will be felt for many turns if they are not dealt with by an opponent.

Weaknesses

Artifacts are very powerful but they have a great deal of fragility. Artifacts are perhaps second only to creatures in their vulnerability to various effects. There are several cards that can decimate artifact-dependent decks such as Shatterstorm or Energy Flux. If these cards are cast and fail to be nullified, then their caster can often eliminate a large portion of an opponent's deck with only a few cards. Thus the use of too many artifacts in a deck can lead to bad card economy on the designer's part.

Enchantments

The last of the seven card types is enchantments. Enchantments are the most common sources of environments in decks. Next to creatures, enchantments are the most common card type. There have been 245 enchantments printed up through the Ice Age set. There are several different types of enchantments and all have their own individual ramifications. There are enchantments which affect the game as a whole, called **independent enchantments** (Power Surge) and enchantments for each of the other permanent card types, called **investment enchantments** (Spirit Link).

Strengths

Perhaps the greatest strength of enchantments is the difficulty inherent in removing them. There are fewer enchantment removal cards than any other form of removal. There are no forms of enchantment removal in black or red and very weak removal in blue. This makes enchantments the most reliable form of permanent and environment alteration. Enchantments do not suffer in loss of strength because of this. This card type provides some of the most powerful non-restricted cards, and they provide the most powerful environments because of this.

Another advantage of enchantments is the range of their effects. **Independent enchantments** can affect the entire game, often wreaking havoc on an opponent. Since a perceptive deck designer will create a deck in which the negative aspects of the enchantment will be nullified, this presents no problem for the enchantment's controller. The result of this is that enchantments can present an often telling advantage for a deck which utilizes them effectively.

Weaknesses

The weaknesses in the enchantment category are more frequently in **investment enchantments** played on a permanent. They are weak according to the order of vulnerability of the permanent they are played on. Creature enchantments are the most dangerous because creatures tend to be the most fragile cards in the game. This can be a source of terrible card economy in a deck. For example, if a player casts a Birds of Paradise and then two Instill Energies on it, he will have created a good source of mana; however, one Lightning Bolt will destroy all three cards. You should remember that when you play an enchantment on a creature, artifact, or land under your own control, you are making an investment in that permanent, and any removal of that permanent allows the destruction of two cards.

Additionally, although enchantments are generally very powerful, they may suffer from the fact that they are often expensive. Although many of the investment enchantments are inexpensive, many of the independent enchantments are very expensive. This means that if they are drawn early in the game they can lead to a slowdown in deck development.

One other problem is enchantments without cumulative effects. Having two of these enchantments in play is no better than having one in play. For example, having two Living Lands in play is no better than having one in play, unless one is hacked. If these enchantments are important to the deck, they will need to be present in numbers to make it statistically probable that they will be drawn, but at the same time duplicates will be a wasted draw.

This concludes the analysis of the seven different card types. When constructing a deck there is typically a mix of these different cards involved, and you should be able to reconcile the character of the deck with the types of cards you employ. The heavier the weight of a particular card type, the more susceptible your deck may be to cards that affect those card types globally.

Chapter 8

Calculations

Once you have decided on the theory and philosophy your deck is going to follow and decided on the basic theme or themes of the deck and what relationships it will employ, it is time to develop the preliminary deck. The act of doing this is essentially a matter of calculating how many of each card should be present in the deck. At this point you are ready to begin assessing the specifics of the deck and seeking to create a preliminary form for your deck. Many times, beginners will make the mistake of putting four of each of the cards they think are integral to the deck into it and usually wind up with an inversatile and ineffective deck. Many factors must be considered before you can add a certain number of any card to your deck.

The most important consideration is exactly what the utility of each card in the deck is. That is, simply, how effective each card is in an overall perspective. If you consider your deck to be a blank slate onto which you will be placing cards, you must now choose the configuration which will lead to the greatest effectiveness within the theme and philosophy of the deck. You begin with this blank slate and add cards until you have achieved a full deck, which will hopefully be the most effective incarnation of the theme, philosophy, and theory of the deck. As you add each card, you must consider several factors in order to find the cards which lead to the closest approximation to the optimum deck of this form.

First off, you must assess whether the addition of each card is giving you the greatest **additive marginal utility**. This simply means assessing whether adding this card greatly increases the power of your deck. More importantly, is there some other card that could better increase the strength of your deck? This can often be choosing the best creature that fits your colors, or finding an enchantment that works well within your theme. Each time you add a card, you should essentially be seeking the card out of all the legal cards that will lead to the greatest increase in the power of the deck. For example, consider a deck in which you have already placed two Disintegrates and three Lightning Bolts. You are working with a great deal of direct damage and intend to add one more of these cards. You must now assess which of these gives you the greatest additive marginal utility. If you are using Mana Flares and will have surplus mana, the Disintegrates probably have the best utility in this case since you will probably be able to do more damage with essentially the same cost in necessary mana as the Lightning Bolt. At the same time, if your deck relies on speed and you are seeking to function with a small amount of mana, then the Lightning Bolt probably has greater additive marginal utility. Assessing which cards have the greatest additive marginal utility in your deck at each stage of development will net you a more powerful deck than simply adding four of each important card to it.

In the case above, one reason that the Lightning Bolt is preferable in the second instance is due to the **diminishing marginal utility** of adding another Disintegrate. This is another important concept in deck construction. Whenever you add a card, you must consider whether this card is as valuable as the last one of the same type which you added. For example, many enchantments' effects are global and are not cumulative. This means that if you draw two of them, the second one has no value unless the first one is countered or destroyed. This is an example of diminishing marginal utility. Had there only been one of these enchantments in the deck, it would have been good to get it at any time. However the second one is not useful since the results are not cumulative. Thus you not only must consider the additive properties of the addition of a card, but also the detrimental aspects of including it.

For every card except basic lands and limited cards, you may have one, two, three, or four instances of them in your deck. Each number says something about the importance and playability of the card, and it is important to understand these distinctions when developing a deck.

When you include four of a card in a deck you are either saying that this card is absolutely necessary or this card is intrinsically powerful. With four of a card in a deck you have created a relatively probable possibility that you will draw two of them in your starting hand. Additionally, your opponent will come to expect these cards and be prepared. He or she will know whether these are important cards to counter and whether there are other cards that relate to these cards which should be dealt with. By suffering these adversities you are either saying that these cards contain a great deal of power and are good regardless of how many you get of them, or that these cards are essential and the risk of wasted draws and predictable plays is well worth it to get these cards. Generally speaking, if you are using four of a card, this would generally indicate that you would like to use even more. For example a Kird Ape is a good example of a card that might be used in groups of four. Kird Apes contain a great deal of power and are very easy to cast. This means that drawing them is very rarely a wasted draw. However, having four reduces surprise value and versatility. Thus it is necessary that they also be well suited with the deck and have importance in the roads to victory.

Including three of a card is generally a good idea if the card is an important card in the deck. Three is a good number for several reasons. First of all, you are still relatively likely to draw cards which are included in threes, and thus you are not giving up too much in the way of deck consistency. At the same time in the same space you fit three groups of four, you can now fit four groups of three. This is an incredible boon to the surprise value and versatility of the deck. Think of what having one more consistent card can mean to your deck. It is one more effect that you can generate without giving up too much probability that you will be able to generate the other effects. Thus three is a versatile number of cards to include in a deck and is commonly used.

Having two of a card in a deck usually indicates that it is not particularly good in multiples, but at the same time you would strongly like to see it during the course of the game. However, if only two of a card are included they should not be essential, because it is not improbable that these cards will not show up. Oftentimes these are cards like Disintegrates and Fireballs in decks that do not rely on direct damage. Inclusion of the two instances of these cards helps broaden the versatility of the deck and at the same time does not interfere too much with the other workings of the deck. Inclusion of two of the same card is usually a good idea if the effect is desirable but not intrinsically necessary for the deck to function in its intended fashion.

Inclusion of one of a card an excellent way to increase deck diversity and versatility. If only one of a card is included, this indicates that the card is generally either ultra powerful or simply works well with the theme of the deck. At the same time, these cards are usually either restricted or useless in multiples. By including only one of these cards you net several advantages. First of all, you can cause your opponent to make sideboarding mistakes, such as sideboarding to deal with a card that will probably not even show up next game. By only including one of several cards you can create incredible versatility, especially when these cards are combined with a Demonic Tutor. This means that if the deck is well constructed, when you draw the Tutor you will have whatever you need. This is due to the fact that by only including one instance of these cards you have created room to include many varieties of card types and effects. Thus by combining all of these levels of inclusion you can create decks that are simultaneously versatile and surprising and also consistent and reliable.

Implications of Card Inclusion

Four - Card is essential to the deck. Usually good in multiples and generally high both in combinational and standalone value.

Three - A fundamental card in the deck. Useful in most situations and a key part of the deck synergy.

Two - A solid card but generally not good in multiples. Usually useful, but not always. Not a key element of the deck.

One - Surprise value. Usually is an intrinsically powerful card and may or may not fit into deck synergy.

Mana Calculations:

After the inclusion of the spells for a deck have been made, it is time to create the mana foundation to support it. In considering mana sources, several decisions have to be made and several factors have to be noted. How much mana is necessary for the deck? What kind of mana will be used and how much of each specific color? To answer these questions you must look at the weight of each color in the deck and also the importance of the cards of each color.

Calculating the number of cards in your deck that should be mana producers is not an easy task. You must consider several factors in deciding the number of mana-producing cards to have in your deck. Several aspects must be analyzed before a value can be arrived at and like all things in deck design will probably be altered during the testing phase. At this point you simply seek to get a starting number that you hope will eventually lead you to the right answers.

The first aspect with which you must concern yourself is the implication of drawing too much mana. That is, what are the effects on your deck of having too much mana in your hand or in play? For example, the White Flash does not need more than one or two mana in play at most times, and thus you would much rather draw a creature than a land at most times in the game. This points toward utilizing a lower percentage of mana cards in the deck, occasionally as low as fifteen or sixteen cards. At the same time decks which include many X casting cost spells or creatures with Firebreathing and other uses for spare mana do not suffer from the same problems, and usually whenever mana is drawn it can be put to a good use. These decks can often go as high as twenty-nine or thirty mana producers in their deck.

Mana production should be assessed in consideration of several things. Most obviously the main consideration is the casting cost of the cards in the deck. If there are many cards with a high casting cost or which require a great deal of colored mana, then a higher percentage may be necessary. The number of colors in the deck is also of great concern. The more colors a deck has, the more lands that will be necessary. Another consideration is whether the lands can serve another purpose besides generating mana. For example, with a Dark Heart of the Woods, a forest can also serve as a heal. This could lead to a higher percentage of mana in the deck. One simple equation to find a starting number of mana-producing cards is:

number of mana producers = 15 + highest # of colored mana + number of colors + (highest casting cost/2)

This can give you a good idea of what number of mana producers to start with. You then should determine what type of other mana you will use—Moxes, other artifact mana, or mixed lands—and in what distributions. Usually this decision is a function of deck theme and theory. Faster decks will require more fast mana, while slower decks will gain less benefit from it. The theme of the deck may be hostile to some kinds of mana: for example, Blood Moon with mixed lands. Thus you should analyze what types of mana are appropriate on an individual deck basis.

To calculate mana distribution you must first assess how many **mana slots** you have in your deck. These are not the same as mana-producing cards, because some mana-producing cards have two slots and others none. First you must decide whether you will be using Moxes, mixed lands, or other artifact mana, and how many. Then you must determine how many slots you have. Mixed lands have two slots since they can hold two different colors, while Moxes and basic lands have only one. After you deduce how many slots you will have it is time to determine what colors to place in them.

Color distribution is usually a matter of working with the deck to perfect the balance. However when the deck is being constructed, a good way to assess how much of each color of mana to include is the following process:

1. Divide the cards into colors and assign each card an importance value from one to three.
2. Sum the totals of the colored mana in each card and the importance value of that card. Then divide by the square root of the number of cards of that color. Do this for each color in the deck.
3. Take a ratio of each of these determined values and allot the mana slots in your deck in the same proportion.

Example:

Consider a deck with twenty-two mana production cards and two colors. The mana sources will include two Moxes and four mixed lands. The rest will be basic lands. The mixed lands each have two slots while the rest of the cards have only one; thus the total number of slots is:

$$4 * 2 + 2 + 16 = 26 \text{ mana slots}$$

Now the other cards in the deck are distributed with the following importance and colored mana requirements:

Black: 4 x (3/2), 8 x (2/2), 10 x (2/1), 3 (1/1)
Green: 4 x (2/2), 6 x (2/1), 3 (1/2)

Thus the respective ratio values for each color are:

$$\frac{\text{Black: } 4 \times (5) + 8 \times (4) + 10 \times (3) + 3 \times (2)}{\text{Sqrt }(25)} = 17.6$$

$$\frac{\text{Green: } 4 \times (4) + 6 \times (3) + 3 \times (3)}{\text{Sqrt }(13)} = 11.9$$

Taking a ratio of these results, black/green = 17.6/11.9 = 1.5

This means you should begin with a roughly 1.5 black/green mana ratio. With the twenty-six mana this equals:

1.5 (x) + (x) = 26
2.5 (x) = 26
x = 10.4

Where x = the number of green mana.

Thus as a starting point we might try:

1 Mox Emerald	4 Forest
1 Mox Jet	12 Swamp
4 Bayou	

Then if you find yourself needing one color or the other you can slowly shift them from the excesses to the deficiencies.

The purpose of this method is only to give you a starting place. It is certainly not a hard and fast equation. By using this method, however, you may find yourself getting to an optimum mix of mana more quickly during the testing process, since it gives you a good starting point, which takes into account the major aspects of mana balance.

Thus many calculations are necessary each time a deck is made. Some players prefer to go on intuition, while others prefer to use hard calculations. Whichever way you choose, you must follow this with rigorous testing of design changes in order to come closer to the optimum deck in your theme.

Chapter 9

Modifications and Enhancements

After you have designed your deck and gone through the first six steps in the deck design procedure you should be ready to cut the deck for greater efficiency. It is very unlikely that your first attempt at putting the deck together will result in an optimum, or even close to optimum configuration of the deck. In order to begin moving closer to finding this optimum you must begin to test this deck against others, starting with the five basic decks. After you have played against the five basic decks you can identify weaknesses that you need to overcome and you should be able to identify unneeded cards in your deck and any oversights you may have made.

There are a number of questions that you should ask after play-testing the deck.

How Good is the Mana Distribution?

The first aspect of your deck that you should analyze is the effectiveness of the mana distribution. This is often one of the most frequently altered aspects of the deck, as players make slight modifications in hopes of improving their chances of having appropriate mana at the correct time. There are two main factors to consider when asking this question. The first is how your opening hands look. Do you have enough mana-producing cards in your

After play-testing the deck, ask yourself the following questions:

1. How good is the mana distribution? Can sixty-five percent of the deck's spells be cast with the mana available in the opening hand? In the late game, is land often drawn when other cards are needed?

2. How good is the deck's synergy? Do all of the cards perform well together? How fragile are the card combinations?

3. How effective are the roads to victory? Are there enough? What cards could be added or removed to improve each road's efficiency?

4. Is the deck fast enough? Can its speed be improved without cost to its efficiency?

5. How heavy is the deck's reaction capability? Is the deck reliant upon reaction?

opening hand to cast at least sixty-five percent of the spells? This question is important because if you do not you may suffer from a great deal of slowdown and card-holding in your deck. If you are unable to cast a large number of the spells in your deck with your opening mana, if you encounter any forms of land destruction you will almost certainly end up holding many cards, and you may even without land destruction's hindrance. If you find that you are encountering this problem, it is generally a good idea to increase the actual percentage of mana in the deck in order to be better able to cast your spells. There are, of course, exceptions to this number and times when you will be able to get by without being able to cast many of your spells early in the game. For example, some decks work on the premise that they will get out one extremely damaging combination, and since they will have to wait for that combination anyway, it is acceptable not to have the necessary mana for some things at the beginning of the game. Additionally, many decks actually use lands such as Mishra's Factories and Strip Mines as active cards, which means that you are generating action even if you are unable to cast some of your spells. The percentage of spells that you are able to cast with your initial mana is an important concern when attempting to improve the caliber of your deck.

The second major factor to consider when revising a deck's mana distribution is how often land is drawn in the later game when other cards are needed. That is, how often is useless land drawn. There are some ways around this problem, but you may find that everyone suffers from this problem in one fashion or another. The degree to which it occurs is what you really must consider and attempt to minimize. If you have a really high mana distribution in your deck, you may find that you enjoy some greater margin of success in the early game, but later you might find that your deck sputters out as you continually draw lands instead of cards that can move you closer to victory. If you concentrate your deck's power into a small number of high casting cost cards, a higher mana-to-spell ratio is often necessary but it does cause a higher degree of variability in the late game. In order to minimize the amount of land drawn in the late game, you should analyze several aspects. First of all, you should make sure that in an attempt to avoid this you do not make yourself vulnerable to land destruction. It is often the case that players will cut their mana as thin as possible in order to escape useless late game draws and in the process cause their decks to be decimated by land destruction decks. If in testing your deck you find that you are drawing **superfluous mana**, mana which serves no real purpose, it is a good idea to cut the number of mana-producing cards in your deck. Generally, however, this should not be done in large increments. Removing one land can make a much bigger difference than you think. Also the first deck you should test it against after you make these modifications is the land destruction deck.

Finding a good balance of mana in your deck is essential in creating an effective deck. Mana is necessary for almost every card in the game, but at the same time it suffers from a strong decrease in marginal utility during the game. Thus it is necessary to form a balance between the threat of useless draws and the threat of bad opening hands. However, great pains should be taken to try to create a deck which has low probability of both.

How Good is the Deck's Synergy?

When analyzing a deck's synergy you need to determine if all of the deck's cards work well in conjunction with one another. That is, do your cards increase your other cards' power, and do you avoid relationships which are detrimental to power? Your cards should typically not interfere with one another, except in very special cases. Most players recognize this, but one should realize that in many cases there are even more efficient cards to replace others and still conform to the deck's synergy. Creating good synergy in a deck is one of the best methods to create strong decks, since a unified front among your cards makes each of them more powerful in their own right.

Some cards may not perform in concordance with the deck's synergy. In many decks the effect of a card actually works in opposition to the deck's synergy. You may question whether the advantages that these cards provide is worth their break in the deck's consistency. Generally, when these types of situations arise it is best to seek a card that has more synergy with the deck and has a similar effect. For example, a Black Vise is a very powerful card and an integral part of many decks; however, it is certainly not applicable to all decks. Some players include the Black Vise and the Rack in the same deck in order to increase the chances of doing damage to their opponents. This shows a lack of synergy in the deck. If the deck contained more synergy there would be a method by which the deck would force an opponent either to have many cards or few cards, and thus either the Vise or the Rack would be useless. If you find you have cards that are at odds with other cards in your deck it is generally a good indication that your deck is suffering from a lack of synergy. There are also many cards that perform independently and are neither enhanced nor damaged by other cards incorporated in the deck's synergy.

There are many decks that rely on powerful combinations to overcome an opponent. In some cases these decks are weak until their combinations come into play. This makes them very fragile. After playing against the five basic decks you should have some idea about just how fragile these combinations are. Then you may determine countermeasures to avoid a break in the combination.

Oftentimes these decks are created because of the power of the combination involved, however it turns out that the combination is really impossible to support.

How Effective are the Roads to Victory?

A common problem many decks have is that they lack adequate means for achieving victory. Sometimes they rely too heavily on achieving victory from one type of source, and sometimes their sources are too distributed and unsupported. You must find roads to victory that have synergy with the rest of your deck. By doing this, you create the means to protect your roads and make them more difficult to cut.

The number and strength of the roads to victory in a deck are usually the greatest concerns. If you have a very limited means to achieve victory, you must protect those means and provide them with support. On the other hand if you have many roads to victory you do not need be overly concerned when one of them is cut off. There are advantages to each type of deck, and usually it is a matter of theme, philosophy, theory, and synergy as to which type is used.

Action decks may have many roads to victory. These decks often seek to overwhelm their opponents by laying so many roads that it is impossible for an opponent to cut them all. Other times they seek to lay one road that is so strong an opponent will not be able to cut it. Examples of these are the small and large creature decks. A small creature deck seeks to have so many potential threats that an opponent cannot deal with them all, while a large creature deck seeks to have one difficult-to-remove creature.

Reaction decks usually utilize limited roads to victory. This is an obvious choice, because the reactive element of the deck is usually able to support the one larger road. Usually, for example, counter-spell decks will have a few large creatures whose removal they prevent by countering any threats to the creature.

Sometimes there is just a small difference between winning and losing with a deck. In some cases, while modifying a deck, you can remove cards that react to an opponent's actions and add cards that not only react to an opponent but increase your chances of achieving victory. For instance if you are playing a deck that has a couple of

Shatters, perhaps you should consider adding Detonates instead. These will also remove artifacts, and they add to the deck's offensive capability. The only loss in the exchange is in the speed reduction: having to go from instant to sorcery speed and sometimes needing more mana. One should always have complete knowledge of the number of cards in a deck that will remove an opponent and what their weaknesses are.

Is the Deck Fast Enough?

In many cases decks suffer because they lack the speed to overcome an opponent or to establish adequate defenses. In other cases decks are laden with cards that add unnecessary fast mana which destroys the deck's potency. When you begin to evaluate a deck's performance after a series of matches you will usually acquire a feel for the deck's tempo. All decks possess a certain speed at which they are best played. Many players believe that decks should be cut so they are as fast as possible; however, many decks require patience rather than great speed to achieve victory. For instance, a counterspell deck does not rely on overwhelming an opponent within the first few rounds of the game. It slowly develops and then reaches a point where it can dominate. Typically you do not look at a counterspell deck and say "How can I make this faster?" since this is not a great concern for the deck. However, if you can speed the deck up without harming its efficiency and reliability, then you should, since you will be able to more effectively counter an opponent's speed in this fashion.

In most cases decks should be cut to be as fast as possible without sacrificing potency. For instance, the original version of Corey's Disk Void deck used Clay Statues (RV4-c). Later the Statues were replaced with Sedge Trolls (RV-r). The Trolls cost one mana less than the Statues and tended to come two or three turns earlier. This speed difference was caused by two factors. The first was simply the creature's casting cost. Though the cost difference between the Statue and the Troll was not that significant (because the Statue only required colorless mana and the Troll required red), the difference in the cost to regenerate the two creatures weighed heavily in the Troll's favor. This is because the Troll only requires one black to regenerate, whereas the Statue requires two colorless. In most cases neither creature would be cast without the appropriate mana to regenerate it. This means that it would take at least four mana for the Troll to be brought into play and six mana for the Statue.

When you cut your deck for speed, not only reconsider your sources of mana or fast mana (Dark Ritual, Wild Growth, artifact mana) but consider the cost and purpose of the creatures you employ.

How Effective is the Deck's Reaction Capability?

There are times when you look at a deck's success record and you notice that you lose to a certain type of deck or you suffer greatly for certain individual cards. In this case it is often wise to prepare some form of reactive defense against such obstacles or to tune your deck to the point that such obstacles pose little or no threat to your victory. Most action-based decks use the latter philosophy and simply rely on their speed to crush opponents. When reaction is added to such decks the results can be variable. In some cases the effectiveness of the assault is diluted by adding cards that may or may not prove to be useful. In other cases these additions remove obstacles to the assault and enhance the offensive value of an attack. It is usually best to experiment with these different combinations to determine the correct mixture for the most effective countermeasures.

Preparing for the Worst

After you have cut the fat out of a deck and added more muscle, you may find that the deck is still not complete. No deck ever seems to be finished. There are always more modifications that can be made. As your opponents and the playing styles around you transform, so too should your deck. Often you will find that a large number of the cards you realize you need in the modification and enhancement stage belong in the deck's sideboard.

Chapter 10

Preparing a Sideboard

After you have modified and enhanced your deck you will find that some cards in your deck are only necessary in some circumstances, and that there are some specific instances in which you need a card that is essentially useless otherwise. In situations like this, these cards typically go to your sideboard and are moved into your deck when you need to confront decks that fall under these specific categories. Constructing a powerful sideboard is paramount to the success of a deck in tournament play, and in friendly play when sideboards are used. Each sideboard is different from deck to deck but in many cases you will find that generally speaking, there are several principles that guide the construction of any sideboard. Choosing a guiding principle by which to construct a sideboard depends upon the deck for which the sideboard is constructed.

Typically sideboards are constructed under one of five basic principles, or specific cards are included to fulfill those functions. The first four of these principles are offensive. They are used to tailor a deck to destroy an opponent. They typically exploit weaknesses and break the synergy of an opponent's deck. The last sideboarding principle is a defensive one. The defensive counter is typically employed when a deck has a fragile architecture and is seriously harmed by certain cards.

The first of the offensive sideboarding principles is the color-specific principle. Color-specific sideboards are constructed to hinder the various colors with color-specific cards. These are

Sideboarding Principles

Offensive:

1. Color-specific—Constructed to hinder different colors by using color specific cards.

2. Type-specific—Constructed to hinder decks that rely heavily on different card types such as mixed lands, Counterspells, or artifacts.

3. Tweak—Constructed to enhance certain elements of a deck that are most effective against an opponent's deck.

4. Transformational—Constructed to change a deck from one form or type to another.

Defensive:

1. Defensive counter—Constructed as a countermeasure against specific cards that weaken the deck potency.

perhaps the most common sideboards. They are typically loaded with cards such as Elemental Blast, Death Grip, Life Force, Tsunami, Gloom, and Flashfire. This type of sideboard is typically nice when your deck is particularly susceptible to a specific color, or when your opponent is depending on one particular color.

The second sideboard variant is the type-specific sideboard. These sideboards are geared to overcome a specific type of deck or decks that are reliant upon a specific type of card. For instance, some sideboards contain additional land or Consecrate Land to overcome land destruction. Others have cards like Blood Moon or Energy Flux to overcome decks that are too reliant upon mixed lands or artifacts. This sideboard type is best when your deck can be overcome by certain types of decks with consistency. All you have to do is isolate a characteristic of these decks and exploit it with your deck. For instance, if your deck performs poorly against a counterspell deck you should look for certain characteristics of a counterspell deck that could be turned against it. Counterspells themselves are reactive cards: they must have a target. If you do not cast anything, the Counterspells in a counter deck will just sit in your opponent's hand. Because you can force a counterspelling opponent to hold cards, he is very susceptible to Black Vises. Because of this you might consider sideboarding in some Black Vises when you face such decks. Then you can patiently wait for your opponent to either die from the Vises or utilize his blue mana to get cards out of his hand. Once he has tapped out his blue mana, you can proceed with your plans in safety. Thus type-specific sideboarding is a good option when your deck is vulnerable to a certain deck. Instead of attempting to work within parameters set by your opponent, you attack the weaknesses of the deck that would be preying on you.

The third offensive sideboarding principle is the tweak principle. The tweak principle is centered on refining and enhancing a deck's pre-existing characteristics that prove to be most effective against the particular configuration of an opposing deck. The least effective components are then reduced for more favorable ones. This method is rather uncommon. It is most often found in decks that lack fragility and are not susceptible to any particular weakness; thus the deck must be strong in the first place in order to utilize this kind of sideboard. On the other hand, elements of this philosophy can usually be found in most sideboards, as in many cases your deck will be effective against an opponent, and thus it will be a good idea to simply highlight the advantages of your deck.

The last and perhaps the rarest of the offensive sideboard principles is the transformational principle. This principle works around the assumption that an opponent will sideboard against your deck after the first match. Between matches you simply sideboard out a major element of the deck and sideboard in a new, totally unrelated theme. This will cause an opponent to suffer from a number of newly sideboarded cards that are now useless to him or her. This can be a devastating weapon, since wasted draws are one of the main things that sideboards should help you to avoid. For instance, if you were playing with a creatureless deck you could simply sideboard out anti-creature cards and sideboard in more creatures. This is a difficult feat to engineer, however, without destroying the synergy of your deck. The results can have excellent surprise value, however, and can often net you a game if you can manage it. Additionally, if the match goes to a third round, then you will have your opponent uncertain and guessing, leading him into possibly making mistakes. Unfortunately, transformational side-boards can sometimes be inversatile. So many cards in your sideboard will be taken up in making the transformation that you will have little room for other cards. This means that if neither form of your deck is particularly effective against your opponent, you will not be able to do anything about it. Thus the various forms of your deck under this philosophy should be very versatile as well. Overall, transformational sideboards can be difficult to create, but the results can be exceptional if the sideboard is well thought out.

The last and the only defensive type of sideboarding principle is the defensive counter. These sideboards are typically constructed for decks that are particularly vulnerable to certain cards. For instance, if your deck has only mixed lands and lacks many alter-nate sources of mana, you may find it beneficial to add Disenchants to the sideboard or Blue Elemental Blasts. These can be effective in a match; however, the difficulty arises from the fact that you gener-ally have to give up a game in order to find out that your opponent is using these cards. That is, you will generally lose the first game if your opponent is using them, so you will have to win the last two. This means your sideboard must be very effective to ensure that you will be able to overcome this difficulty.

Most sideboards contain a mixture of these principles, and usually cards are included for differing reasons. Sideboards are by no means generic and require a great deal of thought to create effectively. They must be tailored to a deck and must match its synergy. They should typically not damage the effectiveness of your deck, only change its direction to one in which it will be more effective against this particular opponent. If they do damage a deck's effectiveness, then they should cause proportionately much greater damage to an opponent or rectify an oversight that is essentially fatal and consistent. Thus the sideboard is essentially a fifteen-card extension of a deck, not a separate entity.

When you construct a deck you should keep the sideboard in mind during the entire process. If you diversify the various ele-ments of your deck it is rather difficult to sideboard against and easier to sideboard with. A single card is difficult if not impossible to effectively sideboard against. For example, if you include one Nether Void in your deck, it may come out in the first match and be damaging to your opponent. However, odds are that the card will not appear during the next game, and any sideboarding your opponent does to counter it will result in wasted card slots. Thus your opponent's potential sideboarding capacity, as well as your own, should also be kept in mind when you are designing your deck and sideboard.

You should try to construct decks so you can easily remove and add cards when facing different decks. It is usually a good idea to predetermine what cards you would remove and what cards you would add to combat the five basic decks. This will prepare you for other decks and will assist you in becoming familiar with your deck's strengths and weaknesses. Generally the decks you will face will have traits in common with the five basic decks, and being prepared to sideboard against them will give you an advantage during play.

This is a typical counterspell/burn deck provided as an example to assist you in predetermining cards to add and remove when facing different decks.

Deck Name: Fire and Ice

Block One	Block Two	Block Three
Pocket 1	Pocket 1	Pocket 1
Counterspell	Nevinyrral's Disk	Island
Counterspell	Nevinyrral's Disk	Island
Counterspell	Nevinyrral's Disk	Island
Counterspell	Nevinyrral's Disk	Island
Pocket 2	Pocket 2	Pocket 2
Power Sink	Incinerate	Island
Power Sink	Incinerate	Island
Power Sink	Incinerate	Island
Power Sink	Incinerate	Island
Pocket 3	Pocket 3	Pocket 3
Spell Blast	Mishra's Factory	Island
Spell Blast	Mishra's Factory	Island
Spell Blast	Mishra's Factory	Island
Mahamoti Djinn	Mishra's Factory	Mountain

Pocket 4	Pocket 4	Pocket 4
Mahamoti Djinn	Strip Mine	Mountain
Mahamoti Djinn	Strip Mine	Mountain
Fireball	Strip Mine	Mountain
Zuran Orb	Strip Mine	Mountain
Pocket 5	Pocket 5	Pocket 5
Lightning Bolt	Earthquake	Mountain
Lightning Bolt	Earthquake	Mountain
Lightning Bolt	Earthquake	Mountain
Lightning Bolt	Island	Mountain

Sideboard

1. Power Surge
2. Power Surge
3. Red Elemental Blast
4. Red Elemental Blast
5. Red Elemental Blast
6. Earthquake
7. Island
8. Island
9. Pyroclasm
10. Pyroclasm
11. Mind Bomb
12. Shatter
13. Energy Flux
14. Energy Flux
15. Energy Flux

Hand Destruction Switches

From sideboard to deck	*From deck to sideboard*
1. Energy Flux	Earthquake
2. Energy Flux	Earthquake
3. Energy Flux	Earthquake
4. Shatter	Nevinyrral's Disk

Most hand destruction decks use the Rack as a major source of damage. When these switches are made, the Racks can be overcome. This is an example of tweaking, because this deck is not particularly vulnerable to hand destruction. The Counterspells are an effective countermeasure to the individual hand destruction spells, but adding the Energy Fluxes and Shatters make it even more capable of dealing with this type of deck.

Land Destruction Switches

From sideboard to deck	*From deck to sideboard*
1. Island	Earthquake
2. Island	Earthquake

Most land destruction decks do not rely heavily on small walking creatures, and this usually allows you to remove the Earthquakes and add the obvious extra land. Land destruction decks are slightly more effective against this deck because if they get going quickly they can make it difficult to get the two blue mana necessary to cast Counterspells. This is an example of defensive sideboarding, using the additional Islands to make your deck less vulnerable to the effects of land destruction.

Burn Deck Switches

From sideboard to deck	*From deck to sideboard*
1. Island	Earthquake
2. Island	Earthquake

Most burn decks rely heavily upon red damage spells. This makes the Earthquake relatively ineffective. In most cases an extra Island will bring about a quicker preparedness for a Counterspell. Since the Counterspells are an excellent defense against the burn spells themselves, increased capacity to cast them is a great boon. This is simply basic type-specific sideboarding, utilizing your sideboard to be just slightly more effective against your opponent.

Counterspell Deck

From sideboard to deck	*From deck to sideboard*
1. Red Elemental Blast	Earthquake
2. Red Elemental Blast	Earthquake
3. Red Elemental Blast	Earthquake
4. Power Surge	Nevinyrral's Disk
5. Power Surge	Nevinyrral's Disk

When facing another counterspell deck there are a number of additions that can be made. Once again the Earthquakes would not be incredibly useful. Power Surges can be well employed against a Counterspell to inflict damage, since counterspellers usually try to leave mana untapped in order to be able to counter. If you choose not to cast many spells, a Power Surge will often eliminate an opposing counterspell deck. In this deck the Power Surge would not prove to be that harmful because all of the untapped lands can be used to turn the Mishra's Factories into creatures multiple times until they are tapped, and the remaining Mishra's Factory can be tapped to make itself bigger. Most counterspell decks do not have a great number of permanents. The Nevinyrral's Disk could be removed to add to the deck's effectiveness in a counter war. The Prodigal Sorcerer would also not yield as much benefit to the deck as another Red Blast, so it can be replaced. This is an example of both type-specific and color-specific sideboarding. In this example you use the Red Blasts because your opponent will be utilizing blue extensively. At the same time the Power Surges are intended to prey on the countering aspect of the deck. The Red Blasts can also be seen as defensive sideboarding. As you can see, many times the philosophies overlap.

Fast Creature Deck

From sideboard to deck	From deck to sideboard
1. Pyroclasm	Blood Lust
2. Pyroclasm	Blood Lust
3. Earthquake	Power Sink
4. Power Surge	Power Sink

You need to react quickly when playing against a fast creature deck. Most Type II fast creature decks are small fast creature decks. For the first few rounds you will generally find that you are trying to survive. This makes cards like Blood Lust ineffective. The Earthquakes, on the other hand, should prove an excellent anti-creature ordinance. The Power Surges will also be of some benefit for the same reason that Power Sinks will be ineffective. Most small fast creature decks rely on very little mana to run their deck. This means that they typically leave a large amount of mana untapped later in the game, making it difficult for Power Sinks to be effective and enhancing the damage potential of Power Surge.

Small creature decks prove to be a great nuisance for counterspell decks, so this one is cut to avoid such a nuisance from the very first game by having a Power Surge and two Earthquakes in the original deck. Both of these cards work well with the deck because they do not disturb its synergy. This is another example of type-specific sideboarding. The deck begins with a capacity to deal with fast creature decks, and the additional cards seek to find the cracks in the defense of the creature deck and assault them.

The major weakness in this deck appears against the Black Vise. This is why the Mind Bomb is added, to assist in escaping the effects of a Black Vise. Once the Mind Bomb is used, this deck can easily remain under five cards in hand. If you challenged a Vise deck with this deck you would most likely cut a Mahamoti and the two Earthquakes. Also, I would consider adding a Shatter to eliminate a Vise, and I would cut a Counterspell. Thus this is an example of defensive sideboarding—considering what your deck is most vulnerable to and including cards to deal with this deficiency.

Hopefully you now have a strong grasp on how to sideboard effectively. Though these are just approximations of how to sideboard against various decks and types of decks, the examples should be applicable to general cases. All decks are different and should be sideboarded against individually. Once you have mastered sideboarding, you will have a great advantage over others who have not acquired this knowledge.

Sideboarding can be of varying importance depending on the tournament structure you participate in. In a Swiss system, the value is reduced because the games count, not matches. This is even more true if the matches are only two games. In one-game round robins, sideboards are virtually useless. Sideboards are generally most effective in a single or double elimination tournament with a standard three-game match.

Chapter 11

Playing Your Deck

As you are going through the process of modifying and enhancing your deck, you will also begin to notice certain aspects of your deck and start making notes about the methods involved in playing your deck. Although designing a strong deck is of great importance and is necessary if you plan to win, being able to properly play your deck is also necessary. There are many traps that you can fall into when playing your deck and many errors you can make. As you are testing your deck, you will often make several observations such as, "I've got to remember to have out my Mishra's Factory or C.O.P. Red before I play my Power Surge." Though this may seem elementary, these kinds of observations are necessary because each deck has its own individual characteristics of game play. For the first several times you play a deck, you will probably learn something new about playing it. Although a large part of acquiring a good understanding of your deck simply comes through practice and play, there are several things you should note and watch for during the testing phase in order to speed the process of learning the little ins and outs of your deck.

One of the first issues you should note in this process is if there are any sequential play elements to the deck. Sequential play elements are simply cards that should be played in a certain order consistently to avoid effects that are at odds with each other. Many times cards in your deck will have a positive relationship if used correctly but a negative relationship if used improperly. For

79

example, Corey's Disk deck contains both Nevinyrral's Disk and Nether Void. When used in the proper sequence, these cards can have a devastating effect; however, if the Nether Void is played first, the Disk will destroy it. When they are played correctly, the Disk will wipe out artifact and creature mana and leave your opponent with nothing but land. Following with the Nether Void will cause your opponent to have difficulty rebuilding after this assault. The inclusion of regenerating creatures in the deck leaves you with a hefty advantage for your opponent to overcome. This is just one example of the need to play many cards in your deck in a certain order. Oftentimes having a large number of sequences in your deck can lead to problems, particularly slowdown and card-holding, but many decks include these sequences because of the power they can bring to a deck. Because sequential plays often take so long to bring about, there is a great danger of one of them being countered or removed and thus breaking the sequence. You must learn how to properly play your deck in order to ensure that you do not sacrifice the power of your deck to improperly played sequences.

Hesitant and Hasty Play

Another important aspect to playing your deck is playing at the proper tempo. This involves playing your cards at the right time in the game, with regard to the turn they are played on. You are seeking to avoid playing in either a hesitant or a hasty fashion. That is, you seek to play your cards at just the right time, so that you maximize the effect from each card. In order to do this you must look at the tradeoffs and contingencies involved. You must analyze what the ramifications of each play are and whether you are capable of dealing with any negative aspects of the play you are considering. This also entails a strong understanding of the deck you are playing.

You must be able to see the ramifications of your play in terms of what both you and your opponent can do. For example, suppose you are holding a Lightning Bolt in your hand and you are trying to decide whether now is a good time to play it in order to do damage to your opponent. Several factors should be considered in this case. The first factor you should consider is whether or not you have an alternate means to eliminate any troublesome creatures that come into play later. If you do have some alternate means of creature destruction you should also consider how many creatures an opponent might have, how large they are, and how close they are to death. If you opponent is at 6 life and you have two Lightning Bolts, it is perhaps best to kill him or her while you have the chance instead of waiting. On the other hand, if you are holding a couple of Lightning Bolts and your opponent has a large fast creature deck and 9 life, it is perhaps best to wait before casting the Bolts their way.

All your decisions about when to play cards must be seen as a contingency. You must realize what impact your play will have over the next few turns. This is an important process in learning to play your deck, because proper timing of spellcasting is imperative in order to win with your deck.

Permanent Timing

Another factor to consider when learning to play your deck is permanent timing. Permanent timing concentrates on the proper timing to use the effects of permanents in play. You must utilize the effects of your cards to their maximum advantage or you are not playing your deck to the utmost. Just as with the utilization of relationships with your cards, in order to win you seek to get more out of each of your cards than your opponent does. In other words you are looking to have higher card economy than your opponent. Thus you must seek to utilize each card to its maximum effect. For instance, when you have a Glasses of Urza it is usually best to use it after your opponent has drawn a card during his draw phase. This is the way to net the most information with the card per phase, and unless you are in desperate need of information it is almost a rule to use it at this time. Another example of proper permanent timing is the use of the Prodigal Sorcerer. If your opponent has a Will-o-the-Wisp and only one source of black mana at the end of his turn, you can kill it if you time your permanents properly. In this case the Sorcerer can tap to do a point of damage to the Wisp at the end of your opponent's turn and then once more to eliminate it.

In order to maximize the effects of your cards you must time them properly. Timing is a key element to successful game play, and it is one of the most important concepts to understand as a playing technique, since most games are essentially defined by when each card is played as well as what cards are played by each player.

Damage Threshold

Another factor that you should be familiar with is your deck's damage threshold. The damage threshold is basically a measure of how much a deck can suffer before victory is at risk. Damage thresholds mainly apply to reaction or denial decks. This is because most action decks do not consider the opponent's effect on their life total—they are primarily concerned with the reduction of an opponent's life total. Many reaction decks expect to take a certain amount of damage before they start to acquire control of the environment and can counter or overcome the actions of an opponent. In other words, these types of decks have to allow for some slack in their life points. When you play your deck, you should note where you enter the danger zone so that you know when to start making sacrifices. For example, suppose your opponent is playing a White Flash type deck with many small white creatures, and you have one Counterspell in your hand. You want to hang on to the Counterspell in order to counter a Crusade, because your opponent will net a lot more damage with that then he will by adding one more creature. However, at some point it becomes necessary to slow the bleeding in order to allow your deck to develop. Thus at some point you must give in and utilize your Counterspell on a small creature. This is simply a matter of necessity, and it is a good idea to be familiar enough with your deck to know when this necessity has arrived.

Thus learning the proper sequence and timing of your deck is essential in playing it properly. At the same time this does not amount to all of the skills necessary for good game play. You must also be able to assimilate information about an opponent's deck and process this information into a plan of action.

Chapter 12

Analyzing and Overcoming Opponents and Their Decks

Analyzing an Opponent's Deck

When you play an opponent, you should use every opportunity you can to accumulate information about his deck and deny him information about your own deck. In order to effectively analyze your opponent's deck, your analysis should be like a reverse deck design process: you dissect the opponent's deck in the reverse fashion of how you put a deck together. You need to find out just how it is cut, with what proportions and what combinations. Of particular interest are the colors, roads to victory, and their reliance on certain cards and combinations.

Note Your Opponent's Colors

The first thing a player should usually note is the color of a deck and the relative strength of each color in the deck. Once you know what colors your opponent is playing, you can narrow down his deck type. For instance, if your opponent is playing without red, you can pretty much rule out a large amount of direct damage in the deck. If you are playing against a blue player you should be wary of

What to Look For When Playing an Opponent

1. Take note of the colors of an opponent's deck.

2. Note the opponent's roads to victory.

3. Note an opponent's combinations and key elements.

4. Determine the opposing player's dependence on specific card types.

Counterspells, as it is infrequent that someone would play blue without including these versatile cards. The analysis of your opponent's colors is perhaps the easiest and fastest means to estimate the contents of an opponent's deck. While you do not glean a great deal of information, you can begin to work with it on the first turn. As soon as your opponent lays a land, you know one color in the deck and can begin to make some estimation as to what elements will be present in the deck. Thus color analysis can be a key element to victory, particularly in your first game against your opponent's deck.

Note Opponent's Roads to Victory

The second element a player should look for is an opponent's roads to victory. This is a very important element to assess, as once these are determined and isolated you can work to eliminate, or if possible, avoid them. Obviously if you can remove or sidestep all of an opponent's roads to victory he cannot win, and if you can eliminate some or many you can drastically slow down his plans. Some decks are cut with a very limited number of roads to victory. If you have the opportunity you should watch as many opponents as you can outside of tournaments and try to figure out their roads to victory. After your matches you might ask an opponent if you could see his deck and then count his roads. This is usually a good exercise to conduct in order to strengthen your ability to break down an opponent's deck. Cutting off an opponent's roads to victory is generally essential in one form or another, so it is fundamentally necessary that you be able to locate and isolate these roads.

Note Opponent's Combinations and Key Elements

Another thing to look for when playing an opponent is the existence of powerful combinations in his deck. Once you discover them, you may find that one break in the combination will lead to the deterioration of the entire chain, since some combinations have members who are very weak individually. Oftentimes destroying an important combination can seriously decrease the power of a deck overall. Many combinations contain cards that can work well independently of one another, and it is important to note when the combination must be dealt with before it reaches critical mass. Dealing with an opponent's combinations is an important skill, as it will help you to diffuse many weapons at once if done properly. This will also help you determine how much time you have before an opponent's full combination is realized and your options will be diminished.

Note Dependence of Specific Card Types

The final basic element to analyze is the reliance of an opponent on certain card types. If your opponent relies heavily on creatures, you may make assumptions about the sequencing of his play. If he relies on artifacts, you may choose to leave your Scavenger Folk untapped to eliminate any major threatening artifact after it has been cast and before it can do its damage. Reliance on a type of card is often a serious deficiency in an opponent's deck. You can often sideboard to make this deficiency consistently telling. A player who relies too heavily on one type of card is in serious trouble if his opponent has the perspicacity to notice this and act on it.

If you are able to determine your opponent's deck composition you can often use your cards to their maximum efficiency against him. For instance, if you face a heavy counterspell deck and your deck contains a large number of instants, you may wait before casting them. Most instants like Lightning Bolts, Disenchants, and Shatters are relatively cheap to cast. Once you have a number of them you can begin to cast them during your opponent's turn, forcing him or her to react then and there and tap mana before your turn. If your opponent lets them go to save his or her counters for your turn, then you get the advantage the instants provide. If your opponent makes the mistake of countering them and taps out, you typically get to cast the spell of your choice during your turn. In either contingency you come out the winner, since you created an undesirable effect in spite of your opponent's counters. Cases like these can only be realized once you understand the nature of an opponent's deck, and that's what makes the skill of assessing an opponent's deck so powerful.

There is, of course, the value of being able to determine what to sideboard against an opponent, but this usually goes without saying. Besides, your sideboard will usually not do you a lot of good in your first game of a match without prior knowledge of your opponent's deck. The strongest of players can take immediate advantage of an opponent's deck composition in a relatively short number of turns in the first match, and you should strive to be able to do this as well.

Playing Against the Opponent

One of the key factors to take into account when playing an opponent is that he is an integral part of how his deck is played. If he is playing a masterfully constructed deck and lacks the skill to match it you can often take advantage of that and capture victory even if his deck is superior.

There are a number of methods you might employ to overcome an opposing player. The first of these is simply the bluff. If your opponent attacks you with a Serra Angel and you manage to block with Scrib Sprite and cast a Giant Growth to kill it, he may think twice before making another assault if you simply hold an extra card. This card may be a land but you can play it up by attacking and then starting to tap a forest to fake the Giant Growth and feign a decision to wait to use it. This tactic has won many a player a number of games. Although considered trickery by some, at the very least, holding cards that do you no good can keep an opponent guessing and often get him to waste hand destruction cards or make mistakes.

Another method for psyching out an opponent is through the additions of red herrings in your deck. When your opponent sees you play a Lightning Bolt or a Counterspell he typically will make

decisions based on you having four of each of these cards in your deck, or at least more than one. By only including one of these in your deck, you can utilize it on the chance it comes up and then simultaneously confuse your opponent. Also, if you only have one of these cards in your deck an opponent will not expect to see it. When it is cast it should bring forth a daunted reaction. This can be both demoralizing and effective in play. Another advantage of the red herring is that it provides excellent support for the bluff.

If you can demoralize an opponent he is more likely to make mistakes. This is a good tactic in tournament play. A demoralizing victory in the first round may lead to an easy victory in the second round, because your opponent will make mistakes. Many action decks have this effect, especially when they perform particularly well. For instance, Juzam Djinn decks have a tendency to intimidate an opponent when a Juzam is cast on the first turn. In some cases it is more beneficial to take some tactical disadvantage if you can increase the demoralization factor to improve your chances in the next game. In most cases when you make such a decision, victory should be well within your sight.

There are also some players that go so far to "talk trash." These players insult or intimidate an opponent into making mistakes by verbally attempting to demoralize him. This is generally not considered good sportsmanship and should be avoided if possible.

Sometimes you can glean information about an opponent's deck by the way he plays it. If he leaves a number of lands untapped you can figure that he is playing some form of reactive deck. If he is continually tapping out to launch offensives, it is usually quite obvious that he is playing an action-type deck.

Once you come to terms with and understand an opponent and his or her deck, you generally can make action predictions. Some decks and even their players are repetitive and make simple plays. When this is the case you should not suffer from any surprises, even when your opponent and his deck are effective. Often you will find yourself predicting cards before they are even played. This information may make the difference in a game or even a match and should therefore be practiced and mastered.

Chapter 13

Type I Tournament Structure

Type I tournaments were the first of the convocation tournament structures. Type I has the largest card base available relative to the other tournament types. With over thirteen hundred cards to choose from, Type I tournaments have the greatest potential for deck diversity. Unfortunately, potential is not always equivalent to fact in many tournaments.

Type I decks vary greatly in power. Many of the more successful tournament decks are loaded with restricted cards.

Restricted Cards Frequently Found in Type I Tournament Decks

1. Ancestral Recall	10. Library of Alexandria
2. Time Walk	11. Mox Emerald
3. Timetwister	12. Mox Jet
4. Recall	13. Mox Sapphire
5. Braingeyser	14. Mox Pearl
6. Wheel of Fortune	15. Mox Ruby
7. Demonic Tutor	16. Black Lotus
8. Mind Twist	17. Ivory Tower
9. Regrowth	18. Chaos Orb

If you were to examine all of the Type I decks that consistently win tournaments you would typically find at least a few of the cards mentioned in this list. This tends to leave very few cards to make an original deck. If you have already filled up twelve card slots it leaves you with only forty-eight slots, and a large portion of those will be filled with land. On the other hand, it is also possible that these decks would be vulnerable to being preyed on by certain decks, since such a high percentage of decks include some of these cards.

The tendency of Type I decks to concentrate on the restricted cards also makes Type I tournaments difficult for new players to be successful in. With the exception of the Ivory Tower and Mind Twist, all of the aforementioned cards are out of print and relatively difficult and expensive to acquire. This makes the winner's circle in Type I rather small and exclusive. On the other hand it is certainly not impossible to obtain these cards, and with some perserverence and a great deal of trading, a neophyte could manage to amass sufficient cards to compete in Type I play.

Another narrowing factor is that as the game progresses and new sets are published it seems that the cards are becoming more balanced. There tends to be a lack of the extremely powerful cards like those that came from Legends, Antiquities, and Arabian Nights. Most of the high-powered out-of-prints like the Juzam Djinn, Diamond Valley, The Abyss, Mana Drain, Living Plane, Nether Void, and the Argivian Archaeologist are just too powerful to compare to cards provided in the newer sets.

Most Type I decks were also laden with twelve to sixteen mixed lands, making them even more difficult to acquire. Each of the rare mixed lands cost a considerable cash investment. This typically drove the price of Type I decks up to at least a hundred dollars in card value. Of course until Revised Four, mixed lands were still in-print cards and could still be acquired by buying booster packs and starter decks.

Because the out-of-print and mixed land cards tend to be difficult and expensive to acquire, many of the more powerful Type I decks have a net value of over $500. This makes many of the more powerful decks much too expensive for any new player to even hope to be able to afford. There is a large amount of new and creative blood that is simply excluded because these new players simply lack the monetary ability to participate in Type I tournaments. At the same time, Type I play can factor in your trading skill. Contrary to popular belief it is possible, if difficult, to trade revised cards for valuable out-of-prints. Doing this, however, may become worthless, since the popularity of Type I play is declining because of the large group of new players who didn't have an opportunity to buy the early sets and are unable to trade for these cards.

Even with a base of over thirteen hundred cards it is often quite typical to see the same cards and decks over and over again. Most of the winning Type I decks are cut either with a large number of Counterspells or land destruction. Though these are often

secondary themes they are in at least eighty percent of the successful Type I decks. Before the recent balance restriction, balance
decks were the third most common winning Type I deck type, but
now it is narrowed to two.

The only chance a new player generally has in Type I is typically
with a small fast creature deck. If these decks are afforded a good
draw or if the opposing player has a poor draw, these decks can
occasionally capture victory. Though there are exceptions, for the
most part these decks do not possess the power or the ability to take
first at a major tournament. The only other possibility is to be very
creative.

It is our belief that Type I tournaments are on their way out.
Though there are a number of out-of-prints that add interest to
Type I tournaments, the unequal balance of card power lends them
a tendency to be overlooked and ignored because of more powerful
cards that demand their space in decks. Type I tournaments will
most likely be replaced by Type II tournaments. Though this may
upset a number of Type I players, it will level the playing field so
the competiton will be more diversified. Some believe at the same
time, however, that the majority of the good players already have
these cards and that Type I play is more interesting since there are
more options from the larger card set. However, Type I is certainly
not applicable for all readers. It is for this reason that the decks we
provide in the appendixes focus on Type II tournament regulations
instead of Type I.

Chapter 14

Type II
Tournament Structure

Fourth Edition and Its Effect on Type II

Type II tournaments are played with the base set and the last two expansion sets. With the release of the Fourth Edition set there were a number of changes to the base set of cards for Type II tournaments. Perhaps the major change was the elimination of mixed lands from the set. Before the release of Fourth Edition, most of the Type II tournament decks were laden with at least a dozen mixed lands. Now that Fourth Edition has returned without mixed lands, an even larger number of people can play Type II tournaments competitively. At the same time, in order to allow more people to play, the variety of the decks was once again sacrificed. Some decks that were good decks just a few days before the release of Revised Four are now impossible to make.

Besides mixed lands, a number of major changes occurred with the introduction of Fourth Edition cards—most notably the reduction of limited cards. The only limited cards left in the Type II card pool are the Balance, Mind Twist, Ivory Tower, Zuran Orb*, and Channel. This will more than likely improve tournaments and reduce the amount of luck involved. People will no

* Although not restricted at the time of writing, it is anticipated that the Zuran Orb will be restricted in the future.

93

longer sigh with regret when an opponent plays a Sol Ring or Ancestral Recall on the first turn.

The restriction of Balance and the addition of many of the more powerful creatures (Killer Bees, Carrion Ants, Clay Statue, Colossus of Sardia) and creature enhancements (Immolation, Blood Lust) tends to suggest that Wizards of the Coast is trying to make creatures more profitable to play. Without Balance as a non-restricted card, the six remaining mass creature destruction spells (Nevinyrral's Disk, Wrath of God, Pestilence, Hurricane, Volcanic Eruption, and Earthquake) cost considerably more. This seems to be a typical example of underpowered cards becoming overpowered. Because creatures were so fragile, Wizards of the Coast is making changes that will help bring them back into popular use, so they will probably swing back. Creatures could always be useful if played correctly, but since such a high percentage of the card pool consists of summon cards, it seems only fair that they should be generally more useful.

Type II Power Decks

Though there are a number of powerful decks in Type II, none seem to greatly overshadow the others. Under the Third Edition, the balance of power leaned toward hand destruction. Instead of diminishing the power of hand destruction, the other deck types simply had their deck strength increased.

With the addition of Strip Mines, Blights, Icequakes, and Thermokarsts, Wizards of the Coast opened up the possibility for light land destruction for Type II. This is perhaps because they wanted to allow it to be used as a secondary deck theme but not a primary one. Blights are not bad cards but they are certainly not as powerful as Sinkholes. It seems that land destruction can now be used more to slow an opponent down instead of simply not allowing him to have enough land to cast any of his spells.

Stasis decks also seem to have gained in power. The addition of Kismet, Twiddle, Zephyr Falcon, Yotian Soldiers, and Time Elementals make Stasis decks some of the most formidable. You can maintain a permanent Stasis with the Time Elemental by using the Elemental to pick up the Stasis at the end of your opponent's turn.

Then you can follow up during your turn by casting the Stasis again. If you have out a Kismet during all of this you will be able to isolate an opponent into having virtually no options. Wizards of the Coast left open the possibility of obtaining a total lock with these additions.

Type II hand destruction decks have always been powerful. The Hymn to Tourach, Mind Twist, Mind Ravel, Mind Warp, and Disrupting Scepter make Type II hand destruction crippling. The Psychic Purge, one of the most powerful anti-hand destruction cards, has been removed, giving these decks a free reign to do their worst without inhibition. These decks become particularly ridiculous with counter magic. Thus if any Type II deck is over-powered it is hand destruction, due to the absence of the Psychic Purge, a malignant side effect of the reduced card set.

Most of the fast creature decks come from either black, white, or green. Black's Dark Ritual and the Mana Vault make it much easier to deploy large creatures early on. Green's Wild Growth, Lanowar Elves, Fyndhorn Elves, Orcish Lumberjacks, Birds of Paradise, and Elves of Deep Shadow make it perhaps the fastest mana-producing color. This makes it particularly easy to generate large creatures quickly like Craw Wurms, Forces of Nature, Scaled Wurms, Lhurgoyfs, Kjeldoran Warriors, and Feral Thallids.

White's small creature deck is also now even more deadly than before. The addition of Tundra Wolves, Land Tax, and Winds of Change make the white/red turbo deck extremely quick. These decks along with the green large creature decks are some of the fastest of the Type II action based decks.

Counter decks were perhaps hurt a bit by the addition of Strip Mines and Mishra's Factories. The introduction of the Strip Mine and Mishra's Factory have added greater diversity to Type II. Type II decks now have a more active role for the land card type, increasing its value as a factor to be considered. The counter decks did benefit from the addition of the Time Elemental. The Elemental's ability to force an opponent to pick up a permanent helps with most counter decks' difficulty in dealing with permanents.

Overall, the changes in Revised Four and the addition of Ice Age did improve Type II play; however, a few changes harmed its diversity. Blue suffered a minor decrease in power, essentially reducing it to an all-counterspell color. Many new players will find it easy to compete in Type II tournaments without a large investment in cards, but many proponents of Type I are dissatisfied with the new emphasis on Type II. Thus the changes in Revised Four were mixed in nature.

Chapter 15

Conclusion

You have now reached the end of a long course of advice, exhortation, and instruction. It may seem that you have been given too much information to be able to apply all of it at once to your current designs for a strong tournament deck. Or again you may think that you have been told many useful things but not the details that you need to immediately improve your deck-designing skills. Either way, your study of this book has not been in vain. Hopefully you have begun to analyze your normal habits and can now reflect on the questions this book has brought to mind.

You probably had a number of your own ideas about deck design before reading this book, and now those views are either reinforced or challenged. In any case you are focused on improving your decks and understanding the game. This is what this book is intended to induce—critical analysis of deck design. We are still learning and still searching to learn faster, stronger, and more effective means to construct the most powerful of decks.

Deck design is a science, and like other sciences you can reach an understanding of it through experimentation, study, and observation. Though there is an element of randomness to Magic, the challenge is to reduce that random factor to a minimum until consistency begins to flood out the chaos. Whether you play Type II, I, or even III, you will find that the majority of the basic rules are consistent from one tournament type to another. Even if you feel you have an understanding of all of the possible relationships, combinations, and play tactics, you will find that there are different ways of amalgamating the skills and knowledge to take an even greater step toward to being the ultimate deck architect.

Appendix A

Type I Decks

This appendix contains representations of the five basic decks for Type I and five tournament-quality deck examples. The five basic decks are for design testing and are not intended as tournament decks. They are made to draw out flaws in deck design. The other decks are actual tournament decks played at one time by different highly skilled players. The tournament decks are shown as examples of applications of the principles stated earlier in this book.

FBD Type I Burn decks

In Type I tournaments burn decks are not as common as they used to be. This is because they are usually easily overcome by white/blue decks with a large number of Counterspells and C.O.P. Reds in the sideboard. Though the Fireballs, Disintegrates, Lightning Bolts, and Chain Lightnings provide a good defense for a well constructed burn deck, they are usually weak to many decks.

It is rare to find an experienced player using a burn deck. Most experienced players shun burn decks for more complicated and intricate decks. Burn decks are usually very narrow in scope and suffer from too narrow roads to victory.

These decks can be devastating, however, against any deck that is not prepared to face them. Though these decks will not win tournaments, they will knock out some unsuspecting players early on. It is generally wise to test your deck against one of these red menaces to ensure that you will not fall prey to them.

As with the other members of the five basic decks, these are mainly included not so much as examples but as good decks to make sure your deck is not susceptible to this kind of attack. They seek to point out weaknesses in your deck and highlight them so you can correct them. Generally a burn deck, unless very well constructed, will not win without some other side theme present in the deck.

Deck Name: FBD Type I: Burn Deck

Block One	Block Two	Block Three
Pocket 1	Pocket 1	Pocket 1
Fireball	Candelabra of Tawnos	Mox Sapphire
Fireball	Wheel of Fortune	Mox Ruby
Fireball	Sol Ring	Mox Pearl
Incinerate	Fork	Mountain
Pocket 2	Pocket 2	Pocket 2
Incinerate	Incinerate	Plateau
Disintegrate	Incinerate	Plateau
Disintegrate	Mana Flare	Plateau
Disintegrate	Mana Flare	Plateau
Pocket 3	Pocket 3	Pocket 3
Earthquake	Disenchant	Savannah
Earthquake	Disenchant	Savannah
Earthquake	Disenchant	Savannah
Hurricane	Lotus	Savannah
Pocket 4	Pocket 4	Pocket 4
Lightning Bolt	Fastbond	Taiga
Lightning Bolt	Fastbond	Taiga
Lightning Bolt	Fastbond	Taiga
Lightning Bolt	Howling Mine	Taiga
Pocket 5	Pocket 5	Pocket 5
Chain Lightning	Howling Mine	Mountain
Chain Lightning	Howling Mine	Mountain

| Chain Lightning | Mox Jet | Forest |
| Chain Lightning | Mox Emerald | Forest |

Sideboard

1. Land Tax	6. Red Elemental Blast	11. Tsunami
2. Land Tax	7. Red Elemental Blast	12. Black Vise
3. Land Tax	8. Hurricane	13. Black Vise
4. Red Elemental Blast	9. Disenchant	14. Black Vise
5. Red Elemental Blast	10. Tsunami	15. Black Vise

FBD: Counterspell Decks (Type I)

Though counterspell decks are weak in Type II they are one of the most powerful deck types in Type I. In Type I the counterspell decks are more powerful because they have the extra power of Mana Drains which add speed and development power. These decks are also called sit and wait decks. If you have four mana available you don't rush to play a Juggernaut if one is in your hand. You generally wait until you have enough mana to cast a Counterspell and a Juggernaut so you can protect it once it comes into play.

Mana Drains make these decks extremely deadly. For instance, if an opponent casts a spell that costs four mana, a Mana Drain will allow you to play a Juggernaut for virtually nothing.

In most cases these decks fare well against all of the deck types, with the exception of small fast creature decks. Though these decks can be overcome with a small addition of red mana for Earthquakes or Pyroclasms, they can often claim victory in the first game of a match. Land destruction decks are also somewhat troublesome for counterspell decks. If a land destruction deck uses Black Vises and Strip Mines, it can be particularly annoying for a counterspell deck. If the counterspell deck is allowed to have over three sources of blue mana there is a very small chance that the land destruction deck will be able to slip in more land destruction unless the counterspell deck's controller makes some fatal error.

Deck Name: FBD Type I: Counterspell Deck

Block One	Block Two	Block Three
Pocket 1	**Pocket 1**	**Pocket 1**
Counterspell	Control Magic	Sol Ring
Counterspell	Control Magic	Black Lotus
Counterspell	Control Magic	Island
Counterspell	Glasses of Urza	Island
Pocket 2	**Pocket 2**	**Pocket 2**
Mana Drain	Mahamoti Djinn	Island
Mana Drain	Mahamoti Djinn	Island
Mana Drain	Mahamoti Djinn	Island
Mana Drain	Chaos Orb	Island
Pocket 3	**Pocket 3**	**Pocket 3**
Power Sink	Juggernaut	Island
Power Sink	Juggernaut	Island
Time Elemental	Juggernaut	Island
Time Elemental	Juggernaut	Island
Pocket 4	**Pocket 4**	**Pocket 4**
Blood Moon	Icy Manipulator	Island
Earthquake	Icy Manipulator	Island
Earthquake	Icy Manipulator	Mountain
Timetwister	Mox Jet	Mountain
Pocket 5	**Pocket 5**	**Pocket 5**
Time Walk	Mox Pearl	Volcanic Island
Ancestral Recall	Mox Sapphire	Volcanic Island
Ancestral Recall	Mox Ruby	Volcanic Island
Jayemdae Tome	Mox Emerald	Volcanic Island

Sideboard

1. Island
2. Island
3. Island
4. Earthquake
5. Earthquake
6. Power Sink
7. Power Sink
8. Pyroblast
9. Pyroblast
10. Blood Moon
11. Blood Moon
12. Strip Mine
13. Strip Mine
14. Strip Mine
15. Strip Mine

FBD Type I: Fast Creature Decks

There are many strategies in Magic to achieve the most effective deck. The most common and reliable effective tournament decks are the action-based fast decks. These decks are designed to eliminate an opponent before he or she can develop. There are numerous ways to go about constructing this type of deck. Most action-based fast decks are creature decks.

There are two different widely used strategies for the construction of fast action-based creature decks. The first is the multiple small fast creature deck and the second is the singular large fast creature deck. Both types of decks can be very effective and deal a large amount of damage early in the game. If a fast deck plays for longer than ten rounds, then it has probably failed in its ability to inflict damage on an opponent. All fast action-based creature decks are designed for a quick kill and often have manifest weaknesses that will become evident if your opponent survives to exploit them.

FBD Type I: Fast Creature (Large)

The large fast creature deck is usually not as common as the small fast creature deck because of its expense. These decks tend to make a large investment in cards in the form of fast mana to summon a large creature early in the game. These creatures tend to have a greater durability than their smaller counterparts but they also have a tendency to be isolated and more susceptible to one-shot elimination. Cards like Swords to Plowshares, Unsummon, and Paralyze are typically great obstacles for large fast creature decks.

These decks typically rely on an opponent's inability to respond to their attacks. This particular large fast creature deck is modeled after one designed by Robert Utley. The Swords to Plowshares and Lightning Bolts are usually used to eliminate an opponent's blockers so the large creatures can get through to their controllers.

Deck Name: FBD Type I: Fast Creature 1

Block One	Block Two	Block Three
Pocket 1	Pocket 1	Pocket 1
Juzam Djinn	Strip Mine	Underground Sea
Juzam Djinn	Strip Mine	Underground Sea
Juzam Djinn	Strip Mine	Underground Sea
Juzam Djinn	Strip Mine	Underground Sea
Pocket 2	Pocket 2	Pocket 2
Juggernaut	Mishra's Factory	Badlands
Juggernaut	Mishra's Factory	Badlands
Juggernaut	Mishra's Factory	Badlands
Juggernaut	Mishra's Factory	Badlands
Pocket 3	Pocket 3	Pocket 3
Lightning Bolt	Mind Twist	Scrubland
Lightning Bolt	Spirit Link	Scrubland
Lightning Bolt	Spirit Link	Scrubland
Vampire	Spirit Link	Scrubland
Pocket 4	Pocket 4	Pocket 4
Vampire	Disenchant	Plateau
Swords to Plowshares	Disenchant	Plateau
Swords to Plowshares	Disenchant	Swamp
Swords to Plowshares	Chaos Orb	Mox Jet
Pocket 5	Pocket 5	Pocket 5
Dark Ritual	Sol Ring	Mox Ruby
Dark Ritual	Black Lotus	Mox Emerald
Dark Ritual	Ancestral Recall	Mox Sapphire
Dark Ritual	Time Walk	Mox Pearl

Sideboard

1. Disenchant
2. Swords to Plowshares
3. Lightning Bolt
4. Pyroblast
5. Pyroblast
6. Pyroblast
7. Disintegrate
8. Disintegrate
9. Disintegrate
10. Black Vise
11. Black Vise
12. Black Vise
13. Hurkyl's Recall
14. Earthquake
15. Earthquake

FBD Type I: Fast Creature Deck (Small)

Fast small creatures decks in Type I are typically not as effective as they are in Type II. The difference between the two is not really that great. In Type II you have many of the same cards without the spoilers.

Also in Type II there are not as many mass creature destruction cards like the Drop of Honey and Abyss. These cards typically can prevent small creature decks from having successful assaults.

This particular small creature deck is rather simple. It is cut so you deploy as many creatures as you can and swamp your opponent. The Lightning Bolts, Incinerates, and Chain Lightning are used to eliminate an opponent's creatures. There are no flying creatures in this deck and there is often a need to sideboard in Hurricanes.

Deck Name: FBD Type I: Fast Creature Deck II

Block One	Block Two	Block Three
Pocket 1	Pocket 1	Pocket 1
Kird Ape	Wyluli Wolf	Chain Lightning
Kird Ape	Wyluli Wolf	Chain Lightning
Kird Ape	Wyluli Wolf	Black Lotus
Kird Ape	Wyluli Wolf	Mox Sapphire
Pocket 2	Pocket 2	Pocket 2
Elvish Archers	Storm Bind	Mox Emerald
Elvish Archers	Storm Bind	Mox Ruby
Elvish Archers	Winter Orb	Forest
Wheel of Fortune	Winter Orb	Mountain
Pocket 3	Pocket 3	Pocket 3
Thallid	Incinerate	Taiga
Thallid	Incinerate	Taiga
Thallid	Incinerate	Taiga
Thallid	Incinerate	Taiga
Pocket 4	Pocket 4	Pocket 4
Scavenger Folk	Regrowth	Volcanic Island
Scavenger Folk	Time Walk	Volcanic Island
Scavenger Folk	Ancestral Recall	Volcanic Island
Timber Wolf	Timetwister	Volcanic Island

Pocket 5	Pocket 5	Pocket 5
Timber Wolf	Lightning Bolt	Tropical Island
Atog	Lightning Bolt	Tropical Island
Atog	Lightning Bolt	Forest
Atog	Lightning Bolt	Forest

Sideboard

1. Black Vise
2. Black Vise
3. Black Vise
4. Black Vise
5. Hurricane
6. Winter Orb
7. Chain Lightning
8. Chain Lightning
9. Strip Mine
10. Strip Mine
11. Hydroblast
12. Hydroblast
13. Hydroblast
14. Hydroblast
15. Meekstone

FBD: Hand Destruction Decks (Type I)

Hand destruction is more common in Type II than in Type I. Though hand destruction has grown in power since the introduction of the Hymn to Tourach and the Mindstab Thrull in the Fallen Empires Limited set and the Mind Ravel, Abyssal Specter, and Mind Warp in the Ice Age expansion set, it is still not quite comparable to counter or land destruction decks. In most cases these decks tend to sputter out after the first ten turns. Opponents start to play cards as they draw them. When this occurs cards like the Hymns and Mind Twist tend to be useless. Hand destruction is usually not as effective unless it is supplemented with Counterspells.

Hand destruction decks are usually weaker in Type I than in Type II. The Psychic Purge can often make these decks suffer greatly. The Purge is not quite as much as a threat to a hand destruction deck unless it is in an action-based deck with multiple sources of damage. This particular deck has a number of side items to make it more effective. Hand destruction and Time Elementals or Unsummons can be extremely effective. Also the Racks usually prove to be an effective source of damage. Regardless of these powerful combinations, hand destruction is not particularly common as a major theme in Type I play.

Deck Name: FBD Type I: Hand Destruction Deck

Block One	Block Two	Block Three
Pocket 1	Pocket 1	Pocket 1
Hymn to Tourach	Gwendlyn Di Corci	Mox Jet
Hymn to Tourach	Time Walk	Mox Sapphire
Hymn to Tourach	Recall	Mox Ruby
Hymn to Tourach	Chaos Orb	Sol Ring
Pocket 2	Pocket 2	Pocket 2
Mind Twist	Hypnotic Specter	Lotus
Disrupting Scepter	Hypnotic Specter	Swamp
Disrupting Scepter	Hypnotic Specter	Swamp
Ancestral Recall	Hypnotic Specter	Swamp
Pocket 3	Pocket 3	Pocket 3
Rack	Time Elemental	Underground Sea
Rack	Time Elemental	Underground Sea
Rack	Sedge Troll	Underground Sea
Rack	Sedge Troll	Underground Sea
Pocket 4	Pocket 4	Pocket 4
Dark Ritual	Lightning Bolt	Badlands
Dark Ritual	Lightning Bolt	Badlands
Dark Ritual	Unsummon	Badlands
Dark Ritual	Unsummon	Badlands
Pocket 5	Pocket 5	Pocket 5
Storm World	Mishra's Factory	Volcanic Island
Storm World	Mishra's Factory	Volcanic Island
Vampire	Mishra's Factory	Volcanic Island
Vampire	Mishra's Factory	Volcanic Island

Sideboard

1. Lightning Bolt
2. Lightning Bolt
3. Disintegrate
4. Disintegrate
5. Shatter
6. Shatter
7. Earthquake
8. Earthquake
9. Earthquake
10. Earthquake
11. Unsummon
12. Unsummon
13. Hurkyl's Recall
14. Hurkyl's Recall
15. Sedge Troll

FBD Type I: Land Destruction Decks

In Type I tournaments one of the two most powerful deck types is land destruction. If constructed properly these decks will usually have at least a fifty/fifty chance against any other deck. One of the difficulties that land destruction decks face is that they usually dedicate a large number of cards to land destruction and fast mana to support that land destruction. Usually these decks rely on cards like Black Vises to eliminate an opponent. Sometimes they will add a couple of large creatures to help administer the blow.

A recent trend among land destruction players is the employment of a Nether Void. This Legends enchant world requires that all players' spells from that point on cost three extra mana. When this is combined with land destruction it makes it that much more difficult for an opponent to recover.

In most cases it is best to be able to eliminate an opponent's land on at least the second turn. The addition of Birds of Paradise can usually make this possible. Unfortunately these creatures tend to be the target of early Lightning Bolts and many land destruction proponents question their employment.

Land destruction decks usually have one great problem. They have difficulty in dealing with decks that have small inexpensive creatures. There are a number of methods for overcoming these decks. Some decks use Earthquakes, The Abyss, or Drop of Honey. For the most part, if a land destruction deck is constructed properly, there is little chance that it will be easily defeated by small creature decks.

Deck Name: FBD Type I: Land Destruction

Block One	Block Two	Block Three
Pocket 1	Pocket 1	Pocket 1
Sinkhole	Birds of Paradise	Mox Ruby
Sinkhole	Birds of Paradise	Mox Jet
Sinkhole	Birds of Paradise	Mox Sapphire
Black Vise	Demonic Tutor	Mox Emerald
Pocket 2	Pocket 2	Pocket 2
Black Vise	Time Walk	Mox Pearl

Ice Storm	Lightning Bolt	Sol Ring
Ice Storm	Lightning Bolt	Black Lotus
Ice Storm	Lightning Bolt	Chaos Orb
Pocket 3	Pocket 3	Pocket 3
Black Vise	Shiven Dragon	Bayou
Stone Rain	Shiven Dragon	Bayou
Stone Rain	Shiven Dragon	Bayou
Stone Rain	Ancestral Recall	Bayou
Pocket 4	Pocket 4	Pocket 4
Strip Mine	Timetwister	Badlands
Strip Mine	Wheel of Fortune	Badlands
Strip Mine	Nether Void	Badlands
Strip Mine	Nether Void	Badlands
Pocket 5	Pocket 5	Pocket 5
Detonate	Mishra's Factory	Taiga
Detonate	Mishra's Factory	Taiga
Crumble	Mishra's Factory	Taiga
Crumble	Mishra's Factory	Taiga

Sideboard

1. Crumble
2. Crumble
3. Earthquake
4. Earthquake
5. Earthquake
6. Paralyze
7. Paralyze
8. Paralyze
9. Paralyze
10. Fireball
11. Fireball
12. Black Vise
13. Red Elemental Blast
14. Red Elemental Blast
15. Red Elemental Blast

Granville's Explosion Deck

Granville Wright made perhaps the fastest and most devastating deck ever seen when he put together his explosion deck. It is the ultimate in action-based decks. The creatures it employs are generally very cost-efficient and most of them fly. This means that the majority of them will be difficult to block. Once one got through it would be Giant Growthed, Blood Lusted, and Mutated. Needless to say, the explosion deck's Birds of Paradise could get very nasty.

There was one major problem with the explosion deck—it would fizzle every once in a while. Sometimes you would draw two Unstable Mutations, two Giant Growths, two Tropical Islands, and two Blood Lusts. The explosion deck could probably beat any deck at least thirty-five percent of the time but unfortunately any deck can probably beat the explosion deck fifteen percent of the time. The only major problems that the explosion deck experiences are a few individual cards. These are Fog, Darkness, Holy Day, and Unsummon. These can often make a Giant Growthed, Blood Lusted, Unstably Mutated, Berserking, 22/22 Scrib Sprite look pretty silly.

Deck Name: Granville's Explosion Deck

Block One	Block Two	Block Three
Pocket 1	Pocket 1	Pocket 1
Kird Ape	Unstable Mutation	Pendelhaven
Kird Ape	Unstable Mutation	Volcanic Island
Kird Ape	Unstable Mutation	Volcanic Island
Kird Ape	Unstable Mutation	Volcanic Island
Pocket 2	Pocket 2	Pocket 2
Scrib Sprite	Giant Growth	Tropical Island
Scrib Sprite	Giant Growth	Tropical Island
Scrib Sprite	Giant Growth	Tropical Island
Scrib Sprite	Giant Growth	City of Brass
Pocket 3	Pocket 3	Pocket 3
Flying Man	Birds of Paradise	Island
Flying Man	Birds of Paradise	Island
Flying Man	Birds of Paradise	Forest
Wheel of Fortune	Timetwister	City of Brass
Pocket 4	Pocket 4	Pocket 4
Serendib Efreet	Lightning Bolt	Taiga
Serendib Efreet	Lightning Bolt	Taiga
Serendib Efreet	Lightning Bolt	Taiga
Time Walk	Lightning Bolt	Ancestral Recall
Pocket 5	Pocket 5	Pocket 5
Blood Lust	Chain Lightning	Mox Emerald
Blood Lust	Chain Lightning	Mox Pearl

Blood Lust	Regrowth	Mox Ruby
Blood Lust	Berserk	Black Lotus

Sideboard

1. Blue Elemental Blast
2. Blue Elemental Blast
3. Blue Elemental Blast
4. Red Elemental Blast
5. Red Elemental Blast
6. Red Elemental Blast
7. Strip Mine
8. Strip Mine
9. Concordant Crossroads
10. Concordant Crossroads
11. Concordant Crossroads
12. Chain Lightning
13. Chain Lightning
14. Psionic Blast
15. Psionic Blast

The House of Pain (Type I deck)

The House of Pain upon the first glance may seem to most players just another Djinn deck when in reality it is a roads to victory deck. The deck is loaded with different ways to deal damage. There are sources of damage from all seven card types. An opposing deck might head off one but it will suffer to another. The light mix of land destruction with fast creatures can often devastate an opponent. If a Djinn comes out early, an opponent typically has only four turns to eliminate it. While they are struggling to remove the Djinn, the land destruction typically reduces their reactionary options and slows the speed at which they can get rid of cards. This puts them at the mercy of the Black Vises. Once the Underworld Dreams is in play the Timetwister and Wheel of Fortune become deadly, especially with a number of Vises in play.

Once a number of powerful permanents are in play the Nether Voids make it difficult for the opponent to recover. The Nether Void should be less damaging to the House of Pain than to an opponent's deck for a number of reasons. The first is the fact that the Mishra's Factories and Strip Mines have no casting cost and will be unaffected by the Void. More than likely you have been able to eliminate a number of your opponent's lands, making his or her speed of casting a great deal slower than your own.

The Detonates are usually reserved for eliminating an opponent's artifact mana. These can be devastating because they typically only take one red mana to eliminate a Mox. In the later game they can serve as another source of damage.

Though the Sedge Trolls are good for stopping small creature decks they often prove to be inadequate for eliminating white turbo decks. These decks generally prove to be the greatest difficulty for the House of Pain. When facing them you should add the Glooms, Earthquakes, the Fireball, and extra Lightning Bolts. Also you might lose the Black Vises and Detonates.

Deck Name: House of Pain

Block One	Block Two	Block Three
Pocket 1	Pocket 1	Pocket 1
Juzam Djinn	Timetwister	Mox Jet
Juzam Djinn	Wheel of Fortune	Mox Ruby
Juzam Djinn	Time Walk	Mox Sapphire
Juzam Djinn	Ancestral Recall	Mox Pearl
Pocket 2	Pocket 2	Pocket 2
Sedge Troll	Nether Void	Mox Emerald
Sedge Troll	Nether Void	Lotus
Sedge Troll	Detonate	Sol Ring
Earthquake	Detonate	Chaos Orb
Pocket 3	Pocket 3	Pocket 3
Mishra's Factory	Stone Rain	Badlands
Mishra's Factory	Stone Rain	Badlands
Mishra's Factory	Stone Rain	Badlands
Mishra's Factory	Stone Rain	Badlands
Pocket 4	Pocket 4	Pocket 4
Strip Mine	Sinkhole	Underground Sea
Strip Mine	Sinkhole	Underground Sea
Strip Mine	Lightning Bolt	Underground Sea
Strip Mine	Lightning Bolt	Underground Sea
Pocket 5	Pocket 5	Pocket 5
Black Vise	Lightning Bolt	Demonic Tutor
Black Vise	Dark Ritual	Volcanic Island
Black Vise	Dark Ritual	Volcanic Island
Underworld Dreams	Dark Ritual	Volcanic Island

Sideboard

1. Detonate	6. Fireball	11. Unsummon
2. Shatter	7. Hurkyl's Recall	12. Unsummon
3. Lightning Bolt	8. Gloom	13. Blue Elemental Blast
4. Earthquake	9. Gloom	14. Blue Elemental Blast
5. Earthquake	10. Gloom	15. Blue Elemental Blast

Matt's Eureka Deck (Type I)

Matt Scoggins, a member of the Palace crew, is often searching for an unusual or unique deck. This is one that he put together and enjoyed some measure of success with. The basic idea of the Eureka deck was to play a Eureka and a number of large trampling creatures and then play a Concordant Crossroads and hit an opponent for a large amount of damage.

Generally one round of punishment with the large creatures in this deck is enough to put an opponent out of the game. Simply laying three creatures which do five damage and a Concordant Crossroads to allow them to attack lets you inflict a massive amount of damage on your opponent very quickly.

The deck has enough mana that it can usually cast some of its creatures if a Eureka is not drawn or countered. The Nevinyrral's Disk can help to clear the play area before the Eureka is cast. The major weakness this deck suffers from is counterspell decks. These decks tend to make it very difficult to get the Eureka off, and since the power in this deck is mainly distributed into a few major cards during any given game, countering these specific cards will usually cause serious problems for the Eureka deck.

At the same time, the deck has excellent surprise value and can be very demoralizing to an opponent. Going from a winning position to death in one round can cause your opponent to make mistakes in the next game because he fears the same thing happening again.

Deck Name: Matt's Eureka Deck

Block One	Block Two	Block Three
Pocket 1	Pocket 1	Pocket 1
Eureka	Colossus	Tropical Island
Eureka	Colossus	Tropical Island
Eureka	Colossus	Tropical Island
Eureka	Colossus	Tropical Island
Pocket 2	Pocket 2	Pocket 2
Concordant Crossroads	Nevinyrral's Disk	Forest
Concordant Crossroads	Nevinyrral's Disk	Forest
Concordant Crossroads	Nevinyrral's Disk	Forest
Time Walk	Chaos Orb	Forest
Pocket 3	Pocket 3	Pocket 3
Craw Wurm	Mana Drain	Forest
Craw Wurm	Mana Drain	Forest
Llanowar Elves	Mana Drain	Forest
Llanowar Elves	Mana Drain	Forest
Pocket 4	Pocket 4	Pocket 4
Craw Giant	Clone	Forest
Craw Giant	Clone	Forest
Craw Giant	Mox Sapphire	Island
Craw Giant	Mox Emerald	Island
Pocket 5	Pocket 5	Pocket 5
Regrowth	Sol Ring	Island
Berserk	Lotus	Island
Ancestral Recall	Mishra's Factory	Island
Ancestral Recall	Mishra's Factory	Island

Sideboard

1. Unsummon	6. Clone	11. Crumble
2. Unsummon	7. Energy Flux	12. Strip Mine
3. Unsummon	8. Energy Flux	13. Strip Mine
4. Tranquility	9. Crumble	14. Strip Mine
5. Tranquility	10. Crumble	15. Strip Mine

Corey's Void/Disk Deck (Type I)

Corey Segal took a long time and a great amount of trouble to produce this deck. The original idea behind the Void/Disk deck was to eliminate an opponent's land and then destroy all of his artifact mana and permanents with the Nevinyrral's Disk, leaving him with nothing. After this occurred the Nether Void was to follow in sequence. This deck is an exceptional example of utilizing sequential play.

Later it was suggested that Corey add Rukh Eggs. They would make the Disks just that much more effective and increase the number of the deck's roads to victory. After the Disk goes off Corey simply regenerates his Trolls and then brings two Rukhs into play. The Black Vises and the artifact mana are the only cards that are likely to be damaged by the use of the Disk. In most cases the loss for the Void/Disk's controller is not as significant as the loss experienced by an opponent.

Corey did relatively well in the last few tournaments he played with this deck. The deck tends to do well against all of the five basic deck types, except for decks that use a mixture of hand destruction and counter magic. Like most decks, once the Void/Disk deck begins to lose card economy it becomes very difficult for it to recover.

Deck Name: Corey's Void/Disk Deck

Block One	Block Two	Block Three
Pocket 1	Pocket 1	Pocket 1
Strip Mine	Nevinyrral's Disk	Mox Jet
Strip Mine	Nevinyrral's Disk	Mox Pearl
Strip Mine	Nevinyrral's Disk	Mox Sapphire
Strip Mine	Nevinyrral's Disk	Mox Ruby
Pocket 2	Pocket 2	Pocket 2
Stone Rain	Nether Void	Mox Emerald
Stone Rain	Nether Void	Black Lotus
Stone Rain	Nether Void	Sol Ring
Stone Rain	Mana Drain	Chaos Orb
Pocket 3	Pocket 3	Pocket 3
Sinkhole	Mishra's Factory	Badlands

Sinkhole	Mishra's Factory	Badlands
Sinkhole	Mishra's Factory	Badlands
Sinkhole	Mishra's Factory	Badlands
Pocket 4	Pocket 4	Pocket 4
Rukh Egg	Black Vise	Volcanic Island
Rukh Egg	Black Vise	Volcanic Island
Rukh Egg	Black Vise	Volcanic Island
Mana Drain	Black Vise	Volcanic Island
Pocket 5	Pocket 5	Pocket 5
Mana Drain	Ancestral Recall	Underground Sea
Sedge Troll	Time Walk	Underground Sea
Sedge Troll	Timetwister	Underground Sea
Sedge Troll	Wheel of Fortune	Underground Sea

Sideboard

1. Unsummon
2. Unsummon
3. Unsummon
4. Psychic Purge
5. Psychic Purge
6. Psychic Purge
7. Psychic Purge
8. Gloom
9. Gloom
10. Gloom
11. Gloom
12. Earthquake
13. Earthquake
14. Hurkyl's Recall
15. Hurkyl's Recall

Charles' Lich Deck (Type I)

The Lich deck is typical of one style of deck design. In this design, one combination or relationship is particularly powerful, and the rest of the deck is designed to help develop and protect this combination. In the case of the Lich deck, it is the relationship between the Dark Heart of the Woods, the Lich, and the Fastbond.

Each of these cards works well with the other two, but in combination they allow you to search your entire deck and have a Fireball and enough mana to kill your opponent. To do this, with the Lich out you sacrifice a Forest after tapping it. You now draw three more cards and have one mana in your pool. Now you sacrifice a Mox to Fastbond damage after tapping it and bring more land into play. You must choose between drawing more cards and bringing more mana into your pool as necessary. If done properly, beginning when you have around five lands and a couple of Moxes in play, you can generally draw through your entire deck, finding your Fireball and amassing enough mana to kill any opponent.

Getting these three cards out at the same time is difficult, and so the deck needs side themes to keep an opponent busy. Land destruction and Djinns are both used to achieve this goal. They both fit in well with the main theme of the deck and work well together. An opponent should have to expend all of his or her resources in order to deal with the quickly generated Djinns, and these resources will be depleted by the land destruction. If they manage to overcome this onslaught, they will be just in time to fall victim to the Lich.

It is important that you bring out the last element of the combination, the Lich, on a turn in which your opponent is tapped out or only has a few mana. If he can counter your Lich, or even worse, Disenchant it, you will be in serious trouble.

Deck Name: Charles' Lich Deck

Block One	Block Two	Block Three
Pocket 1	Pocket 1	Pocket 1
Lich	Strip Mine	Black Lotus
Lich	Strip Mine	Underground Sea
Erhnam Djinn	Strip Mine	Underground Sea
Erhnam Djinn	Strip Mine	Underground Sea
Pocket 2	Pocket 2	Pocket 2
Juzam Djinn	Sinkhole	Underground Sea
Juzam Djinn	Sinkhole	Badlands
Juzam Djinn	Crumble	Forest
Juzam Djinn	Fireball	Forest
Pocket 3	Pocket 3	Pocket 3
Time Walk	Fireball	Tropical Island
Timetwister	Fastbond	Tropical Island
Wheel of Fortune	Fastbond	Tropical Island
Ancestral Recall	Fastbond	Tropical Island
Pocket 4	Pocket 4	Pocket 4
Dark Heart of the Woods	Dark Ritual	Taiga
Dark Heart of the Woods	Dark Ritual	Taiga

Dark Heart of the Woods	Sol Ring	Taiga
Demonic Tutor	Mox Ruby	Taiga
Pocket 5	Pocket 5	Pocket 5
Ice Storm	Mox Jet	Bayou
Ice Storm	Mox Emerald	Bayou
Ice Storm	Mox Sapphire	Bayou
Ice Storm	Mox Pearl	Bayou

Sideboard

1. Gloom
2. Gloom
3. Gloom
4. Gloom
5. Black Vise
6. Black Vise
7. Black Vise
8. Black Vise
9. Erhnam Djinn
10. Erhnam Djinn
11. Sandstorm
12. Sandstorm
13. Crumble
14. Crumble
15. Crumble

Type II Decks

This appendix contains a number of different decks for Type II play. The first five are the five basic deck types represented in Type II form. Once again as with the Type I five basic decks, the decks represented with the title of FBD are not considered tournament quality decks but rather decks to use to find weaknesses in your own designs. The rest of the appendix contains ten Type II tournament-quality decks.

FBD Type II Burn Decks

Burn decks are perhaps the simplest of decks. Their objective is simply to use direct damage spells on an opponent until they are defeated. The major problem with burn decks is that they tend to have very narrow roads to victory. Most of these decks are stunted if not totally defeated by the C.O.P. Red. It is necessary to have some form of enchantment removal to add to a burn deck or else you will be in serious trouble.

These decks benefited from the Ice Age set in many ways. With the inclusion of the Incinerate and Lava Burst, these decks were taken one step higher in their level of damage dealing capacity. The burn decks also had anti-circle cards added such as the Ghostly Flame and Anarchy.

Regardless of their shortcomings, these decks tend to do very well against small creature decks. The versatility of damage spells to act as a means to kill creatures and to eliminate an opponent make these decks formidable foes. Outside of the small creature deck, most of the other decks tend to perform well against burn decks if they are well designed.

This example burn deck is for the most part rather simple. The Nevinyrral's Disks provide another means to remove enchantments and other permanents. The only permanents this deck would lose would be Mana Flares or Land Taxes. In most cases your losses will be minimal. There is a sequential element that you should understand when using the Disk. If you are using it to get rid of C.O.P.s and have a Mana Flare in play, you can tap all of your lands while the Flare is out getting its benefits and then blow the Disk. After the C.O.P.s are removed you could then cast a large red damage spell to eliminate your opponent.

Deck Name: FBD Burn Deck

Block One	Block Two	Block Three
Pocket 1	Pocket 1	Pocket 1
Mana Flare	Earthquake	Mountain
Mana Flare	Earthquake	Mountain
Mana Flare	Earthquake	Mountain
Mana Flare	Earthquake	Mountain
Pocket 2	Pocket 2	Pocket 2
Nevinyrral's Disk	Disenchant	Mountain
Nevinyrral's Disk	Disenchant	Mountain
Power Surge	Disenchant	Mountain
Power Surge	Balance	Mountain
Pocket 3	Pocket 3	Pocket 3
Fireball	Incinerate	Mountain
Fireball	Incinerate	Mountain
Fireball	Incinerate	Mountain
Fireball	Incinerate	Mountain
Pocket 4	Pocket 4	Pocket 4
Lightning Bolt	Land Tax	Plains
Lightning Bolt	Land Tax	Plains

Lightning Bolt	Strip Mine	Plains
Lightning Bolt	Strip Mine	Plains
Pocket 5	Pocket 5	Pocket 5
Disintegrate	Mishra's Factory	Plains
Disintegrate	Mishra's Factory	Plains
Disintegrate	Mishra's Factory	Plains
Disintegrate	Mishra's Factory	Plains

Sideboard

1. Disenchant
2. Swords to Plowshares
3. Swords to Plowshares
4. Swords to Plowshares
5. Circle of Protection - Red
6. Circle of Protection - Red
7. Power Surge
8. Power Surge
9. Anarchy
10. Anarchy
11. Red Elemental Blast
12. Black Vise
13. Black Vise
14. Black Vise
15. Black Vise

FBD Type II: Counterspell Decks

The counterspell deck is usually the most common of the reactive decks. Counterspell decks work to maintain the stability of the playing environment until they can create and support an offensive. These decks fall under slow deck theory because they capture victory over a period of time. When supported with a touch of white reactive permanent removal, these decks can be quite effective. The major problem that most counterspell decks experience is that they are fairly susceptible to fast creature decks. Counterspell decks can lose to large fast creature decks if a large creature is deployed in the first couple of turns before it can be countered. The counterspell deck is particularly weak against small fast creature decks because there tend to be too many creatures to counter early on. Also the creatures tend to be cheaper than the Counterspells used to stop them.

Another major weakness that counterspell decks experience is that they fare poorly against decks that use Black Vises. If Vises are cast early on before they can be countered, it is difficult for a counterspell deck to reduce the number of cards in hand. It becomes especially difficult for a counterspell deck to get under a Vise if an opponent will not cast any other cards after the Vise enters play. To avoid this sometimes a Mind Bomb is used. Another particular weakness of a counterspell deck is against the Strip Mine. If, for instance, you tap all of your mana in play but leave enough to cast a Counterspell, that can turn out to be insufficient if your opponent plays the uncounterable Strip Mine and removes one of the two blue mana. Then they are free to cast whatever they wish. Mishra's Factories can also be a problem for counterspell decks because they too cannot be countered, and by the time a blocker can be brought into play the Factories can cause substantial amounts of damage.

This particular deck has a few combinations to it. The Unsummon and Time Elemental obviously can be used to get a second chance at countering one of an opponent's permanents. The Time Elemental is also useful with the control magics because it allows the enchantment's controller to pick up the control magic when his stolen creature takes lethal damage, when it is no longer the best creature in play, or when it is removed from the game.

Counterspell decks are one of the most powerful of the five basic decks. They take some skill to master and if played correctly are difficult to beat. When you face a counterspell deck, one of your best defenses is your instants. In some cases it is wise to save a number of them to cast during your opponent's turn so you might cast a permanent that he will have trouble removing.

Deck Name: FBD Type II: Counterspell Deck

Block One	Block Two	Block Three
Pocket 1	Pocket 1	Pocket 1
Counterspell	Zuran Orb	Land Cap
Counterspell	Control Magic	Land Cap
Counterspell	Control Magic	Plains
Counterspell	Control Magic	Plains
Pocket 2	Pocket 2	Pocket 2
Spell Blast	Disenchant	Island
Spell Blast	Disenchant	Island
Spell Blast	Disenchant	Island
Spell Blast	Time Elemental	Island
Pocket 3	Pocket 3	Pocket 3
Power Sink	Swords to Plowshares	Island

Power Sink	Swords to Plowshares	Island
Power Sink	Swords to Plowshares	Island
Power Sink	Swords to Plowshares	Island
Pocket 4	Pocket 4	Pocket 4
Air Elemental	Mishra's Factory	Island
Air Elemental	Mishra's Factory	Island
Air Elemental	Mishra's Factory	Island
Air Elemental	Mishra's Factory	Island
Pocket 5	Pocket 5	Pocket 5
Mahamoti Djinn	Adarkar Wastes	Island
Mahamoti Djinn	Adarkar Wastes	Island
Glasses of Urza	Adarkar Wastes	Island
Jayemdae Tome	Adarkar Wastes	Island

Sideboard

1. Unsummon
2. Unsummon
3. Land Tax
4. Land Tax
5. Land Tax
6. C.O.P. Red
7. C.O.P. Red
8. C.O.P. White
9. C.O.P. White
10. Mind Bomb
11. Mind Bomb
12. Mind Bomb
13. Mind Bomb
14. Disenchant
15. Time Elemental

Type II FBD: Fast Creature Decks

Fast creature decks are perhaps the most common type of action-based decks and can be divided into two forms—large fast creature decks and small fast creature decks.

Large Fast Creature Decks

These decks make a relatively large investment in cards in order to bring out one large and durable creature. Large fast creature decks, like most decks that work under fast deck theory, tend to lose speed after the first five rounds. They tend to run out of cards. Players of large fast creature decks generally hope that their advantage is large enough at that point that their opponent cannot effectively recover.

This particular deck is rather simple. It uses its fast mana in the form of Dark Rituals and Mana Vaults to deploy a Vampire or Serra Angel within the first three turns. Once the creature is deployed, then all of the creature's obstacles are to be removed with Swords to Plowshares. Damage should also be dealt by the Black Vises. Once a creature is out, the caster should work as quickly as possible to cast another to seal an opponent's fate.

The major weakness behind these decks is their poor card count economy. They typically use two or three cards to deploy one active card. If these cards (the large creatures) are removed, then the deck loses its effectiveness, since three cards were dealt with in one blow. Cards like Unsummon, Swords to Plowshares, and Paralyze tend to seriously harm these decks. For example, let's say you play a Swamp followed by a Dark Ritual, Mana Vault, and then a Vampire on the first turn. If your opponent responds by casting a Paralyze on your Vampire, he or she has effectively countered three of your cards and one of your turns with one card. Your first turn would be wasted along with the Mana Vault, Dark Ritual, and Vampire.

Deck Name: FBD Type II: Fast Creature I

Block One	Block Two	Block Three
Pocket 1	Pocket 1	Pocket 1
Vampire	Strip Mine	Swamp
Vampire	Strip Mine	Swamp
Vampire	Strip Mine	Swamp
Vampire	Strip Mine	Swamp
Pocket 2	Pocket 2	Pocket 2
Serra Angel	Spirit Link	Swamp
Serra Angel	Spirit Link	Swamp
Serra Angel	Disenchant	Swamp
Serra Angel	Disenchant	Swamp
Pocket 3	Pocket 3	Pocket 3
Carrion Ants	Mana Vault	Swamp
Carrion Ants	Mana Vault	Swamp
Clay Statue	Mana Vault	Plains
Clay Statue	Mana Vault	Plains

Pocket 4	Pocket 4	Pocket 4
Mishra's Factory	Dark Ritual	Plains
Mishra's Factory	Dark Ritual	Plains
Mishra's Factory	Dark Ritual	Plains
Mishra's Factory	Dark Ritual	Plains
Pocket 5	Pocket 5	Pocket 5
Black Vise	Swords to Plowshares	Plains
Black Vise	Swords to Plowshares	Plains
Black Vise	Swords to Plowshares	Plains
Black Vise	Swords to Plowshares	Plains

Sideboard

1. Disenchant
2. Disenchant
3. Paralyze
4. Paralyze
5. Paralyze
6. Terror
7. Terror
8. Conversion
9. Death Grip
10. C.O.P. Red
11. C.O.P. Red
12. Savannah Lion
13. Savannah Lion
14. Savannah Lion
15. Savannah Lion

Small Fast Creature Decks

The small fast creature deck usually deploys multiple small creatures and spreads out its investment. Like large fast creature decks, small fast creature decks tend to lose momentum after the first five rounds. Overcoming this is the major challenge. Once a small creature player has dropped his hand he has his entire investment in play. Cards that invoke mass permanent or creature removal tend to be devastating. For instance if you have out a number of small creatures and your opponent plays an Earthquake they can effectively eliminate multiples of your cards with a single card. Once again when these decks face opposing decks with the right cards they tend to suffer immensely.

This particular deck is cut to be as fast as possible without the use of elaborate card combinations. Most of the creatures cost only one white mana. This allows them to be deployed quickly so they can do a large amount of damage before an opponent can deploy adequate defenses. After turns go by the Priests take a more active role. They use excess mana to increase the size of other creatures. The Armageddons can often seal a victory by eliminating an opponent's ability to respond. The Howling Mines are obviously there to reduce the loss of momentum. The Osai Vulture and Mesa Pegasus cards should help to lessen the effects of Earthquakes.

These decks tend to deal well against counterspell decks, land destruction, and other decks that take time to develop before they start to establish dominance. Cards that generally damage or stop small fast creature decks are Earthquake, Hurricane, Nevinyrral's Disk, Wrath of God, and Balance.

Deck Name: FBD Type II: Fast Creature II

Block One	Block Two	Block Three
Pocket 1	Pocket 1	Pocket 1
Savannah Lions	Icatian Priests	Disenchant
Savannah Lions	Icatian Priests	Disenchant
Savannah Lions	Osai Vultures	Plains
Savannah Lions	Osai Vultures	Plains
Pocket 2	Pocket 2	Pocket 2
Tundra Wolves	Mesa Pegasus	Plains
Tundra Wolves	Mesa Pegasus	Plains
Tundra Wolves	Mesa Pegasus	Plains
Tundra Wolves	Mesa Pegasus	Plains
Pocket 3	Pocket 3	Pocket 3
Icatian Infantry	Crusade	Plains
Icatian Infantry	Crusade	Plains
Icatian Infantry	Crusade	Plains
Icatian Infantry	Crusade	Plains
Pocket 4	Pocket 4	Pocket 4
Icatian Javelineers	Armageddon	Plains
Icatian Javelineers	Armageddon	Plains
Icatian Javelineers	Howling Mine	Plains
Icatian Javelineers	Howling Mine	Plains
Pocket 5	Pocket 5	Pocket 5
White Knight	Swords to Plowshares	Plains
White Knight	Swords to Plowshares	Plains
White Knight	Swords to Plowshares	Plains
White Knight	Swords to Plowshares	Plains

Sideboard

1. Disenchant	6. Eye for an Eye	11. Black Vise
2. Disenchant	7. Armageddon	12. Black Vise
3. Eye for an Eye	8. Armageddon	13. Karma
4. Eye for an Eye	9. Black Vise	14. Karma
5. Eye for an Eye	10. Black Vise	15. Plains

FBD Type II: Hand Destruction

In Type II tournaments one of the most common of the more powerful decks is hand destruction. The main reason for this is because in Type II there is little or no adequate defense against hand destruction besides Counterspells and playing your cards as you draw them. In Type I there is at least the Psychic Purge. If the Purge is used in an action-based deck it can devastate a hand destruction deck.

This deck, like all of the five basic decks, is based on the rather simple concept of removing cards from an opponent's hand and making him suffer from Rack damage in the process. The nice element about the Racks is that once a hand is reduced to no cards, it takes three turns and six points of damage without playing any cards to get above a single Rack. This combination is often unsurmountable.

The rest of the deck is self-explanatory. The white serves as support for creature, artifact, and enchantment removal. The Vampires were added as an alternate and somewhat reliable source of damage.

The most threatening decks to hand destruction decks in Type II are probably small fast creature decks. Though these decks tend to suffer from the Racks they can often overrun a hand destruction deck with their horde faster than the Racks can take a large toll. Sometimes counterspell decks fare relatively well against hand destruction decks, but this depends on each player's draw. Often counterspell decks have no way to deal with a first-turn Mindstab Thrull or Hypnotic Specter. Once the counterspell deck has lost the battle for card count economy, the hand destruction deck is likely to dominate the counterspell deck from that point on.

Deck Name: FBD Type II: Hand Destruction

Block One	Block Two	Block Three
Pocket 1	Pocket 1	Pocket 1
Rack	Disrupting Scepter	Plains
Rack	Disrupting Scepter	Plains
Rack	Mana Vault	Plains
Rack	Mana Vault	Plains
Pocket 2	Pocket 2	Pocket 2
Hymn to Tourach	Vampire	Plains
Hymn to Tourach	Vampire	Swamp
Hymn to Tourach	Swords to Plowshares	Swamp
Hymn to Tourach	Swords to Plowshares	Swamp
Pocket 3	Pocket 3	Pocket 3
Hypnotic Specter	Dark Ritual	Swamp
Hypnotic Specter	Dark Ritual	Swamp
Hypnotic Specter	Dark Ritual	Swamp
Hypnotic Specter	Dark Ritual	Swamp
Pocket 4	Pocket 4	Pocket 4
Mindstab Thrull	Mishra's Factory	Swamp
Mindstab Thrull	Mishra's Factory	Swamp
Mindstab Thrull	Mishra's Factory	Swamp
Mindstab Thrull	Mishra's Factory	Swamp
Pocket 5	Pocket 5	Pocket 5
Mind Twist	Strip Mine	Swamp
Disenchant	Strip Mine	Swamp
Disenchant	Strip Mine	Swamp
Disenchant	Zuran Orb	Swamp

Sideboard

1. Disenchant
2. Swords to Plowshares
3. Swords to Plowshares
4. Terror
5. Terror
6. Terror
7. Strip Mine
8. Drain Life
9. Drain Life
10. Disrupting Scepter
11. C.O.P. Red
12. C.O.P. Red
13. C.O.P. Red
14. C.O.P. White
15. C.O.P. White

FBD Type II: Land Destruction

In Type II tournaments, land destruction is very weak compared to Type I land destruction. Type II land destruction lacks the availability of Type I fast artifact mana and the Nether Void. Without these it is difficult for a Type II land destruction deck to maintain the dominance that it enjoys in Type I. Red is the strongest color for land destruction with the Fissure, Conquer, Orcish Squatters, and the Stone Rain. The Strip Mines also can add some degree of speed to Type II land destruction. One of the most difficult problems with Type II land destruction is that it requires fast mana to be effective. Green tends to add that speed with its creature mana, allowing a Stone Rain to be cast on turn two with ease. Before the Ice Age's addition of Conquer, Mole Worms, Icequakes, and Thermokarst, there was no chance for effective Type II land destruction; now they can be produced.

These decks tend to do fairly well. Even though there are not as many land destruction cards available to Type II decks, land destruction is still very difficult to overcome. These decks will usually overcome counterspell decks, but the victory comes down to player skill and the draw. Many fast creature decks fare well against Type II land destruction decks. They can usually overwhelm them before the loss of land is a problem.

There are a few ways in Type II to counter land destruction decks. The first is to use cards like Land Tax, Hallowed Ground, and Equinox. Land Tax is a fine counter to land destruction decks except for the fact that it enables you to draw more cards, which is not always what you want to do because most land destruction decks use Black Vises. The Equinox is fairly good except for the fact that it and the land it is placed on can easily be eliminated with a Strip Mine. Perhaps the easiest way to overcome land destruction decks is to use cards that are relatively cheap so you can establish dominance early on.

Deck Name: FBD Land Destruction

Block One	Block Two	Block Three
Pocket 1	Pocket 1	Pocket 1
Stone Rain	Lanowar Elf	Forest
Stone Rain	Lanowar Elf	Forest
Stone Rain	Black Vise	Forest
Stone Rain	Black Vise	Forest
Pocket 2	Pocket 2	Pocket 2
Strip Mine	Black Vise	Forest
Strip Mine	Zuran Orb	Forest
Strip Mine	Erhnam Djinn	Forest
Strip Mine	Ernham Djinn	Forest
Pocket 3	Pocket 3	Pocket 3
Thermokarst	Erhnam Djinn	Forest
Thermokarst	Erhnam Djinn	Forest
Thermokarst	Jeweled Amulet	Forest
Thermokarst	Jeweled Amulet	Mountain
Pocket 4	Pocket 4	Pocket 4
Lightning Bolt	Incinerate	Mountain
Lightning Bolt	Incinerate	Mountain
Lightning Bolt	Incinerate	Mountain
Lightning Bolt	Orcish Oriflamme	Mountain
Pocket 5	Pocket 5	Pocket 5
Birds of Paradise	Mishra's Factory	Mountain
Birds of Paradise	Mishra's Factory	Mountain
Birds of Paradise	Mishra's Factory	Mountain
Lanowar Elf	Mishra's Factory	Mountain

Sideboard

1. Black Vise — Counterspell / slow decks
2. Red Elemental Blast — Counterspell / blue decks
3. Red Elemental Blast
4. Red Elemental Blast
5. Lightning Bolt — To kill creature mana and Hypnotic Specters and Mindstabs
6. Lightning Bolt
7. Lightning Bolt
8. Lightning Bolt
9. Sandstorm — Fast creature decks
10. Sandstorm
11. Sandstorm
12. Shatter — Artifact removal
13. Shatter
14. Tranquility — Enchantment removal—Land Tax
15. Tranquility

The Stasis Disk Deck (Type II)

The Stasis Disk deck is one of the most versatile and difficult decks to master. The Disks allow the player of the deck the ability to remove all of an opponent's permanents from play. The Disk can also be a method to remove Stasis during an opponent's turn to avoid giving your opponent the opportunity to do as he pleases for that particular turn.

One of the most powerful features of the Stasis Disk deck is that it is inherently powerful against the five basic decks. This is because of the mixture of Nevinyrral's Disks, Black Vises, and Stasis. The Stasis performs well against land destruction decks because it gives its caster the time to lay many lands before an opponent has the opportunity to eliminate them. It also prevents an opponent from using consistent hand destruction turn after turn (Disrupting Scepter/Hypnotic Specter). The Howling Mines also reduce the effects of hand destruction, and once the deck has the ability to counter the Hymns, Amnesias, and Mind Twist it is unlikely that it will suffer from further hand destruction.

The Disks and Stasis will often stop fast creature decks, and when the Earthquakes are added most small creature decks have very little hope of victory. The Black Vises alone will often stop a counterspell deck, and burn decks will suffer to Stasis and Power Sinks. There are not many versions of the five basic decks that will overcome the Stasis Disk deck.

In order for the Stasis Disk deck to work effectively one must learn how to play it correctly. In an ideal situation the cards of the deck would be played in this order: Black Vise, Howling Mine, Nevinyrral's Disk, Stasis. Once this combination is out, the Mines should help draw a number of Islands to maintain the Stasis. Once the mana is needed one simply blows the Disk during an opponent's turn and eliminates the Stasis, allowing him to untap during his untap phase. If a Time Elemental is drawn it can be used to maintain a permanent Stasis by simply picking up the Stasis at the end of the opponent's turn and recasting it. This ties up six mana for the caster but maintains a permanent Stasis and frees up all of the other available mana.

There are a number of cards that work in support of the Disk and Stasis. One is the Hurkyl's Recall. There are three primary uses for the Recall. The first is to use it after the Disk is blown, allowing the caster to save all of his or her artifacts and the Disk. The second use is with the Black Vises. If an opponent has a number of artifacts you can simply make him pick them up during your turn and force him to take a large amount of Vise damage. The third major use for the Hurkyl's Recall is to use it during an opponent's discard phase before you play a Stasis. This forces your opponent to hold these cards without their benefits while the Stasis keeps his lands tapped. The Twiddle is also excellent with the Stasis. If an opponent has a Serra Angel, Yotian Soldier, or Zephyr Falcon that is constantly beating on you while your Stasis is in play, the Twiddle can force him to tap the creature. The Twiddle can also be used to untap a Disk so it can be used on the turn it is cast. The Clay Statues can be used with the Disk because they simply regenerate after the Disk is blown. The Disintegrate can be used to eliminate an opponent's regenerating creatures. There are a number of possibilities with the Stasis Disk deck, making it very enjoyable to play.

Deck Name: The Stasis Disk Deck

Block One	Block Two	Block Three
Pocket 1	Pocket 1	Pocket 1
Nevinyrral's Disk	Hurkyl's Recall	Island
Nevinyrral's Disk	Hurkyl's Recall	Island
Nevinyrral's Disk	Time Elemental	Island
Nevinyrral's Disk	Time Elemental	Island
Pocket 2	Pocket 2	Pocket 2
Black Vise	Stasis	Island
Black Vise	Stasis	Island
Black Vise	Stasis	Island
Black Vise	Clay Statue	Island
Pocket 3	Pocket 3	Pocket 3
Howling Mine	Clay Statue	Island
Howling Mine	Clay Statue	Island
Counterspell	Disintegrate	Island

Counterspell	Disintegrate	Island
Pocket 4	Pocket 4	Pocket 4
Power Sink	Mishra's Factory	Island
Power Sink	Mishra's Factory	Island
Power Sink	Mishra's Factory	Island
Power Sink	Mishra's Factory	Mountain
Pocket 5	Pocket 5	Pocket 5
Twiddle	Strip Mine	Mountain
Mana Vault	Strip Mine	Mountain
Mana Vault	Strip Mine	Mountain
Mana Vault	Strip Mine	Mountain

Sideboard

1. Clay Statue
2. Earthquake
3. Earthquake
4. Earthquake
5. Earthquake
6. Red Elemental Blast
7. Red Elemental Blast
8. Red Elemental Blast
9. Shatter
10. Shatter
11. Shatter
12. Shatter
13. Disintegrate
14. Disintegrate
15. Counterspell

The Lazarus Deck

William Cole sent this deck in response to an online post on the Magic: The Gathering™ Strategy Board. William had not played the deck because it was still in its early stages of design, but its creativity makes it a nice addition to the book.

The idea behind the Lazarus deck is not as straightforward as you might expect. The object is to force or induce an opponent into discarding creatures from his or her hand that are good targets for an Animate Dead. One can do this in a number of ways. The Hymns and Mind Twists can force an opponent to discard creatures, but since these are done at random it is not always likely that you will force your opponent to discard a large creature. The best means for having large creatures enter the graveyard is through the use of either the Mind Bomb or Disrupting Scepter. If your opponent has the chance to decide he would typically prefer discarding a large and expensive creature over having to discard a spell that he could cast early on. This works best if your opponent has no idea what your deck is like. If you draw a Mind Bomb on the first turn and a Colossus or two you can also use the Bomb to get those creatures out of your hand to the graveyard. Once they have reached the graveyard you can animate them.

The Twiddles are very important in William's deck. If you manage to get a Colossus into play you can use the Twiddle to untap it after it has attacked. Early on the Psychic Venoms may be used to slow an opponent down, but you can use the latter in the game as a source of direct damage. If you draw Psychic Venoms later in the game when your opponent has a large amount of land, concentrate them on one land. Then your Twiddles can be used to do 2, 4, 6, and even 8 points of damage. The Psychic Venoms help the Power Sinks to have an added bite.

The rest of the deck is pretty much self-explanatory. The Racks go with the hand destruction. They, the Mishra's Factories, and the Vampires serve as alternative sources of damage.

William's deck is creative and fun, but it will still suffer from a number of problems. The first of of which is its susceptibility to counter magic. Though the hand destruction helps against counter magic, the combinations of the deck are somewhat fragile. The Lazarus deck would also have great problems against a fast creature deck. There is little that the deck can normally do about a Swarm except try and deploy either a Colossus or Vampire early on.

Deck Name: William Cole's Lazarus Deck

Block One	Block Two	Block Three
Pocket 1	Pocket 1	Pocket 1
Dance of the Dead	Twiddle	Mishra's Factory
Dance of the Dead	Twiddle	Swamp
Vampire	Twiddle	Swamp
Vampire	Mind Twist	Swamp
Pocket 2	Pocket 2	Pocket 2
Power Sink	Hymn to Tourach	Swamp
Power Sink	Hymn to Tourach	Swamp
Power Sink	Hymn to Tourach	Swamp
Power Sink	Hymn to Tourach	Swamp

Pocket 3	Pocket 3	Pocket 3
Colossus	Rack	Swamp
Colossus	Rack	Swamp
Colossus	Rack	Swamp
Colossus	Counterspell	Swamp
Pocket 4	Pocket 4	Pocket 4
Animate Dead	Psychic Venom	Island
Animate Dead	Psychic Venom	Island
Animate Dead	Psychic Venom	Island
Animate Dead	Psychic Venom	Island
Pocket 5	Pocket 5	Pocket 5
Mind Bomb	Disrupting Scepter	Island
Mind Bomb	Mishra's Factory	Island
Mind Bomb	Mishra's Factory	Island
Disrupting Scepter	Mishra's Factory	Island

Sideboard

1. Terror — Creature decks
2. Terror
3. Unsummon — Fast creature decks
4. Unsummon
5. Island — Land destruction
6. Island
7. Island
8. Counterspell
9. Death Grip — Green decks
10. Blue Elemental Blast — Red decks
11. Blue Elemental Blast
12. Drudge Skeletons — Small fast creature decks
13. Drudge Skeletons
14. Drudge Skeletons
15. Drudge Skeletons

Quake and Surge (Type II Deck)

The Quake and Surge is a fun and powerful deck. The deck has a number of independent combinational factors. The Power Surge can act as a major source of damage on its own. Sometimes it can be used in much the same way you might use a Fireball because it affects your opponent first and can often finish him or her. But if the Surge does not eliminate your opponent you can avoid damage a number of ways. First, you can tap all of your land and pump the mana through the Mishra's Factories and then tap it to make it a

3/3, thus avoiding all damage. Then there is the obvious method of simply tapping mana to activate the C.O.P. Red to avoid the damage. If the Sunglasses of Urza are in play all land may be tapped to give the Goblin Balloon Brigade flying several times over. Finally all of the land may be tapped to increase the Firebreathing ability of the Dragon or a creature carrying that enchantment.

The Power Surge is obviously not the only card that works well with the C.O.P. Red. There is also the Chaos Lace and the Earthquake. If your opponent has a troublesome source of damage you cannot really avoid, you can simply Chaos Lace it and tap mana to power the C.O.P. to protect yourself. The Earthquakes also work well with the C.O.P. in play. All of this deck's creatures either fly or have the ability to fly and can avoid Earthquake damage. This allows the Quake to do damage to your opponent and kill his ground creatures.

The creatures provide an alternate source of damage and assist in tapping lands out to avoid Surge damage. This deck performs well against most decks but has its greatest trouble against counterspell decks. Counterspells tend to suffer against the Power Surge if it is allowed to be cast. The sideboard is made to eliminate a counterspell deck.

Deck Name: Quake and Surge

Block One	Block Two	Block Three
Pocket 1	Pocket 1	Pocket 1
Power Surge	Goblin Balloon Brigade	Mishra's Factory
Power Surge	Goblin Balloon Brigade	Mountain
Power Surge	Goblin Balloon Brigade	Mountain
Disintegrate	Goblin Balloon Brigade	Mountain
Pocket 2	Pocket 2	Pocket 2
Earthquake	Fireball	Mountain
Earthquake	Fireball	Mountain
Earthquake	Chaos Lace	Mountain
Earthquake	Chaos Lace	Mountain
Pocket 3	Pocket 3	Pocket 3
Firebreathing	C.O.P. Red	Mountain
Firebreathing	C.O.P. Red	Mountain

Swords to Plowshares	C.O.P. Red	Mountain
Disenchant	Disenchant	Plains
Pocket 4	Pocket 4	Pocket 4
Serra Angel	Lightning Bolt	Plains
Serra Angel	Lightning Bolt	Plains
Serra Angel	Lightning Bolt	Plains
Shiven Dragon	Lightning Bolt	Plains
Pocket 5	Pocket 5	Pocket 5
Mesa Pegasus	Sunglasses of Urza	Plains
Mesa Pegasus	Mishra's Factory	Plains
Mesa Pegasus	Mishra's Factory	Plains
Mesa Pegasus	Mishra's Factory	Plains

Sideboard

1. Disenchant
2. Swords to Plowshares
3. Swords to Plowshares
4. Swords to Plowshares
5. Disintegrate
6. Land Tax
7. Land Tax
8. Land Tax
9. Strip Mine
10. Strip Mine
11. Strip Mine
12. Strip Mine
13. Black Vise
14. Black Vise
15. Black Vise

Tab's Green Thing

Tab Dougherty is a friend who attended Texas A&M University. We met one day while playing at one of A&M's local game shops, where he gave a Type II deck being using at the time a sound thrashing with a deck similar to this one. Though it has changed since then, the deck is still a very powerful example of a large fast creature deck.

This deck is simple but effective. It churns out Craw Wurms and other large creatures at a rapid pace. The Green Thing has Hurricanes, Fireballs, and Disintegrates to help quicken the kill. These damage spells also help to preserve the usefulness of mana acquired in the later game. The Desert Twisters work as excellent support for getting rid of any major threats. Their cost is less significant because they can be generated quickly and efficiently.

There are not that many decks this deck has problems with. The only major annoyances the Green Thing suffers from are counterspell and land destruction decks. Counterspell decks, if played correctly, can usually counter all of the effective measures of the deck. Land destruction is usually not as threatening as counterspell decks unless it is coupled with some form of fast damage and the land destruction is used as a slowing measure.

Deck Name: Tab's Green Thing

Block One	Block Two	Block Three
Pocket 1	Pocket 1	Pocket 1
Wild Growth	Fireball	Karplusan Forest
Wild Growth	Fireball	Karplusan Forest
Wild Growth	Disintegrate	Karplusan Forest
Wild Growth	Disintegrate	Karplusan Forest
Pocket 2	Pocket 2	Pocket 2
Lanowar Elf	Ernham Djinn	Timberline Ridge
Lanowar Elf	Ernham Djinn	Timberline Ridge
Lanowar Elf	Ernham Djinn	Mountain
Lanowar Elf	Ernham Djinn	Forest
Pocket 3	Pocket 3	Pocket 3
Mana Vault	Scaled Wurm	Forest
Mana Vault	Scaled Wurm	Forest
Mana Vault	Ley Druid	Forest
Mana Vault	Ley Druid	Forest
Pocket 4	Pocket 4	Pocket 4
Orcish Lumberjack	Desert Twister	Forest
Orcish Lumberjack	Desert Twister	Forest
Orcish Lumberjack	Desert Twister	Forest
Orcish Lumberjack	Channel	Forest
Pocket 5	Pocket 5	Pocket 5
Craw Wurm	Hurricane	Forest
Craw Wurm	Crumble	Forest
Craw Wurm	Mountain	Forest
Craw Wurm	Mountain	Forest

Sideboard

1. Desert Twister — Permanent removal
2. Hurricane — Flying creature removal/damage
3. Fireball — Creature removal/damage
4. Disintegrate — Regenerating creature removal/damage
5. Crumble — Artifact removal
6. Strip Mine — Counterspell decks
7. Strip Mine
8. Strip Mine
9. Tranquility — Massive enchantment removal
10. Tranquility
11. Tranquility
12. Black Vise — Counterspell decks
13. Black Vise
14. Black Vise
15. Black Vise

Ken's Sea of Fire (Type II)

Ken Ellison sent this deck in response to a post on the Internet. Ken said he had quite a bit of success using the Sea of Fire in a number of local tournaments he participated in. The deck uses the Uthden Trolls and Clay Statues to beat on opponents after a Disk is blown. After the Disk goes off, all of an opponent's creatures will be cleaned off the board, but the Statues and Uthden Trolls will simply regenerate. Then during their controller's turn they and the Mishra's Factories can simply attack without anything to block them.

The Disintegrates and Incinerates help to remove an opponent's regenerators that may remain to pose some sort of threat and, of course to knock out an opponent.

Originally Ken said he had a number of problems with fast creature decks. It was suggested he add Unsummons and Earthquakes to his sideboard. He was particularly happy with the results and made them a permanent addition.

The Sea of Fire also has two surprise cards. These are the Twiddle and the Blood Lust. Ken said he had won many games with them because his opponents just were not expecting to see them. Sometimes you can cast one early in a game and your opponent assumes that you have four of them and will make decisions accordingly.

Deck Name: Sea of Fire

Block One	Block Two	Block Three
Pocket 1	Pocket 1	Pocket 1
Counterspell	Uthden Troll	Island
Counterspell	Uthden Troll	Island
Counterspell	Uthden Troll	Island
Counterspell	Uthden Troll	Island
Pocket 2	Pocket 2	Pocket 2
Power Sink	Clay Statue	Island
Power Sink	Clay Statue	Island
Power Sink	Incinerate	Island
Power Sink	Incinerate	Island
Pocket 3	Pocket 3	Pocket 3
Blood Lust	Incinerate	Island
Twiddle	Incinerate	Island
Shiven Dragon	Disintegrate	Island
Mahamoti Djinn	Disintegrate	Island
Pocket 4	Pocket 4	Pocket 4
Nevinyrral's Disk	Strip Mine	Island
Nevinyrral's Disk	Strip Mine	Mountain
Nevinyrral's Disk	Strip Mine	Mountain
Nevinyrral's Disk	Strip Mine	Mountain
Pocket 5	Pocket 5	Pocket 5
Lightning Bolt	Mishra's Factory	Mountain
Lightning Bolt	Mishra's Factory	Mountain
Lightning Bolt	Mishra's Factory	Mountain
Lightning Bolt	Mishra's Factory	Mountain

Sideboard

1. Earthquake
2. Earthquake
3. Earthquake
4. Earthquake
5. Red Elemental Blast
6. Red Elemental Blast
7. Red Elemental Blast
8. Red Elemental Blast
9. Unsummon
10. Unsummon
11. Unsummon
12. Unsummon
13. Blood Lust
14. Blood Lust
15. Twiddle

Maysonet's Amish Deck

This deck was designed by Adam Maysonet, one of the finest players in the country. Adam was one of the great founders of the Rack/Balance decks. His Maysonet Rack Balance deck (MRB) may have been one of the best decks ever designed. Because of the power of Adam's deck and many like it, Balance was restricted to one per deck, and thus the decks are no longer nearly as effective. This particular deck was originally a Balance deck. It has been modified to meet current Type II restrictions.

The Amish deck is peaceful. It, like the people it was named for, will usually win through patience. The deck has no creatures and inflicts no damage whatsoever. This means that all of an opponent's cards that give life or remove creatures are rendered useless.

The deck uses what many tournament players call deck destruction. The objective of this deck is to get the Howling Mines out as soon as possible so you can reach your Island Sanctuaries and Millstones. Once you have gotten to your Island Sanctuaries you can prevent yourself from depleting your deck as quickly as your opponent depletes his. The Millstones just make the process faster. The Island Sanctuary also serves the purpose of maintaining a safe distance from numerous walking creatures. Unfortunately you still have to worry about flying creatures and islandwalkers.

The Counterspells, Disenchants, and Swords to Plowshares act as support cards. Any annoying flying creatures that enter play should be eliminated with Swords to Plowshares or Wrath of God. Your Counterspells should pick up the rest and any direct damage that might come your way. Land destruction decks are somewhat troublesome for this deck. If you face one, the Land Taxes in the sideboard should be added. However, if you are forced to use the Land Tax be careful not to draw unnecessary cards, as they could cost you the game by depleting your deck of the cards you seek to conserve.

Finally, there are a few cards to be very wary of. The first and foremost of these is the Black Vise. If one of these comes out early on, before you are able to counter it, it can be devastating. The second major card threat this deck suffers from is Gloom. If your opponent plays black, you should save a Counterspell for his Gloom.

These can really hurt this deck's performance. Hurkyl's Recall and Energy Flux can also cause problems and should be avoided.

Deck Name: Maysonet's Amish Deck

Block One	Block Two	Block Three
Pocket 1	Pocket 1	Pocket 1
Millstone	Counterspell	Island
Millstone	Counterspell	Island
Millstone	Counterspell	Island
Maze of Ith	Counterspell	Island
Pocket 2	Pocket 2	Pocket 2
Wrath of God	Disenchant	Island
Wrath of God	Disenchant	Island
Zuran Orb	Disenchant	Island
Balance	Fountain of Youth	Island
Pocket 3	Pocket 3	Pocket 3
Island Sanctuary	Jester's Cap	Island
Island Sanctuary	Jester's Cap	Island
Island Sanctuary	Spirit Link	Plains
Fountain of Youth	Spirit Link	Plains
Pocket 4	Pocket 4	Pocket 4
Howling Mine	Swords to Plowshares	Plains
Howling Mine	Swords to Plowshares	Plains
Howling Mine	Swords to Plowshares	Plains
Howling Mine	Swords to Plowshares	Plains
Pocket 5	Pocket 5	Pocket 5
Power Sink	Island	Plains
Power Sink	Island	Plains
Power Sink	Island	Plains
Power Sink	Island	Plains

Sideboard

1. Land Tax
2. Land Tax
3. Land Tax
4. Land Tax
5. Disenchant
6. Fountain of Youth
7. Wrath of God
8. Mana Short
9. Strip Mine
10. Strip Mine
11. Strip Mine
12. Strip Mine
13. C.O.P. Red
14. C.O.P. Red
15. C.O.P. Red

The Black Sea: A Type II Hand Destruction/Counterspell deck

The Black Sea is an example of one of the more powerful decks in Type II, with its driving goal to establish card count superiority and maintain it. The deck is extremely versatile and effective. Once an opponent begins to suffer from the hand destruction and the Sea has the ability to counter, the deck enjoys a virtual lock. Once the Black Sea has acquired enough mana to use both consistent hand destruction cards (Hypnotic Specter or Disrupting Scepter) and a Time Elemental, all of an opponent's permanents can be eliminated once his hand is emptied. The Time Elemental simply forces an opponent to pick up his permanents while the Hypnotic Specter or Disrupting Scepter forces him to discard them.

Once the Black Sea has established card count superiority the Counterspells act kind of like Time Walks. Once an opponent has lost his hand he can only play one card per turn, and if it is not a land it can be countered. When this state is reached the Sea has already won; there is virtually no comeback.

The Sea has one other devastating element to it. It is fast with large creatures. With a Mana Vault, Dark Ritual, and a Swamp, a Vampire can be played on the first turn. Once a Vampire is out an opponent rarely worries about countering hand destruction. He typically becomes interested in eliminating the Vampire.

The Racks are of course to complement the hand destruction. Once one is in play an opponent is forced to either take damage or hold cards until he has at least three. If you have emptied an opponent's hand that gives you another three turns to draw even more hand destruction.

The Black Sea has relatively few weaknesses. The only decks the Sea would have trouble with are the fast creature decks, a struggle for the first match but winable after sideboarding. Another annoyance for the Sea is a fast land destruction deck. This can be overcome by adding a few more Islands so a Counterspell can come online quicker. Finally, another counterspell deck could prove to be troublesome early on. To overcome these the Black Sea simply adds the Strip Mines and Mana Shorts to take an opponent's counter ability offline so hand destruction can be cast.

Deck Name: The Black Sea

Block One	Block Two	Block Three
Pocket 1	Pocket 1	Pocket 1
Counterspell	Dark Ritual	Island
Counterspell	Dark Ritual	Island
Counterspell	Dark Ritual	Island
Counterspell	Dark Ritual	Island
Pocket 2	Pocket 2	Pocket 2
Power Sink	Vampire	Island
Power Sink	Vampire	Island
Power Sink	Vampire	Island
Hypnotic Specter	Vampire	Island
Pocket 3	Pocket 3	Pocket 3
Hypnotic Specter	Mahamoti Djinn	Island
Rack	Mahamoti Djinn	Island
Rack	Glasses of Urza	Swamp
Rack	Time Elemental	Swamp
Pocket 4	Pocket 4	Pocket 4
Hymn to Tourach	Mana Vault	Swamp
Hymn to Tourach	Mana Vault	Swamp
Hymn to Tourach	Mana Vault	Swamp
Hymn to Tourach	Mind Twist	Swamp
Pocket 5	Pocket 5	Pocket 5
Spell Blast	Hypnotic Specter	Swamp
Spell Blast	Island	Swamp
Disrupting Scepter	Island	Swamp
Disrupting Scepter	Island	Swamp

Sideboard

1. Strip Mine — Counterspell decks
2. Strip Mine
3. Strip Mine
4. Mana Short
5. Mana Short
6. Drudge Skeleton — Small creature decks
7. Drudge Skeleton
8. Drudge Skeleton
9. Prodigal Sorcerer
10. Prodigal Sorcerer
11. Unsummon — Large fast creature decks
12. Unsummon
13. Unsummon
14. Island — Land destruction decks
15. Island

The Ping (Type II)

The Ping deck was built after looking at the Psionic Entity and wondering just what it would take to make it work and work well. Obviously there has to be some way to keep it from killing itself. The first addition was of Holy Strength. Since the Entity does five points of damage when it uses its ability—three to itself and two to the opponent—the Spirit Link was added.

There are a number of problems with this combination, though. The first major difficulty is that the combination requires three cards, and if the Entity is eliminated the card economy and turn economy are lost along with it, which can be devastating. This is why the combination is protected by eight counter magic cards.

The rest of the deck is is combination of non-combat creature damage (Prodigal Sorcerers, Javelineers) and first-striking Tundra Wolves, an effective combination. If you have a Tundra Wolf, Javelineers, and two Prodigal Sorcerers you can use them to kill an opponent's Vampire or Serra Angel if they choose to block the Tundra Wolf. The Disrupting Scepter can be used to reduce the number of problems that the Ping has to deal with. This in combination with all of the non-combatal creature damage makes this deck perform relatively well in terms of card economy.

This deck is fun but could have a number of problems with large fast creature decks, burn decks, and possibly land destruction. The large fast creature decks will usually be too fast for the Ping. The burn decks will more than likely eliminate all of the Ping's creatures and win in card economy. The C.O.P. Reds in the sideboard should help against burn decks they will be still be difficult to overcome. Land destruction mixed with Black Vises will more than likely overcome the Ping because of its already slow development.

Deck Name: The Ping

Block One	Block Two	Block Three
Pocket 1	Pocket 1	Pocket 1
Psionic Entity	Zuran Spellcaster	Island
Psionic Entity	Zuran Spellcaster	Island
Psionic Entity	Zuran Spellcaster	Island

Jandor's Saddlebags	Zuran Spellcaster	Island
Pocket 2	Pocket 2	Pocket 2
Prodigal Sorcerer	Disrupting Scepter	Island
Prodigal Sorcerer	Disrupting Scepter	Island
Prodigal Sorcerer	Icatian Javelineers	Island
Prodigal Sorcerer	Icatian Javelineers	Island
Pocket 3	Pocket 3	Pocket 3
Holy Strength	Counterspell	Island
Holy Strength	Counterspell	Island
Holy Strength	Counterspell	Island
Holy Strength	Counterspell	Plains
Pocket 4	Pocket 4	Pocket 4
Serra Angel	Spirit Link	Plains
Serra Angel	Spirit Link	Plains
Spell Blast	Spirit Link	Plains
Spell Blast	Power Sink	Plains
Pocket 5	Pocket 5	Pocket 5
Tundra Wolf	Power Sink	Plains
Tundra Wolf	Island	Plains
Tundra Wolf	Island	Plains
Tundra Wolf	Island	Plains

Sideboard

1. Disenchant
2. Disenchant
3. Disenchant
4. C.O.P. Red
5. C.O.P. Red
6. C.O.P. Red
7. Swords to Plowshares
8. Swords to Plowshares
9. Swords to Plowshares
10. Unsummon
11. Unsummon
12. Unsummon
13. Land Tax
14. Land Tax
15. Land Tax

White Blitzing Winds: Type II Small Creature

White Blitzing Winds is a small fast creature deck. The major difference between White Blitzing Winds and a normal fast creature deck is that the Winds does not slow down in the later game. The Land Tax alone helps to solve this problem. Most of the spells in the deck require only one or two mana. Since this is the case there is no reason to lay more unless you plan on casting an Armageddon. The Land Tax simply fishes out all of the land you don't want to draw in the later game. That means you will only be drawing spells.

The Land Tax is nice on its own, but when mixed with the Winds of Change and the Zuran Orb it is devastating. The Winds in conjunction with Land Taxes become personal Wheels of Fortune. They make it simple to quickly reproduce your creatures. Also the Winds can help get the one Lightning Bolt that would end the game.

The rest of the deck is simple. Many of the white creatures have first strike, which goes well with the Javelineers and Lightning Bolts. For example, a Tundra Wolf can kill a Vampire and survive if it has a Lightning Bolt to support its assault. The Javelineers are often unexpected and can aid in combat and creature removal.

The high concentration of Lightning Bolts and Swords to Plowshares can be used to clear the playing area for the White Winds' attacking creatures. The Armageddons are used when the Wind is working at an advantage over an opponent. The Howling Mines prevent slowdown and maintain a constant flow of creatures.

The one catch about the White Winds is that in most cases the Land Tax has to be used in order to make the red portion of the deck effective. An opponent could eliminate its ability to use its red spells by simply stripping out the mountains. Most opponents will not realize this until after they have been crushed.

The White Winds should have little or no problem against most decks with the exception of those that have a large amount of Gloom. In order to overcome this, you should simply sideboard in the Fireballs and Disintegrates to supplement creatures cast early on. The only other deck that might prove troublesome would be a burn deck. If a burn deck is encountered, the C.O.P. Reds should act as an efficient counter along with the Eye for an Eyes. Usually large Fireballs are cast late in the game after a burn deck has taken a good deal of damage from small creatures, making the Eye for an Eye very deadly.

Deck Name: White Blitzing Winds

Block One	Block Two	Block Three
Pocket 1	Pocket 1	Pocket 1
Savannah Lion	Swords to Plowshares	Swords to Plowshares
Savannah Lion	Swords to Plowshares	Mountain
Savannah Lion	Disenchant	Mountain
Savannah Lion	Disenchant	Plains
Pocket 2	Pocket 2	Pocket 2
Tundra Wolf	Lightning Bolt	Plains
Tundra Wolf	Lightning Bolt	Plains
Tundra Wolf	Lightning Bolt	Plains
Tundra Wolf	Zuran Orb	Plains
Pocket 3	Pocket 3	Pocket 3
Icatian Infantry	Armageddon	Plains
Icatian Infantry	Armageddon	Plains
Icatian Infantry	Land Tax	Plains
Icatian Infantry	Land Tax	Plains
Pocket 4	Pocket 4	Pocket 4
White Knight	Land Tax	Plains
White Knight	Land Tax	Plains
White Knight	Winds of Change	Plains
White Knight	Winds of Change	Plains
Pocket 5	Pocket 5	Pocket 5
Icatian Javelineers	Crusade	Plains
Icatian Javelineers	Crusade	Plains
Icatian Javelineers	Crusade	Plains
Icatian Javelineers	Crusade	Plains

Sideboard

1. Disenchant — Anti-enchantment/artifacts
2. Disenchant
3. Swords to Plowshares — Large creature decks/regeneration decks
4. Spirit Link
5. Fireball — Decks with Gloom
6. Fireball
7. Disintegrate — Decks with Gloom or numerous regenerators
8. Disintegrate
9. Disintegrate
10. Winter Orb — Slow expensive decks
11. C.O.P. Red — Burn decks
12. C.O.P. Red
13. C.O.P. Red
14. Eye for an Eye — Burn decks/slow limited roads to victory decks
15. Eye for an Eye

Appendix C

Deck Design Procedure

     I. Devise a driving idea for your deck
    II. Specify other cards that work well with this idea
   III. Record the deck
   IV. Perform analysis
        A. Calculate mana distribution
        B. Calculate removal capability and importance of removal
        C. Calculate effectiveness versus the five basic decks
    V. Identify weaknesses
   VI. Assemble deck
  VII. Play against the five basic decks
 VIII. Remove unnecessary cards and make appropriate modifications and enhancements
   IX. Assemble sideboard
    X. Record changes
   XI. Return to step IV

Appendix D

Glossary

Action-based decks: Decks that force an opponent to react to his assaults without considerable attention to reaction. Usually manifested through speedy offense.

Burn decks: Decks that utilize direct damage spells as their main form of both offense and defense. Seldom used in isolation.

Card count economy: A measure of card economy in which the number of cards utilized versus the number of cards nullified is measured.

Card economy: The efficiency a card achieves in play, generally used as a comparative term.

Counter deck: A reaction-based deck that utilizes counter magic to attempt to stop an opponent's offensive and break relationships.

Deck design procedure: An organized method through which to go about designing an effective deck.

Deck environment: The global benefits and hindrances a deck creates (e.g., Howling Mine, Land's Edge, Nether Void, etc.).

Draw rule: The general observance that the player who draws more cards will usually have a great advantage.

Draw strength: An estimation of the number of cards in a deck that allow its player to draw more cards.

Fast creature deck: A deck that seeks to overcome its opponent by quickly mounting a creature offensive before its opponent can effectively respond.

Fast deck theory: Theory of deck design based on the premise that the faster you eliminate an opponent, the less ofa chance he has to eliminate you. The key to fast deck theory is the speed at which a deck tries to achieve victory.

Five basic decks (FBD): A group of decks that represent the common themes present in decks. Particularly useful in testing procedures.

Hand destruction decks: Resource denial decks that seek to defeat an opponent by removing cards from his or her hand, and thus options from his or her game.

Land destruction decks: Resource denial decks that seek to defeat an opponent by removing his or her ability to produce mana.

Reaction-based decks: Decks that seek to achieve victory by being prepared for all contingencies and removing an opponent's ability to act.

Resource denial: Theory of deck design in which a deck seeks to achieve victory by refusing to allow an opponent the basic resources of the game, usually cards and mana.

Sixty-card rule: General rule that states one should always play with the minimum required number of cards in a deck in order to decrease randomness. This is usually sixty cards under convocation rules.

Slow deck theory: Theory of decks which generally works toward victory in a slow fashion by establishing control of the environment and reducing an opponent's options.

Turn economy: Measure of card economy based on the number of turns gained or lost by an action.

Utility: Measure of card economy based on the effectiveness of each player's cards.

White turbo deck: Usually a deck based on small white creatures and Crusades. Very common in tournaments, particularly Type II tournaments.

Sideboard Principles

Offensive Sideboarding Principles

- Color-specific—Constructed to hinder different colors by using color specific cards.

- Type-specific—Constructed to hinder decks that rely heavily on different card types such as mixed lands, Counterspells, or artifacts.

- Tweak—Constructed to enhance certain elements of a deck that are most effective against an opponent's deck.

- Transformational—Constructed to change a deck from one form or type to another.

Defensive Sideboarding Principle

- Defensive counter—Constructed as a countermeasure against specific cards that weaken the deck potency.

Appendix F

Deck Construction Worksheet

The following sheet is added for your convenience. Simply copy the page and use it to record any deck concepts you might have. This will make the design process faster and easier to track. It is often a good idea to keep a file of these decks so they may assist you in your future designs.

Deck Name:

Block One	Block Two	Block Three
Pocket 1	Pocket 1	Pocket 1
Pocket 2	Pocket 2	Pocket 2
Pocket 3	Pocket 3	Pocket 3
Pocket 4	Pocket 4	Pocket 4
Pocket 5	Pocket 5	Pocket 5

Sideboard:

1.	6.	11.
2.	7.	12.
3.	8.	13.
4.	9.	14.
5.	10.	15.

Appendix G

The National Championship:
The Pilgrimage to Philadelphia

The ballroom of the Philadelphia convention center was teeming with nervous energy as the eight finalists for the national championship were being informed about the proper behavior they were to display while on camera. Four of the finalists were playing hand destruction decks, three were playing red green burn/vise decks, and one was playing a land destruction fast creature deck.

Because of the Swiss format of the semifinals of the day before, the finalists were all seated next to each other as they worked to qualify. The Swiss system is such that all of the top-ranked players are seated near each other. Some of the finalists simply took a look at what their soon-to-be-opponents were playing and prepared for them by concentrating their decks and sideboards to be in opposition to their opponents'.

Because of this, of the four hand destruction decks that went to the finals, only one made the American team. Pete Leiher of Florida was the only one of the four finalists playing hand destruction who was able to wade through his pre-sideboarded opponents and make the American team. Pete was playing straight black mixed with artifact support.

Deck Name: Pete Leiher's Discard Deck

Block One	Block Two	Block Three
Pocket 1	Pocket 1	Pocket 1
Hypnotic Specter	Dark Banishing	Mishra's Factory
Hypnotic Specter	Dark Banishing	Mishra's Factory
Hypnotic Specter	Disrupting Scepter	Mishra's Factory
Hypnotic Specter	Disrupting Scepter	Swamp
Pocket 2	Pocket 2	Pocket 2
Hymn to Tourach	Aeolipile	Swamp
Hymn to Tourach	Aeolipile	Swamp
Hymn to Tourach	Aeolipile	Swamp
Hymn to Tourach	Nevinyrral's Disk	Swamp
Pocket 3	Pocket 3	Pocket 3
Paralyze	Drain Life	Swamp
Paralyze	Drain Life	Swamp
Paralyze	Drain Life	Swamp
Paralyze	Zuran Orb	Swamp
Pocket 4	Pocket 4	Pocket 4
Rack	Mind Twist	Swamp
Rack	Thrull Retainer	Swamp
Rack	Thrull Retainer	Swamp
Rack	Thrull Retainer	Swamp
Pocket 5	Pocket 5	Pocket 5
Dark Ritual	Black Knight	Swamp
Dark Ritual	Black Knight	Swamp
Dark Ritual	Black Knight	Swamp
Dark Ritual	Black Knight	Swamp

Sideboard

1. Gloom
2. Gloom
3. Gloom
4. Gloom
5. Terror
6. Terror
7. Icy Manipulator
8. Black Vise
9. Black Vise
10. Aeolipile
11. Ivory Tower
12. Jayemdae Tome
13. Drain Life
14. Strip Mine
15. Mishra's Factory

Pete's said that Incinerates proved to be a problem for his deck. He also said that he had trouble with blue/white decks and that he would not use Gloom against a blue/white deck. Pyroclasm also proved to be a problem for Pete's deck. He said that if he suspected his opponent was using Pyroclasm then he would only play one creature at a time. Pete said that the advantages of the deck were obvious. Black is second most durable of the colors. Because of the Dark Rituals, most vice decks proved to be no problem for Pete. His deck is designed simply to take cards out of an opponent's hand and make them suffer to the Rack.

The other finalist who shared the third-place ranking with Pete was Mike Long of Virginia. Mike said that the source of his success was the knowledge he acquired in the open atmosphere of the Game Parlor in Chantilly, Virgina. Mike played a mixture of creatures, creature removal, and land destruction.

Deck Name: Mike Long's Orgg Deck

Block One	Block Two	Block Three
Pocket 1	Pocket 1	Pocket 1
Stone Rain	Fireball	Fellwar Stones
Stone Rain	Fireball	Fellwar Stones
Stone Rain	Black Vise	Swamp
Stone Rain	Black Vise	Mountain
Pocket 2	Pocket 2	Pocket 2
Icequake	Foul Familiar	Sulfurous Springs
Icequake	Foul Familiar	Sulfurous Springs
Icy Manipulator	Foul Familiar	Sulfurous Springs
Icy Manipulator	Foul Familiar	Sulfurous Springs
Pocket 3	Pocket 3	Pocket 3
Strip Mine	Paralyze	Mountain
Strip Mine	Paralyze	Mountain
Strip Mine	Paralyze	Mountain
Strip Mine	Paralyze	Mountain

Pocket 4	Pocket 4	Pocket 4
Incinerate	Orgg	Swamp
Incinerate	Orgg	Swamp
Incinerate	Orgg	Swamp
Incinerate	Mind Twist	Swamp
Pocket 5	Pocket 5	Pocket 5
Lightning Bolt	Dark Ritual	Swamp
Lightning Bolt	Dark Ritual	Swamp
Lightning Bolt	Dark Ritual	Mountain
Lightning Bolt	Dark Ritual	Mountain

Sideboard

1. Gloom
2. Gloom
3. Gloom
4. Rack
5. Rack
6. Rack
7. Hymn to Tourach
8. Hymn to Tourach
9. Hymn to Tourach
10. Pyroclasm
11. Pyroclasm
12. Pyroclasm
13. Shatter
14. Shatter
15. Jester's Cap

Mike did well in the finals but ended up losing to a couple of his opponent's excellent draws. In the first game of his final match he suffered to a third turn Channel Fireball. In the second game he was eliminated by early Vise damage. Mike's deck is constructed to remove an opponent's creatures with Bolts, Incinerates, and Paralyzes while he beats on his opponents with his Orggs and Foul Familiars. This deck also reduces its opponent's options with its land destruction.

The second-place winner was Henry Stern from Los Angeles, California. Henry was playing the Vice Age deck. The Vise Age deck is normally designed around Winter Orbs, Howling Mines, Black Vises, Channel, Orcish Lumberjacks, Jokulhaups, Fireballs, Incinerates, Lightning Bolts, and Howling Mines. This version was modified to fight hand destruction decks.

Deck Name: Henry Stern's Vice Age Deck

Block One	Block Two	Block Three
Pocket 1	Pocket 1	Pocket 1
Fireball	Dragon	Sylvan Library
Fireball	Dragon	Forest
Fireball	Birds of Paradise	Forest
Fireball	Birds of Paradise	Forest
Pocket 2	Pocket 2	Pocket 2
Lightning Bolt	Birds of Paradise	Forest
Lightning Bolt	Stormbind	Forest
Lightning Bolt	Stormbind	Forest
Lightning Bolt	Stormbind	Forest
Pocket 3	Pocket 3	Pocket 3
Howling Mine	Strip Mine	Dwarven Ruins
Howling Mine	Strip Mine	Dwarven Ruins
Howling Mine	Strip Mine	Mountain
Howling Mine	Strip Mine	Mountain
Pocket 4	Pocket 4	Pocket 4
Orcish Lumberjack	Incinerate	Mountain
Orcish Lumberjack	Incinerate	Mountain
Orcish Lumberjack	Incinerate	Mountain
Channel	Incinerate	Mountain
Pocket 5	Pocket 5	Pocket 5
Jokulhaups	Black Vise	Karplusan Forest
Jokulhaups	Black Vise	Karplusan Forest
Lifeforce	Black Vise	Karplusan Forest
Shatter	Black Vise	Karplusan Forest

Sideboard

1. Shatter
2. Shatter
3. Whirling Dervish
4. Whirling Dervish
5. Whirling Dervish
6. Whirling Dervish
7. Lifeforce
8. Lifeforce
9. Pyroclasm
10. Pyroclasm
11. Pyroclasm
12. Anarchy
13. Anarchy
14. Pyroblast
15. Pyroblast

Mark Justice of Salt Lake City, Utah, winner of the United States Championship, managed to win because he took a risk. Mark constructed his deck on the premise that he knew what the majority of his opponents were playing. He knew that his opponents would rely heavily on artifacts, so he used several anti-artifact cards. He knew that several of his opponents were playing black discard, so he prepared for them with Whirling Dervishes and Lifeforces. This is why it is good to bring two different decks in case you qualify and then go on to the finals.

Mark said that he simply took the risk and played against his opponents instead of trying to build the most universally effective deck. The lesson to be learned is that you should avoid playing one type of deck exclusively and have an extra deck ready so that an opponent cannot prepare for you beforehand.

Deck Name: Mark Justice's Red/Green Deck

Block One	Block Two	Block Three
Pocket 1	Pocket 1	Pocket 1
Whirling Dervish	Strip Mine	Karplusan Forest
Whirling Dervish	Strip Mine	Karplusan Forest
Whirling Dervish	Strip Mine	Karplusan Forest
Whirling Dervish	Strip Mine	Karplusan Forest
Pocket 2	Pocket 2	Pocket 2
Lifeforce	Johtoll Wurm	Mountain
Lifeforce	Zuran Orb	Mountain
Shivan Dragon	Zuran Orb	Mountain
Orgg	Channel	Mountain
Pocket 3	Pocket 3	Pocket 3
Incinerate	Tranquility	Forest
Incinerate	Pyroclasm	Forest
Incinerate	Pyroclasm	Forest
Incinerate	Timberline Ridge	Forest
Pocket 4	Pocket 4	Pocket 4
Lighting Bolt	Crumble	Mountain
Lighting Bolt	Crumble	Mountain

Lighting Bolt	Crumble	Mountain
Lighting Bolt	Crumble	Mountain
Pocket 5	Pocket 5	Pocket 5
Black Vise	Fireball	Forest
Black Vise	Fireball	Forest
Ivory Tower	Fireball	Forest
Rack	Fireball	Forest

Sideboard

1. Pyroclasm
2. Pyroclasm
3. Earthquake
4. Earthquake
5. Rack
6. Hurricane
7. Lifeforce
8. Lifeforce
9. Tranquility
10. Tranquility
11. Jayemdae Tome
12. Disrupting Scepter
13. Disrupting Scepter
14. Shatter
15. Shatter

List of Cards
Sorted by Card Type

This list is constructed solely for players. The list is intended to assist players in designing and constructing decks. For instance, if you are building a Goblin deck and would like to review all of the Goblins the game has to offer, they are all sorted so one may view them as a group. After some study of this list a player can also improve his or her power to predict the likelihood of different effects by analyzing the different card types.

Land

Card	Type	Cost	Power/ Toughness	Description
Adarkar Wastes	Land	--	--	Tap to add 1 colorless to your mana pool or tap to add W to your mana pool and suffer 1 damage or tap to add U to your mana pool and suffer 1 damage.
Adventurers' Guildhouse	Land	--	--	Your green legends may band with other legends.
Badlands	Land	--	--	Tap to add R or B to your mana pool.
Bayou	Land	--	--	Tap to add B or G to your mana pool.

Card	Type	Cost	Power/ Toughness	Description
Bazaar of Baghdad	Land	--	--	Tap to draw 2 cards and immediately discard 3.
Bottomless Vault	Land	--	--	Comes into play tapped. May leave tapped to add 1 storage counter. Tap and remove X storage counters to add X B to your mana pool.
Brushland	Land	--	--	Tap to add 1 colorless to your mana pool or tap to add W to your mana pool and suffer 1 damage or tap to add G to your mana pool and suffer 1 damage.
Cathedral of Serra	Land	--	--	Your white legends may band with other legends.
City of Brass	Land	--	--	Tap for 1 mana of any color. Take 1 damage whenever tapped.
City of Shadows	Land	--	--	Tap and sacrifice one of your creatures andremove it from the game instead. Put a counter on City of Shadows. Tap to add colorless mana equal to the number of counters on City of Shadows.
Desert	Land	--	--	Tap to do 1 damage to attacking creature after it has dealt damage.
Diamond Valley	Land	--	--	Tap to sacrifice a creature to gain its toughness in life.
Dwarven Hold	Land	--	--	Comes into play tapped. May leave tapped to add 1 storage counter. Tap and remove X storage counters to add X R to your mana pool.
Dwarven Ruins	Land	--	--	Comes into play tapped. Tap to add R to your mana pool. Tap and sacrifice to add RR to your mana pool.
Ebon Stronghold	Land	--	--	Comes into play tapped. Tap to add B to your mana pool. Tap and sacrifice to add BB to your mana pool.
Elephant Graveyard	Land	--	--	Tap to add 1 colorless to pool or to regenerate target elephant or mammoth.
Forest	Land	--	--	Tap to add ʿG to your mana pool.

Card	Type	Cost	Power/ Toughness	Description
Glacial Chasm	Land	--	--	Cumulative upkeep of 2 life. Sacrifice a land when it comes into play. Your creatures cannot attack and all damage dealt to you is reduced to 0.
Halls of Mist	Land	--	--	Cumulative upkeep of 1. No creatures can attack if they attacked during their controller's last turn.
Havenwood Battleground	Land	--	--	Comes into play tapped. Tap to add G to your mana pool. Tap and sacrifice to add GG to your mana pool.
Hollow Trees	Land	--	--	Comes into play tapped. May leave tapped to add 1 storage counter. Tap and remove X storage counters to add X G to your mana pool.
Icatian Store	Land	--	--	Comes into play tapped. May leave tapped to add 1 storage counter. Tap and remove X storage counters to add X W to your mana pool.
Ice Floe	Land	--	--	You may choose not to untap Ice Floe during your untap phase. Tap to tap target creature without flying ability that attacks you. As long as Ice Floe remains tapped so does the creature it tapped.
Island	Land	--	--	Tap to add U to your mana pool.
Island of Wak-Wak	Land	--	--	Tap to reduce target flying creature's power to 0 until end of turn.
Karplusan Forest	Land	--	--	Tap to add 1 colorless to your mana pool or tap to add R to your mana pool and suffer 1 damage or tap to add G to your mana pool and suffer 1 damage.
Land Cap	Land	--	--	Does not untap during its controller's untap phase if it has a depletion counter on it. During upkeep remove 1 counter if Land Cap has one present. Tap to add W to your mana pool and add a depletion counter to Land Cap or tap to add U to your mana pool and add a depletion counter to it.

Card	Type	Cost	Power/Toughness	Description
Lava Tubes	Land	--	--	Does not untap if it has a depletion counter on it. During upkeep remove 1 depletion counter. Tap to add B to your mana pool and put one depletion counter on Lava Tubes or tap to add R to your mana pool and put one depletion counter on it.
Library of Alexandria	Land	--	--	Tap to add 1 colorless mana to your pool or tap to draw 1 card, but only if you have 7 cards in your hand.
Maze of Ith	Land	--	--	Tap to untap target attacking creature. Treat creature as if it had never attacked.
Mishra's Factory	Land	--	--	Tap to add 1 colorless mana to your pool. (1) Mishra's Factory becomes an assembly worker until end of turn. Tap to add +1/+1 to any assembly worker until end of turn.
Mishra's Workshop	Land	--	--	Tap to add 3 colorless mana which can only be used to cast artifacts.
Mountain	Land	--	--	Tap to add R to your mana pool.
Mountain Stronghold	Land	--	--	Your red legends may band with other legends.
Oasis	Land	--	--	Tap to prevent 1 damage to any creature.
Plains	Land	--	--	Tap to add W to your mana pool.
Plateau	Land	--	--	Tap to add R or W to your mana pool.
Rainbow Vale	Land	--	--	Tap to add 1 mana of any color to your mana pool, but control of Rainbow Vale then passes to opponent.
River Delta	Land	--	--	Does not untap if it has a depletion counter on it. During upkeep remove 1 depletion counter. Tap to add U or B to your mana pool and put one depletion counter on it.
Ruins of Trokair	Land	--	--	Comes into play tapped. Tap to add W to your mana pool. Tap and sacrifice to add WW to your mana pool.

Card	Type	Cost	Power/ Toughness	Description
Safe Haven	Land	--	--	Tap+(2) to remove 1 creature you control from the game. This ability may be played as an interrupt. During upkeep sacrifice to return all creatures removed from the game by Safe Haven to game. Treat these creatures as if they were just summoned.
Sand Silos	Land	--	--	Comes into play tapped. You may choose not to untap to add a storage counter. Tap and remove X storage counters to add X U to your mana pool.
Savannah	Land	--	--	Tap to add G or W to your mana pool.
Scrubland	Land	--	--	Tap to add B or W to your mana pool.
Seafarer's Quay	Land	--	--	All your blue legends may band with other legends.
Snow-Covered Forest	Land	--	--	Tap to add G to your mana pool.
Snow-Covered Island	Land	--	--	Tap to add U to your mana pool.
Snow-Covered Mountain	Land	--	--	Tap to add R to your mana pool.
Snow-Covered Plains	Land	--	--	Tap to add W to your mana pool.
Snow-Covered Swamp	Land	--	--	Tap to add B to your mana pool.
Sorrow's Path	Land	--	--	Tap to exchange 2 of opponent's blocking creatures. This exchange may not create an illegal block. Sorrow's Path does 2 damage to you and 2 damage to each creature you control when it is tapped.
Strip Mine	Land	--	--	Tap to add 1 colorless mana to your pool. Tap and sacrifice to destroy any one land.
Sulfurous Springs	Land	--	--	Tap to add 1 to your mana pool or tap to add B or R to your mana pool and does 1 damage to you.
Svyelunite Temple	Land	--	--	Comes into play tapped. Tap to add U to your mana pool. Sacrifice and tap to add UU to your mana pool.
Swamp	Land	--	--	Tap to add B to your mana pool.
Taiga	Land	--	--	Tap to add G or R to your mana pool.

Card	Type	Cost	Power/ Toughness	Description
Timberline Ridge	Land	--	--	Does not untap if it has depletion counter on it. Remove 1 depletion counter during upkeep. Tap to add R or G to your mana pool and put 1 depletion counter on it.
Tropical Island	Land	--	--	Tap to add G or U to your mana pool.
Tundra	Land	--	--	Tap to add U or W to your mana pool.
Underground River	Land	--	--	Tap to add 1 to your mana pool or tap to add U or B to your mana pool and does 1 damage to you.
Underground Sea	Land	--	--	Tap to add B or U to your mana pool.
Unholy Citadel	Land	--	--	All your black legends may band with other legends.
Urza's Mine	Land	--	--	Tap to add 1 colorless mana to your pool. If you also control Urza's Power Plant and Urza's Tower, tap to add 2 colorless mana to your pool.
Urza's Power Plant	Land	--	--	Tap to add 1 colorless mana to your pool. If you also control Urza's Mine and Urza's Tower, tap to add 2 colorless mana to your pool.
Urza's Tower	Land	--	--	Tap to add 1 colorless mana to your pool. If you also control Urza's Mine and Urza's Power Plant, tap to add 3 colorless mana to your pool.
Veldt	Land	--	--	Does not untap if it has depletion counter on it. During upkeep remove 1 depletion counter. Tap to add W or G to your mana pool and place 1 depletion counter on it.
Volcanic Island	Land	--	--	Tap to add R or U to your mana pool.
Hammerheim	Legendary Land	--	--	Tap to add R to your mana pool or tap to remove landwalking ability from 1 creature until end of turn.
Karakas	Legendary Land	--	--	Tap to add W to your mana pool or tap to return 1 legend from play to its owner's hand.
Pendelhaven	Legendary Land	--	--	Tap to add G to your mana pool or tap to add +1/+2 to any 1/1 creature until end of turn.

Card	Type	Cost	Power/ Toughness	Description
The Tabernacle at Pendrell Vale	Legendary Land	--	--	While Tabernacle is in play all creatures in play have an additional upkeep cost of 1 colorless mana.
Tolaria	Legendary Land	--	--	Tap to add U to your mana pool or tap to remove banding or bands with other from a creature until end of turn.
Urborg	Legendary Land	--	--	Tap to add B to your mana pool or tap to remove first strike or swamp-walk from one creature until end of turn.

Artifacts

Card	Type	Cost	Power/ Toughness	Description
Aeolipile	Artifact	2	--	Tap+(1) Sacrifice to do 2 damage to any target.
Aegis of the Meek	Artifact	3	--	Tap+(1) Target 1/1 creature gains +1/+2.
Al-abara's Carpet	Artifact	5	--	Tap+(5) to prevent all damage done by non-flying creatures until end of turn.
Aladdin's Lamp	Artifact	10	--	Tap+(X) Instead of drawing a card during your draw phase draw X cards during upkeep and keep only one.
Aladdin's Ring	Artifact	8	--	Tap+(8) Do 4 damage to any target.
Alchor's Tomb	Artifact	4	--	Tap+(2) Change color of any of your permanents in play.
Amulet of Kroog	Artifact	2	--	Tap+(2) Prevent 1 damage to any target.
Amulet of Quoz	Artifact	6	--	Use only if playing for ante. Tap+(0): Sacrifice Amulet of Quoz and flip a coin. Your favor: opponent loses. Opponent's favor: you lose. Opponent can ante another card to counter this effect.
Ankh of Mishra	Artifact	2	--	Any time any player brings a land into play, does 2 points of damage to that player.

Card	Type	Cost	Power/Toughness	Description
Arcum's Sleigh	Artifact	1	--	Tap+(2) Attacking this turn does not cause target creature to tap. You may not use this ability if defending player has no snow-covered lands in play.
Arcum's Weathervane	Artifact	2	--	Tap+(2) Make a snow-covered land non-snow-covered or vice versa. Mark this change with a counter.
Arcum's Whistle	Artifact	3	--	Tap+(3) Target non-wall creature must attack. At end of turn, destroy if it was unable attack. Use this ability only during the creature controller's turn before he or she declares an attack. The creature's controller may counter by paying the creature's casting cost. Does not affect creatures brought into play that turn.
Arena of the Ancients	Artifact	3	--	Taps all legends as they enter play, legends do not untap as normal.
Armageddon Clock	Artifact	6	--	Add 1 counter each upkeep. Does 1 damage to each player for each counter at end of upkeep. Any player may remove a counter during upkeep for 4 mana.
Ashnod's Altar	Artifact	3	--	0: Sacrifice a creature to gain 2 colorless mana.
Ashnod's Battle Gear	Artifact	2	--	Tap+(2) Give creature +2/-2. Effect remains until untapped. May choose not to untap.
Ashnod's Transmogrant	Artifact	1	--	Sacrifice Transmogrant to give any creature +1/+1 and make it an artifact creature.
Balm of Restoration	Artifact	2	--	Tap+(1) Sacrifice to gain 2 life or prevent 2 damage to any player or creature.
Barbed Sextant	Artifact	1	--	Tap+(1) Sacrifice to add 1 mana of any color to your pool and play as an interrupt. Draw a card at the beginning of the next turn's upkeep.
Barl's Cage	Artifact	4	--	3: Target creature does not untap as normal during its controller's next untap phase.

Card	Type	Cost	Power/ Toughness	Description
Basalt Monolith	Artifact	3	--	Tap to add 3 colorless mana to your mana pool. Does not untap as normal. Pay 3 to untap Monolith.
Baton of Morale	Artifact	2	--	2: Target creature gains banding ability until the end of the turn.
Black Lotus	Artifact	0	--	Tap and sacrifice to add 3 mana of any color to your mana pool.
Black Mana Battery	Artifact	4	--	Tap+(2) add a token to Battery. Tap to add B to your mana pool. Also can convert tokens to B.
Black Vise	Artifact	1	--	During your opponent's upkeep, does 1 damage to opponent for each card in their hand above 4.
Blue Mana Battery	Artifact	4	--	Tap+(2) add a token to Battery. Tap to add U to your mana pool. Also can convert tokens to U.
Bone Flute	Artifact	3	--	Tap+(2) All creatures in play get -1/-0.
Book of Raas	Artifact	6	--	2: Pay 2 life to draw one card. Damage may not be prevented or redirected.
Bottle of Suleiman	Artifact	4	--	1: Sacrifice and flip a coin. If you win you get a 5/5 flying artifact creature; if you lose you take 5 damage.
Bronze Tablet	Artifact	6	--	Tap+(4) Swap Tablet w/any card in play. Effect is permanent but may be countered with a loss of 10 life. Ante games only.
Candelabra of Tawnos	Artifact	1	--	X: Untap X lands.
Celestial Prism	Artifact	3	--	Tap+(2) Add 1 mana of any color to your mana pool.
Celestial Sword	Artifact	6	--	Tap+(3) Target creature you control gets +3/+3 until the end of the turn, then bury that target creature.
Chaos Orb	Artifact	2	--	1: Drop card on table from a height of at least 1 foot. Must rotate 360 degrees. Orb and cards touched by Orb are destroyed.
City in a Bottle	Artifact	1	--	Removes all Arabian Nights cards from play and prevents new ones from being brought into play.

Card	Type	Cost	Power/Toughness	Description
Conch Horn	Artifact	2	--	Tap+(1) Sacrifice and draw 2 cards. Return any card from your hand to deck.
Conservator	Artifact	4	--	Tap+(3) Prevent the loss of 2 life.
Copper Tablet	Artifact	1	--	Does 1 point of damage to each player during their upkeep.
Coral Helm	Artifact	3	--	3: Discard a card at random from your hand. Add +2/+2 to any creature until end of turn.
Crown of the Ages	Artifact	2	--	Tap+(4) Switch target enchantment from one creature to another legal target. The controller does not change. Treat target enchantment as though it were just cast on the new target.
Crystal Rod	Artifact	1	--	1: Gain 1 life whenever a blue spell is cast.
Cursed Rack	Artifact	4	--	Your opponent must discard down to 4 cards at the end of their discard phase.
Cyclopean Tomb	Artifact	4	--	Tap+(2) Change any land in play to swamp during your upkeep. Lands revert at one per turn when Tomb is destroyed.
Dark Sphere	Artifact	0	--	Tap to sacrifice and prevent half the damage done to you from one single source rounded down.
Delif's Cone	Artifact	0	--	Tap and sacrifice this card. If creature you control attacks and is not blocked you may choose not to deal damage with this creature and gain life equal to its power.
Delif's Cube	Artifact	1	--	Tap+(2) If target creature you control attacks and is not blocked instead of doing damage you gain a cube counter. 2: Remove a token to regenerate target creature.
Despotic Scepter	Artifact	1	--	Tap to bury a target permanent you control.
Dingus Egg	Artifact	4	--	When any land is destroyed controller takes 2 points of damage.
Disrupting Scepter	Artifact	3	--	Tap+(3) Opponent must discard a card of his or her choice. This may only be used during controller's turn.

Card	Type	Cost	Power/Toughness	Description
Draconian Cylix	Artifact	3	--	Tap+(2) Discard a card at random from your hand to regenerate target creature.
Ebony Horse	Artifact	3	--	Tap+(2) Attacking creature escapes after defense is chosen.
Elkin Bottle	Artifact	3	--	Tap+(3) Turn the top card of your library face up in front of you and play it as if it were in your hand; you must play the card by end of turn or discard.
Elven Lyre	Artifact	2	--	Tap+(1) and sacrifice to give target creature +2/+2 until end of turn.
Feldon's Cane	Artifact	1	--	Tap to reshuffle your graveyard into your library. Remove Cane from the game.
Fellwar Stone	Artifact	2	--	Tap to add 1 mana to your pool of any color that an opponents' land can generate. This ability is played as an interrupt.
Flying Carpet	Artifact	4	--	Tap+(2) Gives flying to target creature until end of turn. Destroyed if target is destroyed while using it.
Forcefield	Artifact	3	--	1: Lose only 1 life to an unblocked creature.
Forethought Amulet	Artifact	5	--	Reduces damage done by sorceries and instants to 2, pay 3 during upkeep or it is destroyed.
Fountain of Youth	Artifact	0	--	Tap+(2) Gain 1 life.
Fyndhorn Bow	Artifact	2	--	Tap+(3) Target creature gains first strike ability until the end of turn.
Gauntlet of Might	Artifact	4	--	All red creatures in play gain +1/+1 and all mountains produce 1 extra red mana.
Gauntlets of Chaos	Artifact	5	--	5: Sacrifice to swap permanent you control with opponent's land, creature, or artifact until end of game. Any enchantments on these cards are destroyed.
Glasses of Urza	Artifact	1	--	Tap to look at opponent's hand.

Card	Type	Cost	Power/ Toughness	Description
Goblin Lyre	Artifact	3	--	0: Sacrifice Goblin Lyre. Flip a coin. Opponent wins: does X damage to you where X is number of creatures opponent controls. You win: Does X damage to opponent where X is the number of creatures you control.
Golgothian Sylex	Artifact	4	--	1: Destroys all Antiquities cards in play including itself.
Green Mana Battery	Artifact	4	--	Tap+(2) Add a token to Battery. Tap to add G to your mana pool. Can also convert tokens to G.
Helm of Chatzuk	Artifact	1	--	Tap+(1) Gives target creature banding until end of turn.
Hematite Talisman	Artifact	2	--	3: Untap target permanent in play. Use this ability only when a red spell is cast successfully and only once for each red spell cast.
Hive, The	Artifact	5	--	Tap+(5) Make a 1/1 flying wasp counter.
Horn of Deafening	Artifact	4	--	Tap+(2) Makes creature deal no damage this turn.
Howling Mine	Artifact	2	--	Each player must draw an additional card during his draw phase.
Ice Cauldron	Artifact	4	--	Tap+(X) Put a charge counter on Cauldron and place a spell card face up on it. Note the type and amount of mana for activation cost. Use this ability only if there are no charge counters on Ice Cauldron. You may play that card as though it were in your hand. Tap to remove the charge counter from Ice Cauldron to add mana of the type and amount used to pay activation cost to your pool. This mana may only be used to cast spell on the Ice Cauldron.
Icy Manipulator	Artifact	4	--	Tap+(1) Tap any creature, land, or artifact in play. No effects are generated from this card.
Illusionary Mask	Artifact	2	--	X: summon any creature face down for casting cost + X. Creature becomes face up when damaged or used.

Card	Type	Cost	Power/ Toughness	Description
Implements of Sacrifice	Artifact	2	--	Tap+(1) Sacrifice to add 2 mana of any color to your pool. Play this ability as an interrupt.
Infinite Hourglass	Artifact	4	--	During your upkeep, put a time counter on Hourglass. During any upkeep, a player may pay 3 colorless to remove a time counter from Infinite Hourglass. All creatures gain +1/+0 for each time counter remaining on the Hourglass.
Iron Star	Artifact	1	--	1: Gain 1 life whenever a red spell is cast.
Ivory Cup	Artifact	1	--	1: Gain 1 life whenever a white spell is cast.
Ivory Tower	Artifact	1	--	During your upkeep you gain 1 life for each card over 4 in your hand.
Jade Monolith	Artifact	4	--	1: Transfer damage to self from creature.
Jade Statue	Artifact	4	--	2: Becomes a creature for the duration of one attack or defense.
Jalum Tome	Artifact	3	--	Tap+(2) Draw a card and then discard a card of your choice.
Jandor's Ring	Artifact	6	--	Tap+(2) Discard the card you just drew and draw another.
Jandor's Saddlebags	Artifact	2	--	Tap+(3) Untap a creature.
Jayemdae Tome	Artifact	4	--	Tap+(4) Draw a card.
Jester's Cap	Artifact	4	--	Tap+(2) Sacrifice to search target player's library and remove 3 cards from the game. Reshuffle after.
Jester's Mask	Artifact	5	--	Comes into play tapped. Tap+(1) Sacrifice to look at opponent's hand and library. Replace hand with same number of cards. Reshuffle.
Jeweled Amulet	Artifact	0	--	Tap+(1) Put charge counter on Amulet. Tap to remove charge counter to add 1 mana of type used to place counter to pool. Play as an interrupt.
Jeweled Bird	Artifact	1	--	Tap to exchange for your ante and draw a new card. Bury old ante.

Card	Type	Cost	Power/ Toughness	Description
Knowledge Vault	Artifact	4	--	Tap+(2) Put a card from your library face down under Vault. Sacrifice Vault and your entire hand to take cards under Vault as your hand.
Kormus Bell	Artifact	4	--	All swamps in play are considered 1/1 creatures.
Kry Shield	Artifact	2	--	Tap+(2) Give +0/+X to a creature where X is its casting cost.
Lapis Lazuli Talisman	Artifact	2	--	3: Untap a target permanent in play. Use only when blue spells are cast and only once for each.
Library of Leng	Artifact	1	--	Skip discard phase. Discard to top of library.
Life Chisel	Artifact	4	--	Sacrifice a creature during your upkeep to gain its toughness in life.
Life Matrix	Artifact	4	--	Tap+(4) Add a regeneration token to a creature. May only be used during your upkeep.
Living Armor	Artifact	4	--	Tap to sacrifice Living Armor to put +0/+X token on target creature.
Malachite Talisman	Artifact	2	--	3: Untap target permanent in play. Use only when green spells are cast and only once for each.
Mana Matrix	Artifact	6	--	You may pay up to 2 less on the colorless part of any instant, interrupt, or enchantment.
Mana Vault	Artifact	1	--	Tap to add 3 to your mana pool. Untap for 4 mana during your upkeep or take 1 damage.
Meekstone	Artifact	1	--	Creatures with power greater than 2 do not untap as normal.
Mightstone	Artifact	4	--	+1/+0 to all attacking creatures.
Millstone	Artifact	2	--	Tap+(2) Opponent discards 2 cards from top of library.
Mirror Universe	Artifact	6	--	Tap and sacrifice this card during upkeep to switch life with your opponent. May not be prevented or redirected.
Mox Emerald	Artifact	0	--	Tap to add G to your mana pool.
Mox Jet	Artifact	0	--	Tap to add B to your mana pool.
Mox Pearl	Artifact	0	--	Tap to add W to your mana pool.
Mox Ruby	Artifact	0	--	Tap to add R to your mana pool.

Card	Type	Cost	Power/ Toughness	Description
Mox Sapphire	Artifact	0	--	Tap to add U to your mana pool.
Nacre Talisman	Artifact	2	--	3: Untap target permanent in play. Use only when white spells are cast and only once for each.
Naked Singularity	Artifact	5	--	Cumulative upkeep: 3. Instead of producing their normal mana, plains produce R mana, islands produce G mana, swamps produce W mana, mountains produce U mana, and forests produce B mana.
Nevinyrral's Disk	Artifact	4	--	Tap+(1) Destroys all creatures, artifacts, and enchantments in play. Comes into play tapped.
North Star	Artifact	4	--	Tap+(4) Cast a spell with any color mana.
Nova Pentacle	Artifact	4	--	Tap+(3) Redirect damage done to from one source to a creature of opponent's choice.
Obelisk of Undoing	Artifact	1	--	6: Return one of your permanents in play to your hand.
Onyx Talisman	Artifact	2	--	3: Untap target permanent in play. Use this ability only when black spells are cast and only once for each black spell cast.
Pentagram of the Ages	Artifact	4	--	Tap+(4) Prevent all damage dealt to you from one source. Does not prevent same source form damaging you again this round.
Pit Trap	Artifact	2	--	Tap+(2) Sacrifice to bury non-flying target creature that is attacking you this turn.
Planar Gate	Artifact	6	--	You may pay up to 2 less of the colorless mana part of summon spells.
Pyramids	Artifact	6	--	2: Prevent land from being destroyed or destroy enchantment on land.
Rack, The	Artifact	1	--	Opponent takes 1 damage for each card less than 3 in his or her hand.
Rakalite	Artifact	6	--	2: Prevent 1 damage to any target. Returns to hand on turn in which it is used.

Card	Type	Cost	Power/ Toughness	Description
Red Mana Battery	Artifact	4	--	Tap+(2) Add a token to Battery or tap to add R to your mana pool. Can convert counters to R.
Reflecting Mirror	Artifact	4	--	Tap+(X) Where X is 2 times casting cost of target spell. Target spell which targets you targets player of your choice instead. This ability is played as an interrupt.
Relic Barrier	Artifact	2	--	Tap to tap target artifact.
Ring of Immortals	Artifact	5	--	Tap+(3) Counter interrupt or enchantment that targets one of your permanents.
Ring of Ma'ruf	Artifact	5	--	5: Sacrifice Ring to select a card from outside of the game instead of drawing.
Ring of Renewal	Artifact	5	--	Tap+(5) Discard a card at random from your hand and draw 2 cards.
Rocket Launcher	Artifact	4	--	2: Do 1 damage to any target. Goes to graveyard at end of turn used. Cannot be used on turn it is brought into play.
Rod of Ruin	Artifact	4	--	Tap+(3) Do 1 damage to any target.
Runed Arch	Artifact	3	--	Comes into play tapped. Tap+(X) Sacrifice Runed Arch. X target creatures with power no greater than 2 cannot be blocked this turn. Later effect may increase target's powers.
Runesword	Artifact	6	--	Tap+(3) Attacking creature gains +2/+0 until end of turn. Any creature damaged by target creature may not regenerate. If a creature is placed in graveyard this turn it is removed from the game. If target creature leaves play this turn then Runesword is buried.
Sandals of Abdallah	Artifact	4	--	Tap+(2) Gives target creature islandwalk for one turn. Discard if target is destroyed while using Sandals.
Serpent Generator	Artifact	6	--	Tap+(4) Create a 1/1 poisoned snake token creature. If snake damages opponent give opponent poison counter. If opponent has 10 or more poison counters he or she loses.

Card	Type	Cost	Power/Toughness	Description
Shield of the Ages	Artifact	2	--	2: Prevent 1 damage to you.
Skull Catapult	Artifact	4	--	Tap+(1) Sacrifice a creature to have Skull Catapult deal 2 damage to a target.
Skull of Orm	Artifact	3	--	Tap+(5) Bring an enchantment card from graveyard to your hand.
Sol Ring	Artifact	1	--	Tap to add 2 to your pool.
Soul Net	Artifact	1	--	1: Gain 1 life whenever a creature goes to the graveyard.
Spirit Shield	Artifact	3	--	Tap+(2) Target creature gets +0/+2 as long as Spirit Shield remains tapped. You may choose not to untap Shield as normal during your untap phase.
Staff of the Ages	Artifact	3	--	Creatures with any landwalking ability may be blocked as if they did not have any landwalking abilities.
Staff of Zegon	Artifact	4	--	3: -2/-0 to target until end of turn.
Standing Stones	Artifact	3	--	Tap+(1) Add 1 mana of any color to your pool, this ability may be played as an interrupt. Damage cannot be redirected or prevented.
Stone Calendar	Artifact	5	--	Your spells cost up to 1 less to cast. Casting cost cannot go below 0.
Sunglasses of Urza	Artifact	3	--	Allows white mana to be used as red mana.
Sunstone	Artifact	3	--	2: Sacrifice a snow-covered land in play to have all creatures in play deal no damage during combat this turn.
Sword of the Ages	Artifact	6	--	Tap and sacrifice this card and as many of your creatures as you want to do damage to any target equal to the sum of the power of all creatures sacrificed.
Tablet of Epityr	Artifact	1	--	1: Gain 1 life when an artifact goes to the graveyard.
Tawnos's Coffin	Artifact	2	--	Tap+(3) Remove creature from the game. Effect remains as long as Coffin is tapped. May choose not to untap.

Card	Type	Cost	Power/ Toughness	Description
Tawnos's Wand	Artifact	4	--	Tap+(2) Makes a creature of power less than 2 blockable only by artifact creatures until end of turn.
Tawnos's Weaponry	Artifact	2	--	Tap+(2) Add +1/+1 to target creature. Effect remains until untapped. May choose not to untap.
Throne of Bone	Artifact	1	--	1: Gain 1 life whenever a black spell is cast.
Time Bomb	Artifact	4	--	During your upkeep, gains a time counter. Tap+(1) Sacrifice to deal X damage to each creature and player where X is the number of time counters on it.
Time Vault	Artifact	2	--	Tap to take an extra turn after this one. Comes into play tapped. Does not untap as normal. You must skip a turn to untap Time Vault.
Tormod's Crypt	Artifact	0	--	Tap and sacrifice Tormad's Crypt to remove all cards in target player's graveyard from the game.
Tower of Coireall	Artifact	4	--	Tap: Target creature cannot be blocked by wall until end of turn.
Triassic Egg	Artifact	4	--	Tap+(3) Put one counter on Egg. Sacrifice Egg with 2 or more counters and bring any creature from your hand or graveyard directly into play.
Urza's Bauble	Artifact	0	--	Tap and sacrifice Urza's Bauble to choose a card at random from target player's hand and look at it. Draw a card at the beginning of the next turn's upkeep.
Urza's Chalice	Artifact	1	--	1: Gain 1 life whenever an artifact is brought into play.
Urza's Miter	Artifact	3	--	3: Whenever an artifact of yours goes to the graveyard you may draw a card.
Vexing Arcanix	Artifact	4	--	Tap+(3) Target player names a card and turns over top card of his library. If is named card it goes to player's hand, otherwise goes to graveyard and Arcanix does 2 damage to target player.

Card	Type	Cost	Power/ Toughness	Description
Vibrating Sphere	Artifact	4	--	During your turn, all creatures you control get a +2/+0 bonus to their power and toughness. During all other turns, all creatures you control get -0/-2 to their power and toughness.
Voodoo Doll	Artifact	6	--	Add one token each upkeep. Tap+(XX) Do X damage to any target. X is the number of tokens on Voodoo Doll. If Voodoo Doll ends the turn untapped you take X damage and Doll is destroyed.
Wand of Ith	Artifact	4	--	Tap+(3) Look at one card at random from target player's hand. If card is not a land target player must choose either to discard it or lose an amount of life equal to its casting cost. If card is a land target player must choose either to discard it or pay 1 life. Effects that prevent or redirect damage may not be used to counter this loss of life.
War Barge	Artifact	4	--	3: Give target creature islandwalk ability until end of turn. If War Barge leaves play this turn target creature is buried.
War Chariot	Artifact	3	--	Tap+(3) Target creature gains trample until end of turn.
Weakstone	Artifact	4	--	All attacking creatures lose -1/-0.
Whalebone Glider	Artifact	2	--	Tap+(2) Target creature with power no greater than 3 gains flying until end of turn. Power may be increased afterwards.
White Mana Battery	Artifact	4	--	Tap+(2) Add 1 token to Battery. Tap to add W to your mana pool. Can convert tokens to W.
Winter Orb	Artifact	2	--	Each player may only untap one land during their untap phase.
Wooden Sphere	Artifact	1	--	1: Gain 1 life each time a green spell is cast.
Zelyon Sword	Artifact	3	--	Tap+(3) Target creature gets +2/+0 as long as Zelyon Sword is tapped. You may choose not to untap.
Zuran Orb	Artifact	0	--	0: Sacrifice a land to gain 2 life.

Card	Type	Cost	Power/ Toughness	Description
Adarkar Sentinel	Artifact Creature	5	3/3	1: +0/+1 bonus to toughness until end of turn.
Battering Ram	Artifact Creature	2	1/1	Bands only when attacking. Destroys blocking walls.
Brass Man	Artifact Creature	1	1/3	Does not untap as normal. Pay 1 to untap during your upkeep.
Bronze Horse	Artifact Creature	7	4/4	Trample. Not damaged by targeted spells if you have other creatures in play.
Clay Statue	Artifact Creature	4	3/1	2: Regenerates.
Clockwork Avian	Artifact Creature	5	0/4	Flying. Starts with 4 +1/+0 counters on it. Remove 1 counter whenever it attacks or defends. Can replace tokens during upkeep for 1 each but this taps the Avian.
Clockwork Beast	Artifact Creature	6	0/4	Starts with 7 +1/+0 counters on it. Remove 1 counter whenever it attacks or defends. Can replace tokens for 1 during upkeep but this taps the Beast.
Coal Golem	Artifact Creature	5	3/3	3: Sacrifice Coal Golem to add RRR to your mana pool.
Colossus of Sardia	Artifact Creature	9	9/9	Trample. Does not untap as normal. Must pay 9 during your upkeep to untap.
Dancing Scimitar	Artifact Creature	4	1/5	Flying.
Diabolic Machine	Artifact Creature	7	4/4	3: Regenerates.
Dragon Engine	Artifact Creature	3	1/3	2: +1/+0 until end of turn.
Grapeshot Catapult	Artifact Creature	4	2/3	Tap to do 1 damage to any flying creature.
Juggernaut	Artifact Creature	4	5/3	Must attack if possible. Cannot be blocked by walls.
Living Wall	Artifact Creature	4	0/6	Counts as a wall. 1: Regenerates.
Marble Priest	Artifact Creature	5	3/3	All walls able to block Priest must do so. Does not take damage from walls.

Card	Type	Cost	Power/Toughness	Description
Mishra's War Machine	Artifact Creature	7	5/5	During your upkeep you must discard a card from your hand. If you do not you take 3 damage and it becomes tapped.
Necropolis	Artifact Creature	5	0/1	Counts as a wall. Take any creatures from your graveyard and remove them from the game. Add X +0/+1 counters where X is the removed creature's casting cost.
Obsianus Golem	Artifact Creature	6	4/6	
Onulet	Artifact Creature	3	2/2	If Onulet dies you gain 2 life.
Ornithopter	Artifact Creature	0	0/2	Flying.
Primal Clay	Artifact Creature	4	*/*	When brought into play caster must select if it is a 1/6 wall, a 3/3 walker, or a 2/2 flyer.
Scarecrow	Artifact Creature	5	2/2	Tap+(6) Prevents all damage done to you by flying creatures until end of turn.
Sentinal	Artifact Creature	4	1/*	Where * is 1 at the time of casting but can be changed to X+1 during combat. X is the power of a creature blocking or blocked by Sentinel.
Shapeshifter	Artifact Creature	6	*/7-*	Where * is chosen on casting and during each of controller's upkeeps.
Snow Fortress	Artifact Creature	5	0/4	Counts as a wall. 1: +1/+0 to Snow Fortress' power until end of turn. 1: +0/+1 to Snow Fortress' toughness until end of turn. 3: Deal 1 damage to target creature without flying that is attacking you.
Soldevi Golem	Artifact Creature	4	5/3	Soldevi Golem does not untap during your untap phase. 0: Untap target creature opponent controls to untap Soldevi Golem at the end of your upkeep. Use this ability only during your upkeep.
Soldevi Simulacrum	Artifact Creature	4	2/4	Cumulative upkeep: 1. 1: +1/+0 to Soldevi Simulacrum's power until end of turn.
Su-Chi	Artifact Creature	4	4/4	If Su-Chi goes to graveyard add 4 colorless mana to your pool.

Card	Type	Cost	Power/ Toughness	Description
Tetravus	Artifact Creature	6	1/1	Flying. Starts with 3 +1/+1 tokens on it. During upkeep can convert tokens to or from 1/1 flying artifact creatures which cannot be enchanted.
Triskelion	Artifact Creature	6	1/1	Begins with 3 +1/+1 counters. May remove a counter at any time to do 1 damage to any target.
Urza's Avenger	Artifact Creature	6	4/4	Each upkeep give bands, flying, trample, and or first strike at -1/-1 for each.
Walking Wall	Artifact Creature	4	0/6	Counts as a wall. 3: Gets +3/-1 to walking wall's power and toughness until end of turn and can attack this turn. Cannot attack the turn it comes under your control and use this ability only once per turn.
Wall of Shields	Artifact Creature	3	0/4	Counts as a wall, banding.
Wall of Spears	Artifact Creature	3	2/3	Counts as wall. First strike.
Yotian Soldier	Artifact Creature	3	1/4	Does not tap when attacking.

White

White Enchantments

Card	Type	Cost	Power/Toughness	Description
Enchant Creatures				
Armor of Faith	Enchant Creature	W	--	Target creature gets +1/+1. W: Enchanted creature gets +0/+1 until end of turn.
Artifact Ward	Enchant Creature	W	--	Target creature cannot be blocked by artifact creatures, does not take damage from artifact sources and ignores artifact effects that target it.
Black Scarab	Enchant Creature	W	--	Target creature gets +2/+2 as long as opponent controls any black cards and cannot be blocked by black cards.
Black Ward	Enchant Creature	W	--	Target creature gains protection from black.
Blessing	Enchant Creature	WW	--	W: Target creature gains +1/+1 until end of turn.
Blue Scarab	Enchant Creature	W	--	Target creature gets +2/+2 as long as opponent controls any blue cards and cannot be blocked by blue creatures.
Blue Ward	Enchant Creature	W	--	Target creature gains protection from blue.
Brainwash	Enchant Creature	W	--	Target creature cannot attack unless its controller pays 3 in addition to any other costs.
Cooperation	Enchant Creature	W2	--	Target creature gains banding.
Divine Transformation	Enchant Creature	WW2	--	Target creature gains +3/+3.
Farrel's Mantle	Enchant Creature	W2	--	If target creature attacks and is not blocked, it may deal X+2 damage to any other creature where X is the power of the creature it enchants. If it does so it does not damage opponent this turn.
Fylgja	Enchant Creature	W	--	When it comes into play put 4 healing counters on it. 0: Remove a counter to prevent 1 damage to creature it enchants. W2: Put a healing counter on Flygja.

Card	Type	Cost	Power/Toughness	Description
Green Scarab	Enchant Creature	W	--	Target creature gets +2/+2 as long as opponent controls any green cards and cannot be blocked by green creatures.
Green Ward	Enchant Creature	W	--	Target creature gains protection from green.
Holy Armor	Enchant Creature	W	--	Target creature gains +0/+2 and W: +0/+1 until end of turn.
Holy Strength	Enchant Creature	W	--	Target creature gains +1/+2
Infinite Authority	Enchant Creature	WWW	--	Destroys all creatures with a toughness < 4 that block it. Gets +1/+1 at end of turn for each creature that it sends to the graveyard.
Lance	Enchant Creature	W	--	Target creature gains first strike.
Prismatic Ward	Enchant Creature	W1	--	When it comes into play choose a color. Damage done to target creature by that color is reduced to 0.
Red Scarab	Enchant Creature	W	--	Target creature gets +2/+2 as long as opponent has red cards in play and cannot be blocked by red creatures.
Red Ward	Enchant Creature	W	--	Target creature gains protection from red.
Seeker	Enchant Creature	WW2	--	Target creature may only be blocked by white and artifact creatures.
Spirit Link	Enchant Creature	W	--	For each point of damage target creature does controller gains 1 life.
White Scarab	Enchant Creature	W	--	Target creature gets +2/+2 as long as opponent controls white cards and cannot be blocked by white creatures.
White Ward	Enchant Creature	W	--	Target creature gains protection from white.
Enchant Lands				
Caribou Range	Enchant Land	WW2	--	WW: Tap land it enchants to put a 0/1 white Caribou token into play. 0: Sacrifice a Caribou token to gain 1 life.

Card	Type	Cost	Power/ Toughness	Description
Consecrate Land	Enchant Land	W	--	Target land cannot be destroyed while enchanted. Any other enchantments on land are destroyed and no new enchantments may be played on it.
Equinox	Enchant Land	W	--	Tap land Equinox enchants to counter a land destruction spell that affects one or more of your lands.
Farmstead	Enchant Land	WWW	--	WW: Gain 1 life. May only be used once per turn.
Enchant Walls				
Animate Wall	Enchant Wall	W	--	Target wall can now attack.
Independent Enchantments				
Angelic Voices	Enchantment	WW2	--	+1/+1 to all your creatures as long as they are all white or artifact creatures.
Arenson's Aura	Enchantment	W2	--	W: Sacrifice an enchantment to destroy target enchantment in play. UU3: Counter target enchantment as it is cast.
Call to Arms	Enchantment	W1	--	Choose a color. As long as target opponent controls more cards of that color than any other, all white creatures in play get a +1/+1 bonus added to their power and toughness. If at any time that opponent does not control more cards of that color than any other, bury this card.
Castle	Enchantment	W3	--	All your untapped, non-attacking creatures gain +0/+2.
Circle of Protection: Artifacts	Enchantment	W1	--	2: Reduce the damage done to you from one artifact source to zero.
Circle of Protection: Black	Enchantment	W1	--	1: Prevent damage done to you from one black source.
Circle of Protection: Blue	Enchantment	W1	--	1: Prevent damage done to you from one blue source.
Circle of Protection: Green	Enchantment	W1	--	1: Prevent damage done to you from one green source.
Circle of Protection: Red	Enchantment	W1	--	1: Prevent damage done to you from one red source.
Circle of Protection: White	Enchantment	W1	--	1: Prevent damage done to you from one white source.

Card	Type	Cost	Power/ Toughness	Description
Cold Snap	Enchantment	W2	--	Cumulative upkeep: 2. During each player's upkeep does 1 damage to that player for each snow-covered land he controls.
Conversion	Enchantment	WW2	--	All mountains in play are considered plains. Controller must pay WW during upkeep or is destroyed.
Crusade	Enchantment	WW	--	All white creatures in play gain +1/+1.
Damping Field	Enchantment	W2	--	Players may only untap 1 artifact each turn during untap.
Divine Intervention	Enchantment	WW6	--	Two turns from now game ends as a draw.
Drought	Enchantment	WW2	--	During your upkeep pay WW or is destroyed. For each B in any spell or activation cost, caster or controller must sacrifice one swamp.
Enduring Renewal	Enchantment	WW2	--	Play with the cards in your hand face up. If you draw a creature from your library, discard it. Whenever a creature is removed from player to the graveyard the creature returns to your hand.
Energy Storm	Enchantment	W1	--	Cumulative upkeep: 1. Damage dealt by instants, interrupts, and sorceries is reduced to 0 as long as Energy Storm remains in play.
Fasting	Enchantment	W	--	You may skip your draw phase to gain 2 life. If you draw a card for any reason, Fasting is destroyed. Put a hunger counter on Fasting during your upkeep. When Fasting has 5 counters on it, it is destroyed.
Fortified Area	Enchantment	WW1	--	All your walls gain +1/+0 and banding.
Great Wall	Enchantment	W2	--	Stops all use of plainswalk in play.
Greater Realm of Preservation	Enchantment	W1	--	W1: Reduces all damage from a red or black source to zero.
Hallowed Ground	Enchantment	W1	--	Ww: Return target land you control to owner's hand.
Heroism	Enchantment	W2	--	0: Sacrifice a white creature to have all attacking red creatures deal no damage. Attacking player may spend 2 R to have an attacking creature deal damage as normal.

Card	Type	Cost	Power/ Toughness	Description
Island Sanctuary	Enchantment	W1	--	You may choose not to draw a card to limit attacks on you to creatures that have flying or islandwalk.
Jihad	Enchantment	WWW	--	+2/+1 to white creatures in play while cards of a chosen color are in play. Discard if no cards of that color are in play.
Justice	Enchantment	WW2	--	During your upkeep pay WW or destroy it. When a red spell or creature does damage, Justice does equal damage to its controller. Not affected by subsequent reduction of damage.
Karma	Enchantment	WW2	--	Each player takes 1 damage during his upkeep for each swamp he controls.
Kismet	Enchantment	W3	--	All of opponent's lands, creatures, and artifacts come into play tapped.
Land Tax	Enchantment	W	--	If opponent controls more land than you during your upkeep you may search through your library and withdraw up to three basic lands. Reshuffle your library.
Lifeblood	Enchantment	WW2	--	You gain 1 life each time opponent taps a mountain.
Moat	Enchantment	WW2	--	Non-flying creatures may not attack while Moat is in play.
Presence of the Master	Enchantment	W3	--	Counters all enchantment spells while in play.
Spiritual Sanctuary	Enchantment	WW2	--	Each player who controls plains gains 1 life during upkeep.

White Instants

Card	Type	Cost	Power/ Toughness	Description
Alabaster Potion	Instant	WWX	--	Gain X life or prevent X damage to one target.
Army of Allah	Instant	WW1	--	All attacking creatures gain +2/+0.

Card	Type	Cost	Power/Toughness	Description
Battle Cry	Instant	W2	--	Untap all white cretures in play you control. Any creature that blocks this turn gets a +0/+1 bonus to its toughness until end of the turn.
Blaze of Glory	Instant	W	--	Target defending creature can and must block all attacking creatures.
Blessed Wine	Instant	W1	--	Gain 1 life. Draw a card from the library at the beginning of the next turn's upkeep phase.
Blood of the Martyr	Instant	WWW	--	For the remainder of the turn you may redirect damage done to any of your creatures to yourself.
Death Ward	Instant	W	--	Regenerates target creature.
Disenchant	Instant	W1	--	Destroys target artifact or enchantment in play.
Divine Offering	Instant	W1	--	Destroy target artifact and gain life equal to its casting cost.
Eye for an Eye	Instant	WW	--	Does damage to opponent equal to the amount done to you by one source.
Festival	Instant	W	--	Opponent may not declare an attack this phase. Play during opponent's upkeep.
Formation	Instant	W1	--	Target creature gains banding until end of turn. Draw a card from the library at the beginning of the next turn's upkeep phase.
Fire and Brimstone	Instant	WW3	--	This card does 4 damage to target player and 4 damage to you. May only be used in a turn when target player attacked.
Glyph of Life	Instant	W	--	All damage done to target wall so far this turn is instead added to your life.
Great Defender	Instant	W	--	+0/+N to target creature where N is its casting cost.
Guardian Angel	Instant	WX	--	Prevents X damage to any one target.
Heal	Instant	W	--	Prevent 1 damage to any creature or player. Draw a card from the library at the beginning of the next turn's upkeep phase.
Healing Salve	Instant	W	--	Gain 3 life or prevent 3 damage to one target.

Card	Type	Cost	Power/ Toughness	Description
Heaven's Gate	Instant	W	--	Changes color of any/all creatures to white to end of turn.
Holy Day	Instant	W	--	No creatures deal or take damage from combat this turn.
Holy Light	Instant	W2	--	All non-white creatures get -1/-1 until end of turn.
Indestructible Aura	Instant	W	--	Creature takes no damage for the rest of turn.
Lightening Blow	Instant	W1	--	Target creature gains first strike capability until end of turn. Draw a card at the next turn's upkeep.
Morale	Instant	WW1	--	All attacking creatures gain +1/+1 until end of turn.
Piety	Instant	W2	--	All defending creatures gain +0/+3 until end of turn.
Rally	Instant	WW	--	All blocking creatures in play get a +1/+1 bonus until end of turn.
Rapid Fire	Instant	W3	--	Give a creature first strike and Rampage:2 (if it does not already have rampage) until end of turn. Play before defense is chosen.
Remove Enchantments	Instant	W	--	Bring enchantments you control to your hand and destroy opponent's. Affects all enchantments you control plus all of opponent's enchantments in your territory. Attacking creatures are in your territory.
Reverse Damage	Instant	WW1	--	All damage done to you from one source is instead added to your life.
Reverse Polarity	Instant	WW	--	All damage done to you by artifacts so far this turn is instead added to your life.
Righteousness	Instant	W	--	Target defending creature gains +7/+7.
Sacred Boon	Instant	W1	--	Prevent up to 3 damage to target creature in play. At end of turn, put a +0/+1 bonus counter on that creature for each 1 damage prevented in this way.
Shield Wall	Instant	W1	--	+0/+2 to all your creatures until end of turn.

Card	Type	Cost	Power/ Toughness	Description
Swords to Plowshares	Instant	W	--	Remove target creature from the game. Creature's controller gains life equal to target's power.
Warning	Instant	W	--	Target attacking creature deals no damage in combat this round.

White Interrupts

Card	Type	Cost	Power/ Toughness	Description
Purelace	Interrupt	W	--	Changes color of target permanent to white.

White Sorceries

Card	Type	Cost	Power/ Toughness	Description
Armageddon	Sorcery	W3	--	Destroys all lands in play.
Balance	Sorcery	W1	--	Balance number of creatures, lands, and cards in hand.
Cleanse	Sorcery	WW2	--	Destroys all black creatures in play.
Cleansing	Sorcery	WWW	--	All lands in play are destroyed. Players may prevent a land from being destroyed by paying one life. This loss of life may not be prevented or redirected.
Dust to Dust	Sorcery	WW1	--	Remove 2 target artifacts from the game.
Icatian Town	Sorcery	W5	--	Put 4 citizen tokens in play, treat these as 1/1 white creatures.
Martyr's Cry	Sorcery	WW	--	All white creatures are removed from the game. Players must draw 1 card for each creature that is lost in this manner.
Resurrection	Sorcery	WW2	--	Take a creature from your graveyard and put it directly into play. Treat this creature as if it were just summoned.
Shahrazad	Sorcery	WW	--	Forces a sub-game of Magic. Loser loses 1/2 of his life.
Tivadar's Crusade	Sorcery	WW1	--	All Goblins in play are destroyed.

Card	Type	Cost	Power/ Toughness	Description
Visons	Sorcery	W	--	Look at top 5 cards of any library. Then may choose to reshuffle it.
Wrath of God	Sorcery	WW2	--	All creatures in play are destroyed and may not regenerate.

White Summons

Card	Type	Cost	Power/ Toughness	Description
Seraph	Summon Angel	W6	4/4	Flying. Any creature which goes to the graveyard on a turn when damaged by Seraph is put directly into play under Seraph's controller's control at end of turn.
Serra Angel	Summon Angel	WW3	4/4	Flying. Does not tap when attacking.
Argivian Archaeologist	Summon Archaeologist	WW1	1/1	Tap+(WW) Bring artifact from graveyard to hand.
D'Avenant Archer	Summon Archer	W2	1/2	Tap to do 1 damage to an attacking or blocking creature.
Hand of Justice	Summon Avatar	W5	2/6	Tap 3 white creatures you control to destroy target creature.
Personal Incarnation	Summon Avatar	WWW3	6/6	Can redirect damage from it to controller. Controller loses 1/2 of his life if it dies.
Righteous Avengers	Summon Avengers	W4	3/1	Plainswalk.
Enchanted Being	Summon Being	WW1	2/2	Takes no damage from creatures with enchantments on them.
Blinking Spirit	Summon Blinking Spirit	W3	2/2	0: Return Blinking Spirit from play to owner's hand.
Martyrs of Korlis	Summon Bodyguard	WW3	1/6	If untapped, all artifact damage done to controller is transferred to one of controller's Martyrs.
Veteran Bodyguard	Summon Bodyguard	WW3	2/6	When not tapped, takes all damage done to you by creatures.
Camel	Summon Camel	W	0/1	Bands. Gives immunity from damage done by deserts to all creatures in band with it.

Card	Type	Cost	Power/Toughness	Description
Moorish Cavalry	Summon Cavalry	WW2	3/3	Trample.
Elvish Healer	Summon Cleric	W2	1/2	Tap to prevent 1 point of damage to any non-green creature or up to 2 points of damage to any green creature in play.
Farrelite Priest	Summon Cleric	WW1	1/3	1: Add W to your mana pool. If more than 3 is spent in this way then destroy Priest at end of turn.
Icatian Priest	Summon Cleric	W	1/1	WW1: Gives target creature +1/+1 until end of turn.
Order of Leitbur	Summon Clerics	WW	2/1	Protection from black. W: First strike. WW: +1/+0 until end of turn.
Samite Healer	Summon Cleric	W1	1/1	Tap to prevent one point of damage to any target.
Snow Hound	Summon Dog	W2	1/1	Tap+(1): Return Snow Hound to owner's hand from play and target blue or green creature in play you control to owner's hand.
War Elephant	Summon Elephant	W3	2/2	Trample. Bands.
Exorcist	Summon Exorcist	WW	1/1	Tap+(W1) Target black creature is destroyed.
Arctic Foxes	Summon Foxes	W1	1/1	If defending player controls no snow-covered lands
Ivory Guardians	Summon Guardians	WW4	3/3	Protection from red. Gets +1/+1 if opponent has red cards in play.
Banalish Hero	Summon Hero	W	1/1	Banding.
Kjeldoran Warrior	Summon Hero	W	1/1	Banding.
Hipparion	Summon Hipparion	W1	1/3	Must pay 1 to block a creature with power of 3 or greater.
Witch Hunter	Summon Hunter	WW2	1/1	Tap to do 1 damage to any player. Tap+(WW1) Return target creature to owner's hand. All enchantments on creatures are destroyed.
Keepers of the Faith	Summon Keepers	WW1	2/3	
King Suleiman	Summon King	W1	1/1	Tap to destroy an Efreet or Djinn.

Card	Type	Cost	Power/ Toughness	Description
Amrou Kithkin	Summon Kithkin	WW	1/1	Cannot be blocked by creatures with a power greater than 2.
Kjeldoran Knight	Summon Knight	WW	1/1	Banding. W1: +1/+0 until end of turn. WW: +0/+2 until end of turn.
Knights of Thorn	Summon Knights	W3	2/2	Protection from red. Banding.
Lost Order of Jarkeld	Summon Knights	WW2	1+*/1+*	Has power and toughness equal to 1+number of creatures opponent controls.
Order of the White Shield	Summon Knights	WW	2/1	Protection from black. W: First strike until end of turn. WW: +1/+0 until end of turn.
White Knight	Summon Knight	WW	2/2	First strike. Protection from black.
General Jarkeld	Summon Legend	W3	1/2	Tap to switch the blockers of two target attacking creatures. Must remain legal blocks. Use General Jarkels's ability only during combat after defense has been chosen and before damage is dealt.
Akron Legionnaire	Summon Legionnaire	WW6	8/4	None of your non-artifact creatures may attack except Legionnaires.
Abu Ja Far	Summon Leper	W	0/1	If destroyed in combat, all creatures blocked by or blocking it are destroyed.
Savannah Lions	Summon Lions	W	2/1	
Mercenaries	Summon Mercenaries	W3	3/3	Whenever it damages a player, he or she must pay 3 to prevent.
Miracle Worker	Summon Miracle Worker	W	1/1	Destroy target enchantment card on a creature you control.
Angry Mob	Summon Mob	WW2	2+*/2+*	Trample. During your turn, the *'s are equal to the number of swamps all opponents control. During any other player's turn
Northern Paladin	Summon Paladin	WW2	3/3	Tap+(WW) Destroy any black card in play.
Order of the Sacred Torch	Summon Paladin	WW1	2/2	Tap and pay 1 life to counter target black spell. Effects that prevent or redirect damage done in ths way cannot be used to counter this loss of life. Use as an interrupt.

Card	Type	Cost	Power/Toughness	Description
Mesa Pegasus	Summon Pegasus	W1	1/1	Flying. Banding.
Pikemen	Summon Pikemen	W1	1/1	Banding. First strike.
Preacher	Summon Preacher	WW1	1/1	Tap to gain control of one creature opponent chooses. If Preacher becomes untapped you lose control of this creature. You may choose not to untap Preacher as normal during your untap phase. You also lose control of creature if Preacher leaves play or at end of game.
Clergy of the Holy Nimbus	Summon Priest	W	1/1	Always regenerates unless opponent pays 1 colorless mana.
Kelsinko Ranger	Summon Ranger	W	1/1	W1: Target creature gains first strike ability until end of turn.
Argivian Blacksmith	Summon Smith	WW1	2/2	Tap to prevent 2 damage to any artifact creature.
Repentant Blacksmith	Summon Smith	W1	1/2	Protection from red.
Combat Medic	Summon Soldier	W2	0/2	W1: Prevent 1 damage to any player or creature.
Icatian Infantry	Summon Soldiers	W	1/1	1: Bands until end of turn. 1: First strike until end of turn.
Icatian Javelineers	Summon Soldiers	W	1/1	When brought into play put a javelin counter on it. Tap and remove the counter to have Javelineers deal 1 point of damage to any target.
Icatian Lieutenant	Summon Soldier	WW	1/2	W1: Target soldier gets +1/+0 until end of turn.
Icatian Phalanx	Summon Soldiers	W4	2/4	Banding.
Icatian Scout	Summon Soldier	W	1/1	Tap+(1) Target creature gets +1/+1 until end of turn.
Icatian Skirmishers	Summon Soldiers	W3	1/1	Bands. First strike. All creatures that band with Skirmishers gain first strike until end of turn.
Kjeldoran Elite Guard	Summon Soldier	W3	2/2	Tap to give target creature +2/+2 until end of turn. If target leaves play this turn, bury this card too. Use only when attack or defense is announced.

Card	Type	Cost	Power/ Toughness	Description
Kjeldoran Guard	Summon Soldier	W1	1/1	Tap to give target creature +1/+1 until end of turn. If target leaves play this turn, bury this card too. Use only when attack or defense is announced and opponent has no snow-covered lands.
Kjeldoran Phalanx	Summon Soldiers	W5	2/5	Banding
Kjeldoran Royal Guard	Summon Soldiers	WW3	2/5	Tap to redirect all damage done to you from unblocked creatures to Guard.
Kjeldoran Skycaptain	Summon Soldier	W4	2/2	Banding, flying, first strike.
Kjeldoran Skyknight	Summon Soldier	W2	1/1	Banding, flying, first strike.
Shield Bearer	Summon Soldier	W1	0/3	Banding.
Petra Sphinx	Summon Sphinx	WWW2	3/4	Tap to have a player guess the top card of their library. If right he gets the card, if wrong it goes to the graveyard.
Thunder Spirit	Summon Spirit	WW1	2/2	First strike.
Squire	Summon Squire	W1	1/2	
Farrel's Zealot	Summon Townsfolk	WW1	2/2	If Farrel's Zealot attacks and is not blocked, controller may choose to have it deal 3 damage to a target creature. If you do so it deals no damage to opponent this turn.
Icatian Moneychanger	Summon Townsfolk	W	0/2	Moneychanger does 3 damage to you when summoned. Put 3 credit counters on Moneychanger at that time. During your upkeep, put one credit counter on Moneychanger. 0: Sacrifice Moneychanger to gain 1 life for each credit counter on it. Use this ability only during your upkeep.
Adarkar Unicorn	Summon Unicorn	WW1	2/2	Tap to add U or U1 to your mana pool which is only usable to pay cumulative upkeep. Play this ability as an interrupt.
Pearled Unicorn	Summon Unicorn	W2	2/2	

Card	Type	Cost	Power/Toughness	Description
Osai Vultures	Summon Vultures	W1	1/1	Flying. Gains a counter at end of turn if a creature went to the graveyard that turn. May turn in 2 counters for +1/+1 until end of turn.
Wall of Caltrops	Summon Wall	W1	2/1	Wall. Bands only with other walls in defense.
Wall of Light	Summon Wall	W2	1/5	Wall. Protection from black.
Wall of Swords	Summon Wall	W3	3/5	Wall. Flying.
Tundra Wolves	Summon Wolves	W	1/1	First strike.
Elder Land Wurm	Summon Wurm	WWW4	5/5	Cannot attack until it has blocked at least once.

Blue

Blue Enchantments

Card	Type	Cost	Power/ Toughness	Description
Enchant Artifacts				
Animate Artifact	Enchant Artifact	U3	--	Makes a target artifact a */* artifact creature where * is the casting cost of the artifact.
Power Artifact	Enchant Artifact	UU	--	Reduces activation cost of target artifact by 2 to a minimum of 1. Does not affect targets with no activation cost.
Relic Bind	Enchant Artifact	U2	--	Give 1 life or 1 damage to a player whenever target artifact is tapped. Must be cast on opponent's artifact.
Steal Artifact	Enchant Artifact	UU2	--	Target artifact comes under caster's control.
Enchant Creatures				
Blinding Grasp	Enchant Creature	U3	--	During your upkeep pay U1 or bury. Gain control of target creature and it gets +0/+1.
Anti-Magic Aura	Enchant Creature	U2	--	Destroys enchantments on target creature and prevents target from being affected by enchantments, sorceries, or instants.
Backfire	Enchant Creature	U	--	For each point of damage done to you by target creature, Backfire does 1 point of damage to target's controller.
Control Magic	Enchant Creature	UU2	--	Take control of target creature.
Creature Bond	Enchant Creature	U1	--	If target creature goes to the graveyard its controller takes damage equal to its toughness.
Dream Coat	Enchant Creature	U	--	Target creature can change colors once per turn.
Errant Minion	Enchant Creature	U2	--	During target creature's controller's upkeep, Errant Minion deals 2 damage to them. They may pay 1 mana for each damage done in this way they wish to prevent.

Card	Type	Cost	Power/ Toughness	Description
Essence Flare	Enchant Creature	U	--	Target creature gets +2/+0. During each of its controller's upkeeps put a -0/-1 counter on creature which remain even if this card is removed.
Fishliver Oil	Enchant Creature	U1	--	Gives target creature islandwalk.
Flight	Enchant Creature	U	--	Target creature gains flying.
Gaseous Form	Enchant Creature	U2	--	Target creature does not deal or take damage in combat.
Invisibility	Enchant Creature	UU	--	Target creature may only by blocked by walls.
Merseine	Enchant Creature	UU2	--	Put 3 net counters on Merseine when it is brought into play. Target creature Merseine enchants does not untap as normal during its controller's upkeep as long as Merseine has net counters on it. As a fast effect, target creature's controller may pay the creature's casting cost to remove a counter from Merseine.
Puppet Master	Enchant Creature	UUU	--	If target creature goes to the graveyard you may instead return it to your hand. If you pay UUU you may also return Puppet Master to your hand as well.
Snow Devil	Enchant Creature	U1	--	Target creature gains flying. As long as you control any snow-covered lands also gains first strike when blocking.
Spectral Cloak	Enchant Creature	UU	--	Creature may not be the target of instants, sorceries, fast effects, or enchantments as long as it is not tapped.
Tangle Kelp	Enchant Creature	U	--	Target creature may not untap during its upkeep if it attacked during its controller's previous round.
Unstable Mutation	Enchant Creature	U	--	Target creature gains +3/+3. During controller's upkeep put a -1/-1 counter on target. Tokens remain even if enchantment is removed.
Venarian Gold	Enchant Creature	UUX	--	Taps creature and keeps it tapped for X turns.

Card	Type	Cost	Power/ Toughness	Description
Enchant Enchantments				
Feedback	Enchant Enchantment	U2	--	Feedback does 1 damage to target's controller during his or her upkeep.
Power Leak	Enchant Enchantment	U1	--	Target's controller must pay 2 during their upkeep or take 1 damage for each unpaid mana.
Enchant Lands				
Erosion	Enchant Land	UUU	--	During your opponent's upkeep, he must pay 1 mana or 1 life or else target land is destroyed. Damage from this may not be prevented or redirected.
Mystic Might	Enchant Land	U	--	Cumulative upkeep: U1. When it comes into play choose target land you control. 0: Tap enchanted land to give target creature in play +2/+2 until the end of the turn.
Phantasmal Terrain	Enchant Land	UU	--	Target land becomes a basic land of caster's choice.
Psychic Venom	Enchant Land	U1	--	Whenever target land becomes tapped
Enchant Worlds				
Field of Dreams	Enchant World	U	--	Top card of each player's library is always face-up.
In the Eye of Chaos	Enchant World	U2	--	All instants and interrupts are countered unless the spell cost is paid a second time with any color mana.
Independent Enchantments				
Arnjlot's Ascent	Enchantment	UU1	--	Cumulative upkeep: U. 1: Target creature in play gains flying ability until end of turn.
Breath of Dreams	Enchantment	UU2	--	Cumulative upkeep: U. Green creatures in play each require an additional cumulative upkeep of 1 to remain in play.
Copy Artifact	Enchantment	U1	--	Becomes an exact copy of target artifact. Is affected by spells that affect enchantments or artifacts.

Card	Type	Cost	Power/Toughness	Description
Dance of Many	Enchantment	UU	--	Create a token copy of creature in play with all of its characteristics. Controller must pay UU during their upkeep or Dance of Many is buried. If Dance of Many leaves play, token creature is destroyed.
Deep Water	Enchantment	UU	--	If you tap 1 blue, all mana-producing lands produce blue instead of their normal color.
Dreams of the Dead	Enchantment	U3	--	U1: Take target white or black creature from your graveyard and put it directly into play as though it were just summoned. That creature now requires an additional cumulative upkeep: 2. If the creature leaves play, remove it from the game entirely.
Energy Flux	Enchantment	U2	--	Each player must pay 2 for each artifact they control or that artifact is destroyed.
Flood	Enchantment	U	--	UU: Target non-flying creature may not attack this turn.
Homarid Spawning Bed	Enchantment	UU	--	UU1: Sacrifice a blue creature to put X Camarid tokens in play, where X is the casting cost of the creature. Treat these tokens as 1/1 blue creatures.
Iceberg	Enchantment	UUX	--	When comes into play put X ice counters on it. 3: Add an ice counter. 0: Remove an ice counter to add 1 to your mana pool. Use as an interrupt.
Icy Prison	Enchantment	UU	--	When Icy Prison comes into play, remove target creature from the game. When it leaves play, return that creature to play under its owner's control as if it were just summoned. During your upkeep, destroy Icy Prison. Any player may pay 3 to prevent this.
Illusionary Terrain	Enchantment	UU	--	Cumulative upkeep: 2. All basic lands of one type become lands of a different type of your choice as long an Illusionary Terrain remains in play.

Card	Type	Cost	Power/ Toughness	Description
Illusions of Grandeur	Enchantment	U3	--	Cumulative upkeep: 2. When comes into play gain 20 life. When leaves play lose 20 life. Loss of life cannot be prevented.
Invoke Prejudice	Enchantment	UUUU	--	Opponent must pay X additional mana to cast summon spells that are not the same color as one of your creatures. X is the casting cost of the summon spell.
Land Equilibrium	Enchantment	UU2	--	If your opponent controls at least as much land as you do, he or she must sacrifice a land for each land he or she puts into play.
Lifetap	Enchantment	UU	--	You gain 1 life whenever opponent taps a forest.
Mana Vortex	Enchantment	UU1	--	Each player sacrifices one land during their upkeep. If there are no lands in play, Mana Vortex is destroyed. If you do not sacrifice a land when Mana Vortex is cast, it is countered.
Mesmeric Trance	Enchantment	UU1	--	Cumulative upkeep: 1. U: Discard a card from your hand to the graveyard to draw a card.
Mystic Remora	Enchantment	U	--	Cumulative upkeep: 1. When opponent successfully casts a non-creature spell, you may draw an extra card. Opponent may counter this effect by paying 4 colorless.
Psychic Allergy	Enchantment	UU3	--	When you cast Psychic Allergy choose a color. During your opponent's upkeep Psychic Allergy deals 1 damage to opponent for each card he or she controls of that color.
Reality Twist	Enchantment	UUU	--	Cumulative upkeep: UU1. Instead of normal, plains produce R, swamps produce G, mountains produce W, and forests produce B.
Snowfall	Enchantment	U2	--	Cumulative upkeep: U. Islands may produce an additional U when tapped for mana which is usable only for cumulative upkeep. Snow-covered islands may produce an additional UU or U which is only usable for cumulative upkeep.

Card	Type	Cost	Power/Toughness	Description
Soul Barrier	Enchantment	U2	--	Whenever target opponent casts a summon spell, deals 2 damage to him. He may pay 2 to prevent this.
Stasis	Enchantment	U1	--	All players skip their untap phase. Controller must pay U during upkeep or Stasis is destroyed.
Sunken City	Enchantment	UU	--	Adds +1/+1 to all blue creatures in play. Controller must pay UU during upkeep or Sunken City is buried.
Tidal Flats	Enchantment	U	--	UU: All your blocking creatures that are blocking non-flying creatures gain first strike until end of turn. The attacking player may pay 1 for each attacking creature to prevent Tidal Flats from giving that creature's blockers first strike.
Tidal Influence	Enchantment	U2	--	Put a tide counter on Tidal Influence when it is brought into play and during your upkeep. If there is 1 tide counter on Tidal Influence all blue creatures get -2/-0. If there are 3 counters on Tidal Influence all blue creatures get +2/+0. If there are 4 counters on Tidal Influence remove them all. You may not cast Tidal Influence if there is another Tidal Influence already in play.
Wrath of Marit Lage	Enchantment	UU3	--	When comes into play tap all red creatures. Red creatures do not untap during their controller's untap.
Undertow	Enchantment	U2	--	Stops all use of islandwalk in play.
Zur's Weirding	Enchantment	U3	--	All players play with cards in their hands face up. Whenever any player draws a card, any other player may pay 2 life to force the player to discard this card. Damage cannot be prevented.

Blue Instants

Card	Type	Cost	Power/ Toughness	Description
Ancestral Recall	Instant	U	--	Draw 3 cards or force opponent to draw 3 cards.
Boomerang	Instant	UU	--	Return target permanent to owner's hand.
Brainstorm	Instant	B	--	Draw 3 cards then take 2 from hand and place on top of your library.
Clairvoyance	Instant	U	--	Look at target player's hand. Draw a card from the library at the beginning of next turn's upkeep.
Enchantment Alteration	Instant	U	--	Move 1 creature or land enchantment to another creature or land without changing its controller.
Enervate	Instant	U1	--	Tap target artifact, creature, or land in play. Draw a card from the library during the beginning of the next turn's upkeep phase.
Flash Flood	Instant	U	--	Destroys red permanent or sends mountain in play back to its owner's hand.
Glyph of Delusion	Instant	U	--	One creature blocked by target wall becomes tapped for X turns where X is the casting cost of the creature.
High Tide	Instant	U	--	Until end of turn all Islands generate an additional U when tapped for mana.
Hurkyl's Recall	Instant	U1	--	All of target player's artifacts are returned to his or her hand.
Infuse	Instant	U2	--	Untap target artifact, creature, or land in play. Draw a card from the library during the beginning of the next turn's upkeep phase.
Jump	Instant	U	--	Target creature gains flight until end of turn.
Mana Short	Instant	U2	--	All of opponent's land is tapped and their mana pool is emptied.
Psionic Blast	Instant	U2	--	Do 4 damage to any target, and does 2 damage to caster.
Ray of Command	Instant	U3	--	Untap target creature opponent controls and gain control of it until end of turn. That creature can tap this turn. When you lose control of creature it becomes tapped.

Card	Type	Cost	Power/Toughness	Description
Ray of Erasure	Instant	U	--	Target player takes the top card of their library and puts it in graveyard. Draw a card at beginning of next turn's upkeep.
Reverberation	Instant	UU2	--	Redirects damage done by 1 sorcery back at its caster.
Riptide	Instant	U	--	Causes all blue creatures to become tapped.
Sea King's Blessing	Instant	U	--	Changes color of any/all creatures to blue.
Silhouette	Instant	U1	--	Creature is not damaged by spells or effects that target it until end of turn.
Siren's Call	Instant	U	--	All of opponent's non-wall creatures must attack. If a creature is unable to attack, it is destroyed.
Telekinesis	Instant	UU	--	Target creature does not deal damage this turn. Taps it and keeps it tapped for 2 turns.
Teleport	Instant	UUU	--	Makes a creature unblockable until end of turn. Play after attackers are chosen but before blockers are chosen.
Twiddle	Instant	U	--	Tap or untap 1 creature, land, or artifact.
Updraft	Instant	U1	--	Target creature gains flying until end of turn. Draw a card from the library at beginning of next turn's upkeep phase.
Unsummon	Instant	U	--	Return target creature to controller's hand.
Winter's Chill	Instant	UX	--	Cast only during combat before defense is chosen. At end of combat, destroy X attacking creatures in play. X cannot be greater than the number of snow-covered lands you control and have in play. For each attacking creature, opponent may pay 1 or 2 to prevent it from being destroyed. If 1, creature neither deals nor receives damage; if 2, deals and receives as normal.

Card	Type	Cost	Power/ Toughness	Description
Word of Undoing	Instant	U	--	Target creature returns to owner's hand. Any white enchantments that you own on that creature return to your hand.

Blue Interrupts

Card	Type	Cost	Power/ Toughness	Description
Blue Elemental Blast	Interrupt	U	--	Counters target red spell as it is being cast, or destroy target red card in play.
Counterspell	Interrupt	UU	--	Counters target spell.
Deflection	Interrupt	U3	--	Target spell with single target now targets a new target of your choice.
Flash Counter	Interrupt	U1	--	Counters an interrupt or instant.
Force Spike	Interrupt	U	--	Target spell is countered unless caster spends an additional 1 colorless.
Magical Hack	Interrupt	U	--	Change a land reference on one card.
Force Void	Interrupt	U2	--	Counters target spell unless the spell's caster pays 1. Draw a card from the library at the beginning of next turn's upkeep phase.
Hydroblast	Interrupt	U	--	Counter target spell or destroy target permanent in play if red.
Mana Drain	Interrupt	UU	--	Counters target spell and gives X mana to you on your next turn where X is the casting cost of the spell.
Power Sink	Interrupt	UX	--	Target spell is countered unless caster spends an additional X mana. If he or she cannot spend this mana all his or her lands are tapped.
Remove Soul	Interrupt	U1	--	Counters target summon spell as it is being cast.
Reset	Interrupt	UU	--	Untaps all your lands. Played on opponent's turn after his upkeep.
Sleight of Mind	Interrupt	U	--	Changes color reference on a spell or permanent.

Card	Type	Cost	Power/ Toughness	Description
Spell Blast	Interrupt	UX	--	Target spell of casting cost X is countered.
Thoughtlace	Interrupt	U	--	Changes color of one card to blue.

Blue Sorcery

Card	Type	Cost	Power/ Toughness	Description
Acid Rain	Sorcery	U3	--	Destroys all forests in play.
Amnesia	Sorcery	UUU3	--	Look at target player's hand. He must discard all non-land cards in his hand.
Braingeyser	Sorcery	UUX	--	Draw X cards or force opponent to draw X cards.
Drafna's Restoration	Sorcery	U	--	Take any number of artifacts from target player's graveyard and place them in any order on top of his library.
Drain Power	Sorcery	UU	--	Tap all of opponent's land and add this mana to your mana pool.
Energy Tap	Sorcery	U	--	Taps a creature for colorless mana equal to its casting cost.
Juxtapose	Sorcery	U3	--	You and opponent trade control of both your highest casting cost creature and your highest casting cost artifact.
Mind Bomb	Sorcery	U	--	All players must discard 3 cards from their hand or suffer 1 damage for each card they do not discard.
Part Water	Sorcery	UXX	--	Gives X creatures islandwalk.
Portent	Sorcery	U	--	Look at top three cards of target player's library then shuffle it or return the three in any order. Draw a card at beginning of next turn's upkeep.
Psychic Purge	Sorcery	U	--	Do 1 damage to any target. If an opponent's action forces you to discard this card, opponent takes 5 damage.
Recall	Sorcery	UXX	--	Sacrifice X cards from your hand and bring X cards from your graveyard to your hand.

Card	Type	Cost	Power/ Toughness	Description
Reconstruction	Sorcery	U	--	Return artifact from your graveyard to your hand.
Time Walk	Sorcery	U1	--	Take another turn after this one.
Timetwister	Sorcery	U2	--	Shuffle your hand, graveyard, and library together and start a new graveyard with Timetwister. Draw a new hand of 7 cards.
Transmute Artifact	Sorcery	UU	--	Send an artifact in play to the graveyard and bring an artifact from your library into play. You must pay the difference in their casting costs.
Volcanic Eruption	Sorcery	UUUX	--	Destroys X mountains and does X damage to all creatures and players for each mountain destroyed.

Blue Summons

Card	Type	Cost	Power/ Toughness	Description
Balduvian Shaman	Summon Cleric	U	1/1	Tap to permanently change the text of target white enchantment you control that does not have cumulative upkeep by replacing all instances of one color word with another.
Clone	Summon Clone	U3	*/*	Copies the color and abilities of creature.
Dandan	Summon Dandan	UU	4/1	Cannot attack if opponent does not have islands. Destroyed if you have no islands.
Devouring Deep	Summon Devouring Deep	U2	1/2	Islandwalk.
Mahamoti Djinn	Summon Djinn	UU4	5/6	Flying.
Serendib Djinn	Summon Djinn	UU2	5/6	Flying. Destroys a land during upkeep. Take 3 damage if the destroyed land is an island.
Vesuvan Doppelganger	Summon Doppelganger	UU3	*/*	Copies a creature but not color. Can change creature copied during upkeep.

Card	Type	Cost	Power/ Toughness	Description
Azure Drake	Summon Drake	U3	2/4	Flying.
Electric Eel	Summon Eel	U	1/1	Pay RR to give +2/+0 to Electric Eel. Does 1 damage to you. Does 1 damage to you when brought into play.
Serendib Efreet	Summon Efreet	U2	3/4	Flying. Does 1 damage to controller during their upkeep.
Air Elemental	Summon Elemental	UU3	4/4	Flying.
Time Elemental	Summon Elemental	U2	0/2	Tap+(UU2) Send target permanent to owner's hand. Take 5 damage and destroy Elemental if is used to attack or block.
Water Elemental	Summon Elemental	UU3	5/4	
Psionic Entity	Summon Entity	U4	2/2	Tap to do 2 damage to any target, but also does 3 damage to itself.
Silver Erne	Summon Erne	U3	2/2	Flying, trample.
Zephyr Falcon	Summon Falcon	U1	1/1	Flying. Does not tap when attacking.
Flying Men	Summon Flying Men	U	1/1	Flying.
Brine Hag	Summon Hag	UU2	2/2	Creatures which damaged the Hag on the turn it goes to the graveyard become 0/2 creatures.
Deep Spawn	Summon Homarid	UUU5	6/6	Trample. During your upkeep, take two cards from top of your library and put them in your graveyard or destroy Deep Spawn. U: Deep Spawn may not be the target of fast effects or spells until end of turn and does not untap as normal during your next upkeep phase. If Deep Spawn is untapped tap it.
Homarid	Summon Homarid	U2	2/2	Put a token on Homarid when it is brought into play and during your upkeep. If there is 1 counter on Homarid, it gets -1/-1. If there are 3 counters on Homarid it gets +1/+1. If there are 4 counters on Homarid, remove them all.

Card	Type	Cost	Power/ Toughness	Description
Homarid Shaman	Summon Homarid	UU2	2/1	U: Tap a green creature.
Homarid Warrior	Summon Homarid	U4	3/3	U: Warrior may not be the target of spells or fast effects until the end of turn. Does not untap as normal during its controller's next untap phase. If Homarid Warrior is not tapped tap it.
Illusionary Forces	Summon Illusion	U3	4/4	Cumulative upkeep: U. Flying.
Illusionary Presence	Summon Illusion	UU1	2/2	Cumulative upkeep: U. During your upkeep gains a landwalk ability of your choice.
Island Fish Jasconius	Summon Island Fish	UUU4	6/8	Does not untap as normal. Pay UUU during your upkeep to untap Island Fish. Cannot attack if your opponent does not have islands. Destroyed if at any time you don't have islands in play.
Polar Kraken	Summon Kraken	UUU8	11/11	Cumulative upkeep: Sacrifice a land. Trample. Comes into play tapped.
Leviathan	Summon Leviathan	UUU U5	10/10	Trample. When Leviathan comes into play you must sacrifice 2 islands. In order to attack, you must sacrifice 2 islands. To untap you must sacrifice 2 islands.
Segovian Leviathan	Summon Leviathan	U4	3/3	Islandwalk.
Lord of Atlantis	Summon Lord	UU	2/2	Gives all Merfolk in play +1/+1.
Musician	Summon Mage	U2	1/3	Cumulative upkeep: 1. Tap to place a music counter on target creature in play. During that creature's controller's upkeep phase
Old Man of the Sea	Summon Marid	UU1	2/3	Tap to take control of a creature with a power less than or equal to Old Man. Retain control as long as Old Man does not become untapped or leave play. May choose not to untap Old Man.
Merfolk Assassin	Summon Merfolk	UU	1/2	Tap to destroy a creature with islandwalk.
Merfolk of the Pearl Trident	Summon Merfolk	U	1/1	

Card	Type	Cost	Power/ Toughness	Description
River Merfolk	Summon Merfolk	UU	2/1	U: Mountainwalk until end of turn.
Seasinger	Summon Merfolk	UU	10/1	Bury Seasinger if you have no islands in play. Tap to gain control of target creature if its controller controls at least 1 island. You lose control of target creature if Seasinger leaves play, if you lose control of Seasinger, or if it becomes untapped. You may choose not to untap Seasinger as normal during your untap phase.
Svyelunite Priest	Summon Merfolk	U1	1/1	Tap+(UU) Target creature may not be the target of spells or fast effects until end of turn. Use this ability only during your upkeep.
Vodalian Knights	Summon Merfolk	UU1	2/2	First strike. U: Flying until end of turn. Vodalian Knights may not attack unless your opponent controls at least one island. Bury if you control no islands.
Vodalian Mage	Summon Merfolk	U2	1/1	Tap+(U) Counters target spell unless caster of spell spends an additional 1. Play this ability as an interrupt.
Vodalian Soldiers	Summon Merfolk	U1	1/2	
Mistfolk	Summon Mistfolk	UU	1/2	U: Counter target spell that targets it.
Phantasmal Forces	Summon Phantasm	U3	4/1	Flying. Pay U during your upkeep or Phantasmal Forces is destroyed.
Phantom Monster	Summon Phantasm	U3	3/3	Flying.
Phantasmal Mount	Summon Phantasm	U1	1/1	Flying. Tap to give target creature with toughness less than 3 flying and +1/+1 until end of turn. Toughness may subsequently be increased. If either Mount or target leave play other is buried.
Sage of Lat-Nam	Summon Sage	U2	1/2	Tap Sage and sacrifice an artifact to draw a card from your library.
Sea Serpent	Summon Serpent	U5	5/5	May not attack unless opponent controls at least one island. Destroyed if at any time you have no islands in play.

Card	Type	Cost	Power/ Toughness	Description
Giant Shark	Summon Shark	U5	4/4	If Shark blocks or is blocked by a creature that is damaged this turn, Shark gains +2/+0 and trample until end of turn. Shark can only attack if opponent controls at least one island. Buried if at any time controller controls no islands.
Ghost Ship	Summon Ship	UU2	2/4	Flying. UUU: Regenerates.
Merchant Ship	Summon Ship	U	0/2	Controller gains 2 life if Ship attacks and is not blocked. Cannot attack unless opponent controls at least one island. Destroyed if at any time controller controls no islands.
Pirate Ship	Summon Ship	U4	4/3	Tap to do 1 damage to target. Opponent must have islands to attack with this card. Destroyed if you have no islands.
Shyft	Summon Shyft	U4	4/2	During your upkeep may change it to any color or combination of colors.
Sindbad	Summon Sindbad	U1	1/1	Tap to draw 1 card. Discard this card unless it is a land.
Elder Spawn	Summon Spawn	UUU4	6/6	Cannot be blocked by red creatures. Sacrifice an island each turn or take 6 damage and Elder Spawn is destroyed.
Sea Spirit	Summon Spirit	U4	2/3	U: +1/+0 until end of turn.
Sibilant Spirit	Summon Spirit	U5	5/6	Flying. Whenever declared as an attacker, defender may draw a card.
Wind Spirit	Summon Spirit	U4	3/2	Flying. Must be blocked by more than one creature during combat.
Giant Tortoise	Summon Tortoise	U1	1/1	Gains +9/+3 if untapped.
Glacial Wall	Summon Wall	U2	0/7	Wall.
Illusionary Wall	Summon Wall	U4	7/4	Cumulative upkeep: U. Flying, first strike.
Thunder Wall	Summon Wall	UU1	0/2	Flying. U: +1/+1 until end of turn.

Card	Type	Cost	Power/ Toughness	Description
Vodalian War Machine	Summon Wall	UU1	0/4	0: Tap target Merfolk you control to allow Vodalian War Machine to attack this turn or give a +2/+1 until end of turn. If Vodalian War Machine is put in the graveyard, all Merfolk tapped in this manner this turn are destroyed.
Wall of Air	Summon Wall	UU1	1/5	Wall. Flying.
Wall of Vapor	Summon Wall	U3	0/1	Takes no damage when blocking creatures.
Wall of Water	Summon Wall	UU1	0/5	Wall. U: +1/+0
Wall of Wonder	Summon Wall	UU2	1/5	Wall. UU2: +4/-4 and can attack.
Apprentice Wizard	Summon Wizard	UU1	0/1	Tap+(U) add 3 to your mana pool.
Balduvian Conjurer	Summon Wizard	U1	0/2	Tap to turn target snow-covered land into a 2/2 creature. Cannot be tapped for mana if it came into play this turn.
Krovikan Sorcerer	Summon Wizard	U2	1/1	Tap to choose one card from your hand and draw another. If discarded card was black draw two cards instead, keep one and discard the other.
Magus of the Unseen	Summon Wizard	U1	1/1	Tap+U1: Untap target artifact in play opponent controls and gain control of it until end of turn. If that artifact is a creature, it can attack and you may use any abilities that require tapping. When you lose control of it, tap it.
Prodigal Sorcerer	Summon Wizard	U2	1/1	Tap to do 1 damage to any target.
Soldevi Machinist	Summon Wizard	U1	1/1	Tap to add 2 to your mana pool which can only be used for activation costs of an artifact. Use this ability as an interrupt.
Zuran Enchanter	Summon Wizard	U1	1/1	Tap+(2B): Target player chooses and discards one card from his hand. Ignore this ability if target has no cards. Use this ability only during your turn.

Card	Type	Cost	Power/ Toughness	Description
Zuran Spellcaster	Summon Wizard	U2	1/1	Tap to deal one damage to target creature or player.
Water Wurm	Summon Wurm	U	1/1	Water Wurm gains +0/+1 if opponent controls at least 1 island.
Drowned	Summon Zombies	U1	1/1	B: Regenerates.

Black

Black Enchantments

Card	Type	Cost	Power/ Toughness	Description
Enchant Artifacts				
Artifact Possession	Enchant Artifact	B2	--	Does 2 damage to target's controller whenever target is tapped or activated.
Curse Artifact	Enchant Artifact	BB2	--	During upkeep, controller of target may choose to bury target. If controller chooses not to bury artifact, Curse Artifact does 2 damage to him.
Warp Artifact	Enchant Artifact	BB	--	Does 1 damage to target's controller during his upkeep.
Enchant Creatures				
Cloak of Confusion	Enchant Creature	B1	--	If target creature you control that has Cloak of Confusion on it attacks and is not blocked you may choose to have the creature deal no damage and force an opponent to discard a card from his hand at random. This ability is ignored if target opponent has no cards in hand.
Demonic Torment	Enchant Creature	B2	--	Target may not attack and deals no damage during combat.
Fear	Enchant Creature	BB	--	Target may only be blocked by black or artifact creatures.
Imprison	Enchant Creature	B	--	Pay 1 each time target attacks, blocks, or is tapped to counter action. If you do not pay, enchantment is destroyed.
Krovikan Fetish	Enchant Creature	B2	--	Target creature gains a +1/+1 bonus to power and toughess. Draw a card from your library during the next upkeep phase.
Leshrac's Rite	Enchant Creature	B	--	Target creature gains swampwalk ability.
Mind Whip	Enchant Creature	2BB	--	Target creature's controller suffers 2 points of damage dealt by Mind Whip unless he or she pays 3. If Mind Whip damages creature's controller in this manner, tap that creature.

Card	Type	Cost	Power/ Toughness	Description
Paralyze	Enchant Creature	B	--	Taps target creature when cast. Creature does not untap as normal, controller must pay 4 during upkeep to untap.
Seizures	Enchant Creature	B1	--	When target creature becomes tapped, its controller suffers 3 points of damage. This can be prevented by paying 3.
Soul Kiss	Enchant Creature	B2	--	B: Pay 1 life point and target creature enchanted by Soul Kiss gains +2/+2 until end of turn. You may not spend more than BBB each turn. Effects that redirect or prevent damage cannot be used to counter this.
Spirit Shackle	Enchant Creature	BB	--	Target gets a -0/-2 counter each time it is tapped.
Takklemaggot	Enchant Creature	BB2	--	Target gets -0/-1 counter during each upkeep. When target goes to the graveyard, its controller picks another creature to place Takklemaggot on. If there are no creatures in play it becomes an enchantment and does 1 damage each turn to controller of last creature to die.
Thrull Retainer	Enchant Creature	B	--	Target gets +1/+1. Sacrifice Thrull Retainer to regenerate target.
Unholy Strength	Enchant Creature	B	--	Target gains +2/+1.
Weakness	Enchant Creature	B	--	Target gains -2/-1.
Enchant Dead Creatures				
Animate Dead	Enchant Dead Creature	B1	--	Return 1 creature from any graveyard to play under your control at -1 power.

Card	Type	Cost	Power/ Toughness	Description
Dance of the Dead	Enchant Dead Creature	B1	--	Take dead creature from any graveyard and place it in play under your control, tapped with a +1/+1 bonus and treated as if just summoned. That creature does not untap as normal. At the end of its controller's upkeep, may pay an additional B1 to untap that creature. If Dance of Dead is removed from target creature then it is placed in its owner's graveyard.
Enchant Lands				
Blight	Enchant Land	BB	--	If land is tapped it is destroyed at end of turn.
Cursed Land	Enchant Land	BB2	--	Does 1 damage to controller of target during his or her upkeep.
Evil Presence	Enchant Land	B	--	Target land becomes a swamp.
Tourach's Gate	Enchant Land	BB1	--	Can only be played on a target land you control. Sacrifice a Thrull to put 3 time counters on Tourach's Gate. During your upkeep remove a time counter from Tourach's Gate. If there are no counters on Gate, bury it. 0: Tap land Tourach's Gate enchants all your attacking creatures get +2/-1 until end of turn.
Enchant Worlds				
Nether Void	Enchant World	B3	--	Counters all spells unless caster spends an additional 3.
The Abyss	Enchant World	B3	--	All players bury 1 non-artifact creature they control during their upkeep.
Independent Enchantments				
All Hallow's Eve	Enchantment	B2	--	Two turns after casting time all creatures in all graveyards are brought directly into play.
Bad Moon	Enchantment	B1	--	All black creatures in play get +1/+1.
Breeding Pit	Enchantment	B3	--	During your upkeep pay BB or is destroyed. At end of your turn bring a Thrull counter into play. Treat as 0/1 black creature.

Card	Type	Cost	Power/ Toughness	Description
Chains of Mephistopheles	Enchantment	B1	--	All players must discard 1 card for each card they have drawn, other than the first during the draw phase.
Deathgrip	Enchantment	BB	--	BB: Counters a green spell as it is being cast.
Gate to Phyrexia	Enchantment	BB	--	Sacrifice a creature during upkeep to destroy any artifact in play.
Gloom	Enchantment	B2	--	White spells and white enchantments cost 3 more.
Greed	Enchantment	B3	--	B: Draw a card and lose 2 life. Loss of life cannot be prevented or redirected.
Haunting Wind	Enchantment	B3	--	Does 1 damage to anyone who taps or powers an artifact.
Hecatomb	Enchantment	BB1	--	When Hecatomb enters play its caster must sacrafice 4 creatures. 0: Swamps you control may be tapped to have Hecatomb cause 1 point of damage to target creature or player.
Horror of Horrors	Enchantment	BB3	--	Can sacrifice a swamp to regenerate a black creature.
Infernal Darkness	Enchantment	BB2	--	Cumulative upkeep: B and 1 life point. All lands that produce mana now produce B instead of their normal mana type.
Leshrac's Sigil	Enchantment	BB	--	BB: When an opponent successfully casts a green spell, you may look at his hand and choose one card that he must discard. BB: Return Leshrac's Sigil from play to its owner's hand.
Lich	Enchantment	BBBB	--	You have 0 life. Your cards are now your life. If you take damage, you must remove a card from play, if you gain life you may draw that many cards. If you have no cards in play or Lich is destroyed, you lose.
Lim-Dul's Hex	Enchantment	B1	--	During its controller's upkeep Lim-Dul's Hex inflicts 1 point of damage to each player. This damage can be prevented by playing B or 3. By paying this the damage is prevented to the player and not the opponent.

Card	Type	Cost	Power/ Toughness	Description
Necropotence	Enchantment	BBB	--	Once Necropotence is in play you skip your draw phase from that point on. If you discard a card from your hand that card is removed from the game. 0: Pay 1 life and set aside a card from the top of your library and place in your hand at the next discard phase. Damage cannot be redirected or prevented.
Oath of Lim-Dul	Enchantment	B3	--	For each damage you suffer discard a card from play or from your hand. You may not remove Oath of Lim-Dul in this mannner unless you no longer control any permanents and have no cards in your hand except for the Oath of Lim-Dul. BB: Draw a card.
Oubliette	Enchantment	BB1	--	Select a creature in play. Creature is removed from game as long as Oubliette is in play.
Pestilence	Enchantment	BB2	--	B: Does 1 damage to all creatures and all players. Removed from play if there are no creatures in play at end of turn.
Quagmire	Enchantment	B2	--	Stops all use of swampwalk.
Season of the Witch	Enchantment	BBB	--	At end of turn, all untapped creatures that could have attacked but didn't are destroyed. Pay 2 life during your upkeep or is destroyed. Damage cannot be prevented or redirected.
Tourach's Chant	Enchantment	BB1	--	During your upkeep, pay B or destroy Tourach's Chant. Whenever a player puts a forest into play, does 3 damage to him, unless he puts a -1/-1 creature on a creature he controls.
Underworld Dreams	Enchantment	BBB	--	Each time opponent draws a card he takes 1 damage.
Withering Wisps	Enchantment	BB1	--	If at the end of the turn there are no creatures in play destroy Withering Wisps. B: Withering Wisps deal 1 point of damage to each creature and player. Its controller may not spend more B in this manner than his snow-covered swamps.

Card	Type	Cost	Power/ Toughness	Description
Worms of the Earth	Enchantment	BBB2	--	No more land may be brought into play. During any player's turn they may sacrifice two lands or take 5 damage to destroy Worms of the Earth.

Black Instants

Card	Type	Cost	Power/ Toughness	Description
Dark Banishing	Instant	B2	--	Destroy target non-black creature without possibility of regenerating.
Darkness	Instant	B	--	No creatures deal damage in attack phase this turn.
Demonic Consultation	Instant	B	--	Caster names a card and removes the top 6 cards of library. The next card is revealed. If the card is the card named it may be placed in its caster's hand; if not the card is removed from the game. This continues until the card named is revealed.
Glyph of Doom	Instant	B	--	Destroys all creatures blocked by wall at end of combat.
Gravebind	Instant	B	--	Target creature is unable to regenerate this turn. During the next upkeep phase draw a card from your library.
Hell Swarm	Instant	B	--	-1/-0 to all creatures until end of turn.
Howl from Beyond	Instant	BX	--	Target creature gains +X/+0 until end of turn.
Marsh Gas	Instant	B	--	All creatures get -2/-0 until end of turn.
Simulacrum	Instant	B1	--	Transfer all damage done to you so far this turn to a creature.
Terror	Instant	B1	--	Target creature is buried.
Touch of Darkness	Instant	B	--	Changes the color of any creatures in play to black until end of turn.
Transmutation	Instant	B1	--	Switch power and toughness of creature until end of turn. Effects that alter power and toughness are also switched.

Card	Type	Cost	Power/Toughness	Description
Word of Command	Instant	BB	--	Cast one of opponent's spells using his or her mana.

Black Interrupts

Card	Type	Cost	Power/Toughness	Description
Burnt Offering	Interrupt	B	--	Sacrifice a creature under your control to add its casting cost in any combination of red and black mana to your pool.
Dark Ritual	Interrupt	B	--	Add BBB to your mana pool.
Deathlace	Interrupt	B	--	Changes color of target permanent to black.
Sacrifice	Interrupt	B	--	Sacrifice a creature and add its casting cost in black mana to your pool.
Songs of the Damned	Interrupt	B	--	Add B to your mana pool for each creature in your graveyard.
Spoils of Evil	Interrupt	B2	--	Add 1 colorless mana to your pool and gain 1 life for each artifact or creature in opponent's graveyard

Black Sorcery

Card	Type	Cost	Power/Toughness	Description
Ashes to Ashes	Sorcery	BB1	--	Removes 2 target non-artifact creatures from the game and does 5 damage to caster.
Contract from Below	Sorcery	B	--	Discard entire hand. Ante an additional card, and draw 7 new cards into your hand. May only be used in ante games.
Darkpact	Sorcery	BBB	--	Exchange top card from your library with any card in the ante. May only be used in ante games.
Demonic Attorney	Sorcery	BB1	--	All players must ante an additional card or forfeit.

Card	Type	Cost	Power/ Toughness	Description
Demonic Tutor	Sorcery	B1	--	Search through your library for one card and place it in your hand. Reshuffle your library.
Drain Life	Sorcery	B1	--	Does X damage to target and adds X to caster's life. X must be black mana.
Gaze of Pain	Sorcery	B1	--	Unblocked attacking creatures may choose not to attack to deal damage to target creature.
Hellfire	Sorcery	BBB2	--	Destroys all non-black creatures and does 3 damage to you plus 1 damage for each creature that goes to the graveyard.
Hymn to Tourach	Sorcery	BB	--	Target player discards 2 cards from his hand. If he does not have 2 cards, entire hand is discarded.
Icequake	Sorcery	BB1	--	Destroys target land and does 1 damage to controller if target land is snow-covered.
Inquisition	Sorcery	B2	--	Look at target player's hand. Does 1 damage to target for each white card in his hand.
Jovial Evil	Sorcery	B2	--	Opponent takes 2 damage for each white creature controlled.
Mind Ravel	Sorcery	B2	--	Target player discards a card of choice from his hand. Draw a card at the beginning of next turn's upkeep.
Mind Twist	Sorcery	BX	--	Target player must discard X cards. If he does not have X cards, entire hand is discarded.
Mind Warp	Sorcery	B3X	--	Look at target player's hand and force him to discard X cards of your choice.
Pox	Sorcery	BBB	--	Sacrifice, rounding up, 1/3 of life, hand, creatures, and lands in that order. Damage cannot be prevented.
Raise Dead	Sorcery	B	--	Return target creature from graveyard to your hand.
Sinkhole	Sorcery	BB	--	Destroy target land.
Soul Burn	Sorcery	B2	--	Does 1 damage to target for each B or R spent in addition to cost. You gain 1 life for each damage you inflict this way.

Card	Type	Cost	Power/ Toughness	Description
Soul Exchange	Sorcery	BB	--	Sacrifice a creature, but remove it from the game instead of putting it in the graveyard. Remove 1 creature from the graveyard and put it directly into play as if it were just summoned. If sacrificed creature was a Thrull put a +2/+2 on creature.
Spoils of War	Sorcery	BX	--	Put X +1/+1 bonus counters on any number of target creatures in play. X is the number of creatures and artifacts in opponent's graveyard.
Stench of Evil	Sorcery	BB2	--	Destroy all plains. Does 1 damage for each plains destroyed this way to controller. Damage may be prevented for 2 each points.
Syphon Soul	Sorcery	B2	--	Does 2 damage to all players. Caster gains 1 life for each unprevented point of damage.
Touch of Death	Sorcery	B2	--	Deals 1 damage to target player and you gain 1 life. Draw a card at the beginning of the next turn's upkeep.
Word of Binding	Sorcery	BBX	--	X target creatures become tapped.

Black Summons

Card	Type	Cost	Power/ Toughness	Description
Abomination	Summon Abomination	BB3	2/6	Any green or white creature blocked by or blocking it is destroyed at the end of combat.
Fallen Angel	Summon Angel	BB3	3/3	Flying. Sacrifice a creature for +2/+1 until end of turn.
Carrion Ants	Summon Ants	BB2	0/1	1: +1/+1 until end of turn.
Royal Assassin	Summon Assassin	BB1	1/1	Tap to destroy 1 tapped creature.
Ebon Praetor	Summon Avatar	BB4	5/5	Trample. First strike. During your upkeep, put a -2/-2 counter on Ebon Praetor. You may sacrifice 1 creature to remove a -2/-2 counter from Preator. If the creature sacrificed was a Thrull, put a +1/+0 counter on Ebon Praetor.

Card	Type	Cost	Power/ Toughness	Description
Banshee	Summon Banshee	BB2	0/1	Tap+(X) Banshee does X damage, half (rounded up) to you and half (rounded down) to your opponent.
Vampire Bats	Summon Bats	B	0/1	B: +1/+0 until end of turn. Only BB may be spent in this fashion.
Brine Shaman	Summon Cleric	B1	1/1	Tap and sacrifice a creature to give target creature a +2/+2 bonus until end of turn. UU1: Sacrifice a creature in play to counter target summon spell as it is cast.
Initiates of the Ebon Hand	Summon Clerics	B	1/1	1: Add B to your mana pool. If more than 3 is spent in this fashion, Initiates is destroyed at end of turn.
Order of the Ebon Hand	Summon Clerics	BB	2/1	B: First strike BB: +1/+0 Until end of turn.
Priest of Yawgmoth	Summon Cleric	B1	1/2	Tap to sacrifice one of your artifacts for black mana equal to its casting cost.
Kjeldoran Dead	Summon Dead	B	3/1	When it comes into play, sacrifice a creature. B: Regenerate.
Lord of the Pit	Summon Demon	BBB4	7/7	Trample. First strike. Sacrifice 1 creature every upkeep or does seven damage to you.
Minion of Leshrac	Summon Demon	BBB4	5/5	Protection from black. During your upkeep sacrifice a creature or deals 5 damage to you and becomes tapped. Cannot be sacrificed to itself. Tap to destroy a creature or land.
Minion of Tevesh Szat	Summon Demon	BBB4	4/4	During your upkeep, pay BB or deals 2 damage to you. Tap to give target creature +3/-2 until end of turn.
Yawgmoth Demon	Summon Demon	BB4	6/6	Flying. First strike. Sacrifice an artifact during upkeep or take 2 damage and Demon taps.
Demonic Hordes	Summon Demons	BBB3	5/5	Tap to destroy a land. Pay BBB during upkeep or loose a land and Demonic Hordes becomes tapped.
Stone-Throwing Devils	Summon Devils	B	1/1	First strike.
Juzam Djinn	Summon Djinn	BB2	5/5	Does 1 damage to controller during their upkeep.
Eater of the Dead	Summon Eater of the Dead	B4	3/4	0: Remove a creature from any graveyard to untap.

Card	Type	Cost	Power/ Toughness	Description
Janun Efreet	Summon Efreet	BB2	3/3	Flying. Must pay BB during upkeep or is buried.
El-Hajjaj	Summon El-Hajjaj	BB1	1/1	Gain 1 life for each damage El-Hajjaj does to a target.
Evil Eye of Orms-By-Gore	Summon Evil Eye	B4	3/6	May only be blocked by walls. Only your Evil Eyes may attack while Evil Eye is in play.
The Fallen	Summon Fallen	BBB1	2/3	During its controller's upkeep The Fallen does 1 damage to each opponent it has previously damaged.
Moor Fiend	Summon Fiend	B3	3/3	Swampwalk.
Ghosts of the Damned	Summon Ghosts	BB1	0/2	Tap to add -1/-0 to any creature until end of turn.
Ashen Ghoul	Summon Ghoul	B3	3/1	Can attack the turn it comes into play. B: Return to play under your control. Use this ability only at the end of your upkeep and only if it is in your graveyard with 3 creatures above it.
Khabal Ghoul	Summon Ghoul	B2	1/1	Add a +1/+1 counter to Ghoul for each creature that was destroyed at end of turn.
Scavenging Ghoul	Summon Ghoul	B3	2/2	Add 1 token to Ghoul at end of turn for each creature that died during the turn. Remove 1 token to regenerate Ghoul.
Phyrexian Gremlins	Summon Gremlins	B2	1/1	Tap to tap any artifact in play. Artifact remains tapped as long as Gremlins remain tapped. You may choose not to untap Gremlins.
Guardian Beast	Summon Guardian	B3	2/4	While Guardian Beast is in play and untapped, artifacts under your control cannot be stolen or destroyed.
Hell's Caretaker	Summon Hell's Caretaker	B3	1/1	Tap and sacrifice a creature during upkeep to bring a creature from your graveyard directly into play.
Cosmic Horror	Summon Horror	BBB3	7/7	First strike. Pay BBB3 during upkeep or does 7 damage to you and is destroyed.
Headless Horseman	Summon Horseman	B2	2/2	
Bog Imp	Summon Imp	B1	1/1	Flying.

Card	Type	Cost	Power/ Toughness	Description
Nettling Imp	Summon Imp	B2	1/1	Tap to force an opponent's creature to attack. If it cannot attack it is destroyed.
Noritt	Summon Imp	B3	1/1	Tap to untap target blue creature. Tap to force a non-wall creature to attack. If cannot it is destroyed at end of turn.
Infernal Denzien	Summon Infernal Denzien	B7	5/7	During your upkeep sacrifice 2 swamps or becomes tapped and opponent gains control of one of your creatures. Opponent loses control if Denzien leaves play. Tap to take control of target creature. Lose control if Denzien leaves play.
Flow of Maggots	Summon Insects	B2	2/2	Cumulative upkeep: 1. Flow of Maggots cannot be blocked by any non-wall creatures.
Black Knight	Summon Knight	BB	2/2	Protection from white. First strike.
Knight of Stromgald	Summon Knight	BB	2/1	Protection from white. BB: +1/+0 until end of turn. B: First strike until end of turn.
Stromgald Cabal	Summon Knights	BB1	2/2	Tap and pay 1 life to counter target white spell. Damage cannot be prevented. Play as an interrupt.
Hyalopterous Lemure	Summon Lemure	B4	4/3	0: Flying and -0/-1 until end of turn.
Zombie Master	Summon Lord	BB1	2/3	All Zombies in play get swampwalk and regeneration.
Lost Soul	Summon Lost Soul	BB1	2/1	Swampwalk.
Lesser Werewolf	Summon Lycanthrope	B3	2/4	B: When blocking or blocked by creatures, may take -1/-0 until end of turn to give a permanent -1/-0 to creature blocking/blocked by it.
Infernal Medusa	Summon Medusa	BB3	2/4	All creatures blocked by or blocking it are destroyed at end of turn.
Mold Demon	Summon Mold Demon	BB5	6/6	Must sacrifice two swamps when it comes into play.

Card	Type	Cost	Power/ Toughness	Description
Frankenstein's Monster	Summon Monster	BBX	0/1	When Frankenstein's Monster is brought into play, if you do not take X creatures from your graveyard and remove them from the game, Monster is countered. For each creature removed from your graveyard, you may choose to give Frankenstein's Monster a permanent +2/+0, +1/+1, or +0/+2.
Cyclopean Mummy	Summon Mummy	B1	2/1	Is removed from the game when it goes to the graveyard from play.
Murk Dwellers	Summon Murk Dwellers	B3	2/2	When attacking, Murk Dwellers gain +2/+0 if not blocked.
Nameless Race	Summon Nameless Race	B3	*/*	Pay * life when bringing Nameless Race into play. Effects that prevent or redirect damage may not be used to counter this loss of life. When Nameless Race is brought into play, * may not be greater than the number of white cards all opponents have in play and in their graveyard.
Shimian Night Stalker	Summon Night Stalker	BB3	4/4	Tap+(B) Redirect damage done to you by one creature to Stalker.
Nightmare	Summon Nightmare	B5	*/*	Flying. Where * is the number of swamps you have in play.
Hasran Ogress	Summon Ogre	BB	3/2	Pay 2 when it attacks or take 3 damage.
Xenic Poltergeist	Summon Poltergeist	BB1	1/1	Tap to turn an artifact into an artifact creature with power and toughness equal to its casting cost until the beginning of your next turn.
Rag Man	Summon Rag Man	BB2	2/1	Tap+(BBB) Look at opponent's hand; if it contains creatures he must discard one of them at random. This ability may only be used during its controller's turn.
Erg Raiders	Summon Raiders	B1	2/3	If do not attack do 2 damage to controller.
Bog Rats	Summon Rats	B	1/1	Cannot be blocked by walls.
Pestilence Rats	Summon Rats	B2	*/3	Where * is number of other rats in play.
Plague Rats	Summon Rats	B2	*/*	Where * is number of Plague Rats in play.

Card	Type	Cost	Power/ Toughness	Description
Grave Robbers	Summon Robbers	BB1	1/1	Tap+(B) Take an artifact from any graveyard and remove it from the game to gain 2 life.
Pit Scorpion	Summon Scorpion	B2	1/1	Give opponent a poison counter each time it hits opponent. If opponent ever has 10 or more poison counters, he loses.
Frozen Shade	Summon Shade	B2	0/1	B: +1/+1
Hoar Shade	Summon Shade	B3	1/2	B: +1/+1 until end of turn.
Nether Shadow	Summon Shadow	B	1/1	If Nether Shadow is in the graveyard and 3 creatures are above it, then it comes into play during your upkeep phase.
Drudge Skeletons	Summon Skeletons	B1	1/1	B: Regenerates.
Giant Slug	Summon Slug	B1	1/1	5: Gains basic Landwalk ability at the start of your next upkeep until end of that turn.
Sorceress Queen	Summon Sorceress	BB1	1/1	Tap to make a creature 0/2 until end of turn.
Abyssal Specter	Summon Specter	BB2	2/3	Flying. Whenever it damages a player, that player must discard a card of his choice.
Hypnotic Specter	Summon Specter	BB1	2/2	Flying. If Specter damages opponent, he or she must discard one card at random.
Foul Familiar	Summon Spirit	B2	3/1	Cannot block. B: Pay 1 life to return to hand. Damage cannot be prevented.
Armor Thrull	Summon Thrull	B2	1/3	Tap and sacrifice to add a +1/+2 counter to target creature.
Basal Thrull	Summon Thrull	BB	1/2	Tap and sacrifice to add BB to your mana pool.
Derelor	Summon Thrull	B3	4/4	Your black spells cost an additional B to cast.
Mindstab Thrull	Summon Thrull	BB1	2/2	If it attacks and is not blocked you may sacrifice Mindstab to force opponent to discard 3 cards at random from hand. If so it deals no damage during this combat. If player does not have enough cards his entire hand is discarded.

Card	Type	Cost	Power/ Toughness	Description
Necrite	Summon Thrull	BB1	2/2	If Necrite attacks and is not blocked you may sacrifice it to bury target creature controlled by the player it attacked this round. If you do this, Necrite deals no damage in combat this turn.
Thrull Champion	Summon Thrull	B4	2/2	All Thrulls in play gain +1/+1. Tap to take control of target Thrull. You lose control of target Thrull if Champion leaves play or you lose control of Champion.
Thrull Wizard	Summon Thrull	B2	1/1	Counters target black spell unless caster plays an additional B or 3.
Uncle Istvan	Summon Uncle Istvan	BBB1	1/3	All damage done to Uncle Istvan by creatures is reduced to 0.
Krovikan Vampire	Summon Vampire	BB3	3/3	If damages a creature that dies that turn, creature comes into play under your control. If you lose control of Vampire or it leaves play, bury the creature.
Sengir Vampire	Summon Vampire	BB3	4/4	Flying. Gets a +1/+1 token whenever a creature dies in a turn in which Sengir Vampire damaged it.
Walking Dead	Summon Walking Dead	B1	1/1	B: Regenerates.
Drift of the Dead	Summon Wall	B3	*/*	Where * is the number of snow-covered lands you control.
Wall of Bone	Summon Wall	B2	1/4	Wall. B: Regenerates.
Wall of Putrid Flesh	Summon Wall	B2	2/4	Wall. Protection from white. Not damaged by creatures with enchantments on them.
Wall of Shadows	Summon Wall	BB1	0/1	Wall. Takes no damage when blocking creatures. Cannot be targeted by effects that target only walls.
Wall of Tombstones	Summon Wall	B1	0/1+*	Wall. Where * is the number of creatures in the graveyard at the end of your upkeep.

Card	Type	Cost	Power/Toughness	Description
Dread Wight	Summon Wight	BB3	3/4	Any creature that blocks or is blocked by Wight becomes tapped and gets a paralyzation counter. Creature does not untap if it has a counter on it. Target's controller can remove a counter as a fast effect for 4.
Will-O-The-Wisp	Summon Will-O-The-Wisp	B	0/1	Flying. B: Regenerates.
Cuombajj Witches	Summon Witches	BB	1/3	Tap to do 1 damage to any target. Opponent also gets to do 1 damage to any target.
Krovikan Elementalist	Summon Wizard	BB	1/1	R2: Target creature gets +1/+0 bonus to power until end of turn. UU: Target creature you control gains flying ability until end of turn, bury it at end of turn.
Mole Worms	Summon Worms	B2	1/1	You may choose not to untap Mole Worms during untap. Tap to tap target land. As long as Worms remains tapped so does land.
Bog Wraith	Summon Wraith	B3	3/3	Swampwalk.
The Wretched	Summon Wretched	BB3	2/5	At end of turn take control of all creatures which block this card. Lose control of creatures if card leaves play.
Gangrenous Zombies	Summon Zombies	BB1	2/2	Tap and sacrifice to deal 1 damage to each creature and player or 2 damage if you control any snow-covered swamps.
Legions of Lim-Dul	Summon Zombies	BB1	2/3	Snow-covered swampwalk.
Lim-Dul's Cohort	Summon Zombies	BB1	2/3	Creatures blocking/blocked by this creature cannot regenerate this turn.
Scathe Zombies	Summon Zombies	B2	2/2	

Red

Red Enchantments

Card	Type	Cost	Power/ Toughness	Description
Enchant Creatures				
Aggression	Enchant Creature	R2	--	Target non-wall creature in play gains first strike and trample abilities. At the end of its controller's turn destroy if it did not attack that turn.
Brand of Ill Omen	Enchant Creature	R3	--	Cumulative upkeep: R. Target creature's controller cannot cast summons.
Burrowing	Enchant Creature	R	--	Gives target creature mountainwalk.
Earthbind	Enchant Creature	R	--	Target flying creature loses flight and takes 2 points of damage.
Errantry	Enchant Creature	R1	--	Target creature gets +3/+0. If it attacks no other creatures may attack that turn.
Eternal Warrior	Enchant Creature	R	--	Target creature does not tap when attacking.
Firebreathing	Enchant Creature	R	--	R: +1/+0 until end of turn.
Giant Strength	Enchant Creature	RR	--	Target creature gains +2/+2.
Immolation	Enchant Creature	R	--	Target creature gains +2/-2.
Imposing Visage	Enchant Creature	R	--	Target creature can only be blocked by two or more creatures.
Stonehands	Enchant Creature	R2	--	Target creature gains +0/+2. R: +1/+0 until end of turn.
The Brute	Enchant Creature	R1	--	Target creature gains +1/+0 and RRR: Regenerates.
Enchant Lands				
Conquer	Enchant Land	RR3	--	Gain control of target land.
Goblin Caves	Enchant Land	RR1	--	If target land is a basic mountain all Goblins in play gain +0/+2.
Goblin Shrine	Enchant Land	RR1	--	If target land is a basic mountain all goblins in play gain +1/+0. Does 1 damage to all goblins if it leaves play.

Card	Type	Cost	Power/ Toughness	Description
Enchant Worlds				
Caverns of Despair	Enchant World	RR2	--	All players may only attack or block with up to 2 creatures each turn.
Gravity Sphere	Enchant World	R2	--	All creatures lose flying ability.
Land's Edge	Enchant World	RR1	--	Any player may discard a card at any time. If discarded card is a land may do 2 damage to any player.
Storm World	Enchant World	R	--	Each player takes 1 damage for each card in their hand less than 4.
Independent Enchantments				
Blood Moon	Enchantment	R2	--	All non-basic lands in play are now basic mountains.
Chaos Moon	Enchantment	R3	--	If number of permanents is odd all red creatures get +1/+1 and mountains produce an extra R until end of turn. If even all red creatures get -1/-1 and mountains produce colorless mana.
Crevasse	Enchantment	R2	--	Stops use of mountainwalk.
Curse of Marit Lage	Enchantment	RR3	--	When comes into play tap all islands in play. Islands no longer untap during controller's untap phase.
Dwarven Armory	Enchantment	RR2	--	2: Sacrifice a land in play to put a +2/+2 bonus power and toughness counter on target creature. Use only during the upkeep phase.
Glacial Crevasses	Enchantment	R2	--	0: Sacrifice a snow-covered mountain in play. No creatures may deal damage in combat this turn.
Goblin Kites	Enchantment	R1	--	R: A target creature you control which cannot have a toughness greater than 2 gains flying until end of turn. Other effects may later be used to increase the creature's toughness. At end of turn flip a coin, opponent calls heads or tails. If the flip is in opponent's favor bury the creature.
Goblin War Drums	Enchantment	R2	--	Each attacking creature you control that opponent chooses to block may not be blocked with fewer than 2 creatures.

Card	Type	Cost	Power/ Toughness	Description
Goblin Warrens	Enchantment	R2	--	R2: Sacrifice 2 Goblins to put 3 goblin tokens into play, treat these tokens as 1/1 red creatures.
Magnetic Mountain	Enchantment	RR1	--	Blue creatures cost 4 to untap during upkeep.
Mana Flare	Enchantment	R2	--	All mana producing lands produce 1 extra mana.
Manabarbs	Enchantment	R3	--	1 damage to anyone who taps a land.
Melting	Enchantment	R3	--	All snow-covered lands become normal lands.
Mudslide	Enchantment	R2	--	Creatures without flying do not untap as normal. Controller may pay 2 during upkeep to untap a creature.
Orcish Oriflamme	Enchantment	RR1	--	All your attacking creatures gain +1/+0.
Power Surge	Enchantment	RR	--	During upkeep phase, all players take 1 damage per land which was untapped at the beginning of turn.
Raging River	Enchantment	RR	--	Opponents must split ground defenses.
Raiding Party	Enchantment	RR	--	Raiding Party may not be the target of white spells or effects. 0: Sacrifice an Orc to destroy all plains, a player may tap a white crature to prevent up to 2 plains from being destroyed. Any number of creatures may be tapped in this manner.
Smoke	Enchantment	RR	--	Players may only untap 1 creature during untap phase.
Total War	Enchantment	R3	--	Whenever any player declares an attack, all their creatures must attack or die, except walls and creatures not controlled at beginning of turn.

Red Instants

Card	Type	Cost	Power/ Toughness	Description
Active Volcano	Instant	R	--	Destroy blue permanent or return 1 island in play to its owner's hand.
Backdraft	Instant	R1	--	Does 1/2 of damage done by a sorcery back at the caster.

Card	Type	Cost	Power/ Toughness	Description
Battle Frenzy	Instant	R2	--	All green creatures you control get +1/+1 and non-green get +1/+0 until end of turn.
Blood Lust	Instant	R1	--	Target creature gains +4/-4 until end of turn. If this reduces a creature's toughness below 1, its toughness is now 1.
Disharmony	Instant	R2	--	Take control of an attacking creature until end of turn. It comes across untapped.
Dwarven Catapult	Instant	RX	--	Does X damage divided evenly among opponent's creatures, rounded down.
Dwarven Song	Instant	R	--	Change any/all creatures in play to red until end of turn.
False Orders	Instant	R	--	Choose how/if one creature blocks.
Feint	Instant	R	--	Target attacker deals no damage and creatures it blocks deal no damage. Blockers blocking it are tapped.
Fissure	Instant	RR3	--	Bury any land or creature in play.
Flare	Instant	R2	--	Deals 1 damage to target creature or player. Draw a card at the beginning of the next turn's upkeep.
Glyph of Destruction	Instant	R	--	Target blocking wall gains +10/+0 and takes no damage while blocking. Is destroyed at end of turn.
Incinerate	Instant	R1	--	Deals 3 damage to target creature or player. Target cannot regenerate.
Inferno	Instant	RR5	--	Does 6 damage to all creatures and players.
Lightning Bolt	Instant	R	--	Does 3 damage to any target.
Melee	Instant	R4	--	Play when you attack, choose how defenders block. Unblocked attackers are untapped and treated as if they didn't attack.
Panic	Instant	R	--	Target creature cannot block this turn. Draw a card at the beginning of the next turn's upkeep.
Shatter	Instant	R1	--	Destroys target artifact.
Tunnel	Instant	R	--	Buries target wall.

Card	Type	Cost	Power/ Toughness	Description
Vertigo	Instant	R	--	Vertigo deals 2 damage to target creature with flying and it loses flying until end of turn.
Word of Blasting	Instant	R1	--	Bury target wall. Does an amount of damage to controller equal to wall's casting cost.

Red Interrupts

Card	Type	Cost	Power/ Toughness	Description
Artifact Blast	Interrupt	R	--	Counters an artifact as it is being cast.
Chaoslace	Interrupt	R	--	Changes the color of one card in play to red.
Fork	Interrupt	RR	--	Copy sorcery or instant and control the duplicate.
Pyroblast	Interrupt	R	--	Counter target spell if it is blue or destroy permanent if it is blue.
Red Elemental Blast	Interrupt	R	--	Destroys a red card in play or counters a red spell as it is being cast.

Red Sorcery

Card	Type	Cost	Power/ Toughness	Description
Anarchy	Sorcery	RR2	--	Destroy all white permanents in play when cast.
Avalanche	Sorcery	RR2X	--	Destroy X snow-covered lands in play.
Chain Lightning	Sorcery	R	--	Does 3 damage to any target. Player or controller of target may spend RR to pick another target. Repeat.
Detonate	Sorcery	RX	--	Destroys an artifact without regeneration and does X damage to controller. X is casting cost of artifact.
Disintegrate	Sorcery	RX	--	Does X damage to any 1 target. Target cannot regenerate. If dies this turn, leaves game.
Earthquake	Sorcery	RX	--	Does X damage to all players and all non-flying creatures.

Card	Type	Cost	Power/ Toughness	Description
Eternal Flame	Sorcery	RR2	--	Does an amount of damage to your opponent equal to the number of mountains you control, but also does half that amount of damage to you, rounded up.
Falling Star	Sorcery	R2	--	Flip 360 degrees. Does 3 damage to all creatures touched. Does 3 damage to any creature touched but not killed.
Fireball	Sorcery	RX	--	X damage to target each extra target costs one extra mana, split damage evenly, rounded down.
Flashfires	Sorcery	R3	--	Destroys all plains in play.
Game of Chaos	Sorcery	RRR	--	Flip a coin. Your favor: gain 1 life and opponent loses 1 life. Opponent's favor: lose 1 life and opponent gains 1 life. Damage cannot be prevented. Stakes double each round.
Goblin Grenade	Sorcery	R	--	Sacrifice a Goblin to do 5 damage to 1 target.
Jokulhaups	Sorcery	RR4	--	Bury all artifacts, creatures, and lands.
Lava Burst	Sorcery	RX	--	Does X damage to target creature or player. Cannot be prevented or redirected.
Mana Clash	Sorcery	R	--	You and target player each flip a coin. Does 1 damage to any player whose coin comes up tails. Repeat until both player's coins come up heads at the same time.
Meteor Shower	Sorcery	RXX	--	Deals X+1 damage divided among any number of targets.
Pyroclasm	Sorcery	R1	--	Does 2 damage to each creature.
Pyrotechnics	Sorcery	R4	--	Distribute 4 damage among any targets.
Shatterstorm	Sorcery	RR2	--	All artifacts in play are buried.
Stone Rain	Sorcery	R2	--	Destroy any 1 land in play.
Wheel of Fortune	Sorcery	R2	--	Both players discard their hands and draw 7 new cards.
Winds of Change	Sorcery	R	--	Both players shuffle their hands into their library and draw up to the same number of cards as before.

Red Summons

Card	Type	Cost	Power/Toughness	Description
Aladdin	Summon Aladdin	RR2	1/1	Tap+(RR) Take control of 1 of opponent's artifacts.
Ali Baba	Summon Ali Baba	R	1/1	Tap+(R) Tap a wall.
Ali from Cairo	Summon Ali from Cairo	RR2	0/1	You cannot be reduced below 1 life due to damage while Ali is in play.
Kird Ape	Summon Ape	R	1/1	Gains +1/+2 if controller controls at least 1 forest.
Atog	Summon Atog	R1	1/2	Sacrifice an artifact to give Atog +2/+2 until end of turn.
Ball Lightning	Summon Ball Lightning	RRR	6/1	Trample. Can attack on turn it comes into play. Is buried at end of turn it comes into play.
Balduvian Barbarians	Summon Barbarians	RR1	3/2	
Barbarian Guides	Summon Barbarians	B2	1/2	Tap+(R2): Target creature you control gains a snow-covered landwalk ability until end of turn. Return that creature to owner's hand from play at end of turn.
Beasts of Bogardan	Summon Beasts	R4	3/3	Protection from red. Gain +1/+1 if opponent has white cards in play.
Aerathi Berserker	Summon Berserker	RRR2	2/4	Rampage: 3.
Bird Maiden	Summon Bird Maiden	R2	1/2	Flying.
Brothers of Fire	Summon Brothers	RR1	2/2	RR1: Brothers of Fire does 1 damage to any target and 1 damage to you.
Raging Bull	Summon Bull	R2	2/2	
Cave People	Summon Cave People	RR1	1/4	If declared as an attacker gains +1/-2 until end of turn. Tap+(RR1) Target creature gains mountainwalk until end of turn.
Orcish Healer	Summon Cleric	RR	1/1	Tap+(RR): Target creature cannot regenerate this turn. Tap+(RBB) or Tap+(RGG): Regenerate target black or green creature.

Card	Type	Cost	Power/ Toughness	Description
Mijae Djinn	Summon Djinn	RRR	6/3	Flip a coin when attacking. If in opponent's favor Djinn is tapped but does not attack.
Dragon Whelp	Summon Dragon	RR2	2/3	Flying. R: +1/+0 until end of turn. If more than RRR is spent in this way during one turn, Dragon Whelp is destroyed at end of turn.
Shivan Dragon	Summon Dragon	RR4	5/5	Flying. R: +1/+0 until end of turn.
Fire Drake	Summon Drake	RR1	1/2	Flying. R: +1/+0 until end of turn. No more than R may be spent in this way during one turn.
Kobold Drill Sergeant	Summon Drill Sergeant	R1	1/2	Gives all your Kobolds +0/+1 and trample.
Dwarven Armorer	Summon Dwarf	R	0/2	Tap+(R) Discard a card from your hand to put either a +9/+1 or a +1/+0 counter on target creature.
Dwarven Demolition Team	Summon Dwarves	R2	1/1	Tap to destroy a wall.
Dwarven Lieutenant	Summon Dwarf	RR	2/1	R1: Target Dwarf gets +1/+0 until end of turn.
Dwarven Soldier	Summon Dwarf	R1	2/1	If Dwarven Soldier blocks or is blocked by Orcs, it gets +0/+2 until end of turn.
Dwarven Warriors	Summon Dwarves	R2	1/1	Tap to make a creature with a power of 2 or less unblockable until end of turn.
Dwarven Weaponsmith	Summon Dwarf	R1	1/1	Tap and sacrifice artifact during upkeep to give a permanent +1/+1 to target creature.
Blazing Effigy	Summon Effigy	R1	0/3	When put in graveyard from play, you do 3 damage to any creature. If Effigy was killed by another Effigy, you do damage done by the other Effigy plus 3 to the creature.
Tempest Efreet	Summon Efreet	RRR1	3/3	Tap and bury Efreet in opponent's graveyard to take a random card from his hand into yours. Swap is permanent. Can be countered by losing 10 life. Play only in ante games.
Ydwen Efreet	Summon Efreet	RRR	3/6	Flip a coin when blocking, if in opponent's favor does not block and becomes tapped.

Card	Type	Cost	Power/ Toughness	Description
Rukh Egg	Summon Egg	R3	0/3	If Rukh goes to the graveyard from play, a 4/4 flying red Rukh token is put into play at end of turn.
Earth Elemental	Summon Elemental	RR3	4/5	
Fire Elemental	Summon Elemental	RR3	5/4	
Granite Gargoyle	Summon Gargoyle	R2	2/2	Flying. R: Gains +0/+1 until end of turn.
Orc General	Summon General	R2	2/2	Sacrifice one Orc or Goblin to give all Orcs +1/+1 until end of turn.
Bone Shaman	Summon Giant	RR2	3/3	B: Creature damaged by this creature cannot regenerate until end of turn.
Frost Giant	Summon Giant	RRR3	4/4	Rampage: 2.
Hill Giant	Summon Giant	R3	3/3	
Karplusan Giant	Summon Giant	R6	3/3	0: Tap a snow-covered land you control to give +1/+1 until end of turn.
Stone Giant	Summon Giant	RR2	3/4	Tap to make a creature of toughness less than Giant's power flying until end of turn. Target creature is destroyed at end of turn.
Tor Giant	Summon Giant	R3	3/3	
Two-Headed Giant of Foriys	Summon Giant	R4	4/4	Trample. May block 2 attackers.
Quarum Trench Gnomes	Summon Gnomes	R3	1/1	Tap to make 1 plains generate colorless mana instead of white mana for the rest of the game.
Mountain Goat	Summon Goat	R	1/1	Mountainwalk.
Goblin Artisans	Summon Goblins	R	1/1	Tap when you cast an artifact and then flip a coin with opponent calling heads or tails. If in opponent's favor, artifact is countered; if in your favor draw a card.
Goblin Balloon Brigade	Summon Goblins	R	1/1	R: Flying until end of turn.
Goblin Chirurgeon	Summon Goblin	R	0/2	0: Sacrifice a Goblin to regenerate target creature.

Card	Type	Cost	Power/ Toughness	Description
Goblin Digging Team	Summon Goblins	R	1/1	Sacrifice this card to destroy a wall.
Goblin Flotilla	Summon Goblins	R2	2/2	Islandwalk. At the beginning of the attack, pay R or any creatures blocking or blocked by Goblin Flotilla gain first strike until end of turn.
Goblin Hero	Summon Goblin	R2	2/2	
Goblin King	Summon Goblin King	RR1	2/2	All Goblins get +1/+1 and mountainwalk.
Goblin Mutant	Summon Goblin	RR2	5/3	Trample. Cannot attack if defender has an untapped creature with a power greater than 2.
Goblin Sappers	Summon Goblins	R1	1/1	Tap+(RR): Target creature you control cannot be blocked this turn. At the end of turn destroy target and Sappers. Tap+(RRRR): Target creature you control cannot be blocked this turn. Destroy target creature after combat.
Goblin Ski Patrol	Summon Goblins	R1	1/1	R1: Flying and +2/+0. Bury at end of turn. Can only be used if you control snow-covered mountain and can only be used once.
Goblin Snowman	Summon Goblins	R3	1/1	When blocking neither deals nor receives damage. Tap to deal 1 damage to target creature it blocks.
Goblin Wizard	Summon Goblin	RR2	1/1	Tap to take a Goblin from your hand and put it directly into play. Treat this Goblin as if it were just summoned. Tapped target Goblin gains protection from white until end of turn.
Goblins of the Flarg	Summon Goblins	R	1/1	Mountainwalk. This card is buried if controller also controls any Dwarves.
Mons's Goblin Raiders	Summon Goblins	R	1/1	
Balduvian Hydra	Summon Hydra	RRX	0/1	When comes into play put X +1/+0 counters on it. 0: Remove a counter to prevent 1 damage to it. RRR: Put a counter on it that is only usable during your upkeep.
Rock Hydra	Summon Hydra	RRX	0/0	Starts with X +1/+1 tokens. Loses 1 token for each point of damage taken unless R is spent. Pay RRR during upkeep to gain a new token.

Card	Type	Cost	Power/ Toughness	Description
Hurr Jackal	Summon Jackal	R	1/1	Tap to prevent target creature from regenerating this turn.
Crimson Kobolds	Summon Kobolds	0	0/1	Counts as a red card.
Crookshank Kobolds	Summon Kobolds	0	0/1	Counts as a red card.
Kobolds of Kher Keep	Summon Kobolds	0	0/1	Counts as a red card.
Marton Stromgald	Summon Legend	RR2	1/1	If attacking all other attacking creatures gain +*/+* where * is the number of attacking creatures. If blocking all other blockers gain +*/+* where * is the number of blocking creatures.
Chaos Lord	Summon Lord	RRR4	7/7	First strike. Can attack the turn it comes into play on a side except the turn it comes into play. If during your upkeep, the number of permanents under controller's control is even, it switches to opponent's control.
Keldon Warlord	Summon Lord	RR2	*/*	Where * is the number of creatures controller has in play.
Kobold Overlord	Summon Lord	R1	1/2	First strike. Gives all Kobolds first strike.
Crimson Manticore	Summon Manticore	RR2	2/2	Flying. Tap to do 1 damage to attacking or blocking creature.
Hurloon Minotaur	Summon Minotaur	RR1	2/3	
Desert Nomads	Summon Nomads	R2	2/2	Desertwalk. Immune to damage from deserts.
Gray Ogre	Summon Ogre	R2	2/2	
Primordial Ooze	Summon Ooze	R	1/1	Must attack if possible. Get +1/+1 token each upkeep. Must pay 1 mana per token or it taps and you take damage equal to number of tokens.
Brassclaw Orcs	Summon Orcs	R2	3/2	Cannot be assigned to block any creature of power greater than 1.
Ironclaw Orcs	Summon Orcs	R1	2/2	Cannot be assigned to block creatures of power greater than 1.
Orcish Artillery	Summon Orcs	RR1	1/3	Tap to do 2 damage to any target. Then does 3 damage to controller.

Card	Type	Cost	Power/ Toughness	Description
Orcish Cannoneers	Summon Orcs	RR1	1/3	Tap to do 2 damage to any target and 3 damage to you.
Orcish Captain	Summon Orc	R	1/1	1: Choose a target Orc. Flip a coin. If in your favor that Orc gets +2/+0 until end of turn; if in opponent's favor Orc gets -0/-2 until end of turn.
Orcish Conscripts	Summon Orcs	R	2/2	Cannot attack or block unless 2 other creatures are attacking or blocking.
Orcish Farmer	Summon Orc	RR1	2/2	Tap to change target land to a swamp until its controller's next upkeep.
Orcish Librarian	Summon Orc	R1	1/1	Tap+(R): Take the top 8 cards of your library, remove 4 of the 8 at random, and replace remaining 4 in any order on top of library.
Orcish Lumberjack	Summon Orc	R	1/1	Tap and sacrifice a forest to add 3 mana in any combination of red and green to your mana pool. Play as an interrupt.
Orcish Mechanics	Summon Orcs	R2	1/1	Tap and sacrifice an artifact to do 2 damage to any target.
Orcish Spy	Summon Orc	R	1/1	Tap to look at top 3 cards of target player's library and then return them in the same order.
Orcish Squatters	Summon Orcs	R4	2/3	If attacks and not blocked you gain control of target land. Lose if you lose control of Squatters or if they leave play.
Orcish Veteran	Summon Orc	R2	2/2	Cannot be assigned to block any creature of power greater than 1. R: First strike until end of turn.
Orgg	Summon Orgg	RR3	6/6	Trample. Orgg may not attack if opponent controls an untapped creature of power greater than 2. Orgg cannot block any creature of power greater than 2.
Firestorm Phoenix	Summon Phoenix	RR4	3/2	Flying. If in graveyard, return it to owner's hand. May not be summoned against until next turn.
Roc of Kher Ridges	Summon Roc	R3	3/3	Flying.

Card	Type	Cost	Power/ Toughness	Description
Goblin Rock Sled	Summon Rock Sled	R1	3/1	Trample. Opponent must control at least 1 mountain. Does not untap as normal if it attacked during last turn.
Sisters of the Flame	Summon Sisters	RR1	2/2	Tap to add R to your mana pool. This ability may be used as an interrupt.
Hyperion Blacksmith	Summon Smith	RR1	2/2	Tap to tap or untap one of opponent's artifacts.
Flame Spirit	Summon Spirit	R4	2/3	R: +1/+0 until end of turn.
Stone Spirit	Summon Spirit	R4	4/3	Creatures with flying may not block Stone Spirit.
Kobold Taskmaster	Summon Taskmaster	R1	1/2	Gives all Kobolds +1/+0.
Sabretooth Tiger	Summon Tiger	R2	2/1	First strike.
Sedge Troll	Summon Troll	R2	2/2	B: Regenerates. Gains +1/+1 if controller controls at least 1 swamp.
Uthden Troll	Summon Troll	R2	2/2	R: Regenerates.
Spinal Villain	Summon Villain	R2	1/2	Tap to destroy a blue creature.
Wall of Dust	Summon Wall	R2	1/4	Wall. Creatures blocked by wall may not attack next turn.
Wall of Earth	Summon Wall	R1	0/6	Wall.
Wall of Fire	Summon Wall	RR1	0/5	Wall. R: +1/+0 until end of turn.
Wall of Heat	Summon Wall	R2	2/6	Wall.
Wall of Lava	Summon Wall	RR1	1/3	Wall. R: +1/+1 until end of turn.
Wall of Opposition	Summon Wall	RR3	0/6	1: Add +1/+0 to Wall of Opposition until end of turn.
Wall of Stone	Summon Wall	RR1	0/8	Wall.
Grizzled Wolverine	Summon Wolverine	RR1	2/2	R: +2/+0 until end of turn. Can only be used once and only when blocked.
Karplusan Yeti	Summon Yeti	RR3	3/3	Tap to deal/take damage to target creature equal to its power.
Mountain Yeti	Summon Yeti	RR2	3/3	Mountainwalk. Protection from white.

Green

Green Enchantments

Card	Type	Cost	Power/ Toughness	Description
Enchant Artifacts				
Living Artifact	Enchant Artifact	G	--	Put one token on artifact for each life lost. Can convert one token to 1 life during your upkeep.
Enchant Creatures				
Aspect of Wolf	Enchant Creature	G1	--	Gives +*/+* where * is 1/2 number of forests.
Cocoon	Enchant Creature	G	--	Taps creature and holds it tapped for three turns. Then it gets +1/+1 and flying.
Instill Energy	Enchant Creature	G	--	Target creature may untap once during your turn in addition to your untap phase. May attack on the turn it is brought into play.
Lure	Enchant Creature	GG1	--	All creatures able to block target creature must do so.
Maddening Wind	Enchant Creature	G2	--	Cumulative upkeep: G. Does 2 damage to target's controller during upkeep.
Regeneration	Enchant Creature	G1	--	Target creature gains G: Regenerates.
Snowblind	Enchant Creature	G3	--	Target creature get -*/-*. When attacking * = number of snow-covered lands defender controls. All other times * = number of snow-covered lands controller controls.
Venom	Enchant Creature	GG1	--	All non-wall creatures target creature blocks or is blocked by are destroyed at end of combat.
Wanderlust	Enchant Creature	G2	--	Does 1 damage to creature's controller during upkeep.
Web	Enchant Creature	G	--	Target creature gains +0/+2 and may block flying creatures.
Enchant Lands				
Earthlore	Enchant Land	G	--	0: Tap enchanted land to give target blocking creature +1/+2 until end of turn.

Card	Type	Cost	Power/ Toughness	Description
Forbidden Lore	Enchant Land	G2	--	0: Tap enchanted land to give target creature +2/+1 until end of turn.
Hot Springs	Enchant Land	G1	--	0: Tap enchanted land to prevent 1 damage to a target.
Kudzu	Enchant Land	GG1	--	Destroys target land when it is tapped; controller of destroyed land may then place it on another land.
Wild Growth	Enchant Land	G	--	Target land generates an additional G.
Enchant Worlds				
Arboria	Enchant World	GG2	--	If a player does not put a card into play or cast a spell he cannot be attacked until his next turn.
Concordant Crossroads	Enchant World	G	--	Creatures may attack on the turn in which they are summoned.
Living Plane	Enchant World	GG2	--	All lands in play become 1/1 creatures as well as lands and may not be tapped on the turn they come into play.
Revelation	Enchant World	G	--	All players play with hand face up on the table.
Independent Enchantments				
Blizzard	Enchantment	GG	--	Cumulative upkeep: 2. Cannot cast if you don't control snow-covered land. Creatures with flying do not untap as normal.
Cyclone	Enchantment	GG2	--	Gets 1 token each upkeep. Must pay G for each token or is discarded. Does 1 damage per token to all players and creatures.
Deadfall	Enchantment	G2	--	Prevents all forestwalk in play.
Drop of Honey	Enchantment	G	--	During upkeep lowest power creature in play is discarded and may not regenerate.
Elven Fortress	Enchantment	G1	--	G1: Target blocking creature gets +0/+1 until end of turn.
Fastbond	Enchantment	G	--	You may bring as many lands into play as you like during a turn taking 1 damage for each extra land.
Fryalise's Charm	Enchantment	GG	--	GG: When any opponent casts a black spell, draw a card. Can only be used once per spell. GG: Return to owner's hand.

Card	Type	Cost	Power/ Toughness	Description
Freyalise's Wind	Enchantment	GG2	--	Whenever a permanent is tapped, it gets a wind counter. Does not untap if it has a wind counter on it, but removes counter instead.
Fungal Bloom	Enchantment	GG	--	GG: Put a spore counter on a target fungus.
Fyndhorn Pollen	Enchantment	G2	--	Cumulative upkeep: 1. All creatures get -1/-0. G1: All creatures get -1/-0 until end of turn.
Gaea's Touch	Enchantment	GG	--	You may put 1 additional land in play during each of your turns but that land must be a basic forest; you may sacrifice Gaea's Touch to add GG to your mana pool.
Hidden Path	Enchantment	GGGG2	--	All green creatures gain forestwalk.
Lifeforce	Enchantment	GG	--	GG: Counters target black spell as it is being cast.
Living Lands	Enchantment	G3	--	Treat all forests in play as 1/1 creatures.
Night Soil	Enchantment	GG	--	1: Remove 2 creatures in any graveyard from play to put a Saporling token into play. Treat this token as a 1/1 green creature.
Powerleech	Enchantment	GG	--	Gain 1 life whenever opponent taps or powers an artifact.
Ritual of Subdual	Enchantment	GG4	--	Cumulative upkeep: 2. All lands produce colorless mana.
Sylvan Library	Enchantment	G1	--	May draw 2 extra cards during draw then put 2 back on the library in any order. Lose 4 life for each card not put back.
Thelon's Chant	Enchantment	GG1	--	During your upkeep pay G or bury Thelon's Chant. Whenever a player puts a swamp into play Thelon's Chant does 3 damage to him unless he puts a -1/-1 counter onto a creature that he controls.
Thelon's Curse	Enchantment	GG	--	Blue creatures do not untap as normal during their controller's upkeep. During their upkeep controller of these blue creatures may spend an additional U to untap one creature. Each creature may only be untapped in this fashion once.

Card	Type	Cost	Power/ Toughness	Description
Thoughtleech	Enchantment	GG	--	Whenever opponent taps an island gain 1 life.
Titania's Song	Enchantment	G3	--	All artifacts in play become artifact creatures with power and toughness equal to their casting cost. They do not retain their abilities as artifacts.

Green Instants

Card	Type	Cost	Power/ Toughness	Description
Berserk	Instant	G	--	Doubles power of creature and gives trample until end of turn. Creature dies if it attacks.
Camouflage	Instant	G	--	Opponent blocks blindly.
Crumble	Instant	G	--	Buries target artifact and gives controller life equal to its casting cost.
Fanatical Fever	Instant	GG2	--	Target creature gets +3/+0 and trample until end of turn.
Fog	Instant	G	--	Creatures deal and take no damage during combat.
Foxfire	Instant	G2	--	Untap target attacking creature. It neither deals nor receives damage this turn. Draw a card at the beginning of the next turn's upkeep.
Giant Growth	Instant	G	--	Target creature gains +3/3 until end of turn.
Glyph of Reincarnation	Instant	G	--	All creatures which survive being blocked by target wall are buried. Then pull 1 creature of choice out of attacker's graveyard and into play for each one that is buried.
Natural Selection	Instant	G	--	Look at top 3 cards of any library, then rearrange them or reshuffle library.
Reincarnation	Instant	GG1	--	If target creature goes to graveyard this turn you may pull any creature of choice from graveyard.
Sandstorm	Instant	G	--	All attacking creatures take 1 damage.

Card	Type	Cost	Power/ Toughness	Description
Spore Cloud	Instant	GG1	--	Tap all blocking creatures. No creatures deal damage in combat this turn. Neither attacking nor blocking creatures untap as normal during their controller's next untap phase.
Stampede	Instant	GG1	--	All attacking creatures get trample and +1/+0 until end of turn.
Storm Seeker	Instant	G3	--	Opponent takes on damage for each card in their hand.
Subdue	Instant	G	--	Gives a creature +0/+X until end of turn but it deals no damage in combat. X is the casting cost of the creature.
Sylvan Paradise	Instant	G	--	Changes the color of any/all creatures in play to green until end of turn.
Touch of Vitae	Instant	G2	--	Untap target creature. Draw a card at the beginning of the next turn's upkeep.
Trailblazer	Instant	GG2	--	Target creature cannot be blocked this turn.
Venomous Breath	Instant	G3	--	At end of combat
Whiteout	Instant	G1	--	All creatures lose flying until end of turn.

Green Interrupts

Card	Type	Cost	Power/ Toughness	Description
Avoid Fate	Interrupt	G	--	Counters interrupt or enchantment targeted at one of your permanents.
Lifelace	Interrupt	G	--	Changes color of target permanent to green.
Rust	Interrupt	G	--	Counters effect of an artifact with an activation cost.

Green Sorcery

Card	Type	Cost	Power/Toughness	Description
Channel	Sorcery	GG	--	Convert life into colorless mana until end of turn.
Desert Twister	Sorcery	GG4	--	Destroy any one card in play.
Essence Filter	Sorcer	GG1	--	Destroy all enchantments or all non-white enchantments.
Eureka	Sorcery	GG2	--	Players alternate playing permanents from their hand with no casting cost required.
Forgotten Lore	Sorcery	G	--	Opponent chooses a card from your graveyard, you can make him pick another for G, repeating as many times as you like. Place this card in your hand.
Hurricane	Sorcery	GX	--	Does X damage to all players and all flying creatures.
Ice Storm	Sorcery	G2	--	Destroys any 1 land.
Metamorphosis	Sorcery	G	--	Sacrifice creature for casting cost plus one of any color mana. Mana may only be used for summoning spells.
Nature's Lore	Sorcery	G1	--	Search your library for a forest and put it into play. Does not count as your land for the turn.
Rebirth	Sorcery	GGG3	--	Each player may add a card to his ante and be returned to 20 life points. Only used in ante games.
Regrowth	Sorcery	G1	--	Return any card from graveyard to hand.
Stream of Life	Sorcery	GX	--	Target player gains X life.
Stunted Growth	Sorcery	GG3	--	Target player takes 3 cards from hand and puts them on top of library in any order.
Thermokarst	Sorcery	GG1	--	Destroy target land. If it is snow-covered gain 1 life.
Tranquility	Sorcery	G2	--	Destroys all enchantments in play.
Tsunami	Sorcery	G3	--	Destroys all islands in play.
Typhoon	Sorcery	G2	--	Opponent takes 1 damage for each island he or she has.
Untamed Wilds	Sorcery	G2	--	Bring one basic land from library into play.

Card	Type	Cost	Power/Toughness	Description
Winter Blast	Sorcery	GX	--	Taps X creatures and does 2 damage to each of them that has flying ability.

Green Summons

Card	Type	Cost	Power/Toughness	Description
Barbary Apes	Summon Apes	G1	2/2	
Nafs Asp	Summon Asp	G	1/1	If damages opponent, he must pay 1 during his next upkeep or take an additional damage.
Aurochs	Summon Aurochs	G3	2/3	Trample. When attacking, gets a +1/+0 bonus for each of the other Aurochs that attack.
Scarwood Bandits	Summon Bandits	GG2	2/2	Tap+(G2) Take control of target artifact. Opponent may counter action by paying 2. You lose control of artifact if Scarwood Bandits leaves play or at end of game.
Thicket Basilisk	Summon Basilisk	GG3	2/4	All non-wall creatures blocking or blocked by Basilisk are destroyed at the end of combat.
Balduvian Bears	Summon Bears	G1	2/2	
Grizzly Bears	Summon Bears	G1	2/2	
Pale Bears	Summon Bears	G2	2/2	Islandwalk.
Killer Bees	Summon Bees	GG1	0/1	Flying. G: +1/+1 until end of turn.
Durkwood Boars	Summon Boars	G4	4/4	
Fyndhorn Brownie	Summon Brownie	G2	1/1	Tap+(G2): Untap target creature.
Cat Warriors	Summon Cat Warriors	GG1	2/2	Forestwalk.
Elder Druid	Summon Cleric	G3	2/2	Tap+(G3): Elder Druid taps or untaps target artifact, creature, or land.

Card	Type	Cost	Power/Toughness	Description
Freyalise Supplicant	Summon Cleric	G1	1/1	Tap and sacrifice a red or white creature to deal half the creature's power, rounded down, to any target.
Juniper Order Druid	Summon Cleric	G2	1/1	Tap to untap target land. Use this ability as an interrupt.
Ley Druid	Summon Cleric	G2	1/1	Tap to untap any 1 land in play.
Thelonite Druid	Summon Cleric	G2	1/1	Tap+(G1) Sacrifice a creature to turn all you forests into 2/3 creatures until end of turn. The forests still count as lands but may not be tapped for mana if they were brought into play this turn.
Thelonite Monk	Summon Cleric	GG2	1/2	Tap to sacrifice a green creature to turn a target land into a basic forest. Mark changed land with a counter.
Hornet Cobra	Summon Cobra	GG1	2/1	First strike.
Cockatrice	Summon Cockatrice	GG3	2/4	Flying. Any non-wall creatures blocking or blocked by Cockatrice are destroyed at end of combat.
Whirling Dervish	Summon Dervish	GG	1/1	Protection from black. Gets a +1/+1 token each time it damages opponent.
Pygmy Allosaurus	Summon Dinosaur	G2	2/2	Swampwalk.
Ernham Djinn	Summon Djinn	G3	4/5	Each upkeep, gives one of opponent's creatures forestwalk until next upkeep.
Emerald Dragonfly	Summon Dragonfly	G1	1/1	Flying. GG: First strike until end of turn.
Citanul Druid	Summon Druid	G1	1/1	Gets a +1/+1 counter each time opponent casts an artifact.
Ichneumon Druid	Summon Druid	GG1	1/1	Opponent takes 4 damage for each instant past the first one he casts each turn.
Folk of the Pines	Summon Dryads	G4	2/5	G1: +1/+0 until end of turn.
Rime Dryad	Summon Dryad	G	1/2	Snow-covered forestwalk.
Ifh-Biff Efreet	Summon Efreet	GG2	3/3	Flying. Any player may pay G to do 1 damage to all flying creatures and all players.
Wood Elemental	Summon Elemental	G3	*/*	Where * is the number of untapped forests sacrificed when Wood Elemental is brought into play.

Card	Type	Cost	Power/ Toughness	Description
Elves of Deep Shadow	Summon Elves	G	1/1	Tap to add B to your mana pool and Elves of Deep Shadow does 1 damage to you.
Elvish Archers	Summon Elves	G1	2/1	First strike.
Elvish Farmer	Summon Elf	G1	0/2	During your upkeep put a spore counter on Elvish Farmer. 0: Remove 3 spore counters from Elvish Farmer to put a Saporling token into play. Threat this token as a 1/1 green creature. 0: Sacrifice a Saporling to gain 2 life.
Elvish Hunter	Summon Elf	G1	1/1	Tap+(G1) Keep opponent's creature tapped next turn.
Elvish Scout	Summon Elf	G	1/1	Tap+(G) Untap a target attacking creature you control. That creature neither deals nor receives damage during combat this turn.
Fyndhorn Elder	Summon Elf	G2	1/1	Tap to add GG to your mana pool.
Fyndhorn Elves	Summon Elves	G	1/1	Tap to add G to your mana pool.
Llanowar Elves	Summon Elves	G	1/1	Tap to add G to your mana pool.
Savaen Elves	Summon Elves	G	1/1	Tap+(GG) Target enchant land is destroyed.
Verduran Enchantress	Summon Enchantress	GG1	0/2	While Enchantress is in play, you may draw a card whenever you cast an enchantment.
Aisling Leprechaun	Summon Faerie	G	1/1	Turns all creatures blocking or blocked by it green.
Argothian Pixies	Summon Faeries	G1	2/1	Cannot be blocked by artifact creatures. Ignores damage from artifact sources.
Fire Sprites	Summon Faeries	G1	1/1	Flying. Tap+(G) Add R to your mana pool.
Scryb Sprites	Summon Faeries	G	1/1	Flying.
Shelkin Brownie	Summon Faerie	G1	1/1	Tap to remove bands with other ability from a creature until end of turn.
Force of Nature	Summon Force	GGG G2	8/8	Trample. Controller must pay GGGG during upkeep or Force of Nature does 8 damage to him or her.

Card	Type	Cost	Power/ Toughness	Description
Feral Thallid	Summon Fungus	GGG3	6/3	During your upkeep, put a spore counter on Feral Thallid. 0: Remove 3 spore counters from Feral Thallid to regenerate it.
Spore Flower	Summon Fungus	GG	0/1	During your upkeep, put a spore counter on Spore Flower. 0: Remove 3 spore counters from Spore Flower. No creatures deal damage in combat this turn.
Thallid	Summon Fungus	G	1/1	During your upkeep, put a spore counter on Thallid. 0: Remove 3 spore counters from Thallid to put a Saporling token into play. Treat this token as a 1/1 green creature.
Thallid Devourer	Summon Fungus	GG1	2/2	During your upkeep, put a spore counter on Thallid Devourer. 0: Remove 3 spore counters from Thallid Devourer to put a Saporling token into play. Treat this token as a 1/1 green creature. 0: Sacrifice a Saporling to give Thallid Devourer +1/+2 until end of turn.
Thorn Thallid	Summon Fungus	GG1	2/2	During your upkeep, put a spore counter on Thorn Thallid. 0: Remove 3 spore counters from Thorn Thallid to do 1 damage to any target.
Fungusaur	Summon Fungusaur	G3	2/2	Gets a +1/+1 token when damaged and not killed.
Gaea's Avenger	Summon Gaea's Avenger	GG1	*+1/*+1	Where * is the number of artifacts opponent has in play.
Gaea's Leige	Summon Gaea's Leige	GGG3	*/*	Where * is number of forests opponent has in play when attacking and is number of forests controller has at all other times. Tap to turn any land in play into a forest.
Craw Giant	Summon Giant	GGG G3	6/4	Trample. Rampage: 2.
Gorilla Pack	Summon Gorilla Pack	G2	3/3	Cannot attack if opponent has no forests. Bury if you have no forests.
Pradesh Gypsies	Summon Gypsies	G2	1/1	Tap+(G1) Give a creature -2/-0 until end of turn.

Card	Type	Cost	Power/ Toughness	Description
Scarwood Hag	Summon Hag	G1	1/1	Tap+(GGGG) Target creature gains forestwalk until end of turn or target creature loses forestwalk until end of turn.
Yavimaya Gnats	Summon Insects	G2	0/1	Flying. G: Regenerate.
Land Leeches	Summon Leeches	GG1	2/2	First strike.
Lhurgoyf	Summon Lhurgoyf	GG2	*/1+*	Where * is the number of creatures in all graveyards.
Lurker	Summon Lurker	G2	2/3	Lurker may not be the target of any spell unless Lurker was declared as an attacker or blocker this turn.
War Mammoth	Summon Mammoth	G3	3/3	Trample.
Woolly Mammoths	Summon Mammoths	GG1	3/2	Gains trample as long as you have any snow-covered lands.
Birds of Paradise	Summon Mana Birds	G	0/1	Flying. Tap to add 1 mana of any color to your mana pool.
Master of the Hunt	Summon Master	GG2	2/2	GG2: Creates 1/1 green Wolves of the Hunt token creature which can bands with other Wolves of the Hunt.
Moss Monster	Summon Monster	GG3	3/6	
Niall Silvain	Summon Niall Silvain	GGG	2/2	Tap+(GGGG) Target creature is regenerated.
Shanodin Dryads	Summon Nymphs	G	1/1	Forestwalk.
Ghazban Ogre	Summon Ogre	G	2/2	During controller's upkeep, player with highest life total gains control of Ghazban Ogre.
Brown Ouphe	Summon Ouphe	G	1/1	Tap+(G1): Target artifact ability which requires an activation cost. Use as an interrupt.
People of the Woods	Summon People of the Woods	GG	1/*	Where * is number of forests controlled by People of the Wood's controller.
Pixie Queen	Summon Pixie Queen	GG2	1/1	Flying. Tap+(GGG) give other creature flying.
Pyknite	Summon Pyknite	G2	1/1	Draw a card at the beginning of the next turn's upkeep after summoning.

Card	Type	Cost	Power/ Toughness	Description
Elven Riders	Summon Riders	GG3	3/3	Only blockable by walls and flying creatures.
Willow Satyr	Summon Satyr	GG2	1/1	Tap to take control of a Legend. May chose not to untap. Lose control of Legend if Satyr becomes untapped or leaves play.
Scavenger Folk	Summon Scavenger Folk	G	1/1	Tap+(G) Sacrifice Scavenger Folk to destroy target artifact.
Singing Tree	Summon Singing Tree	G3	0/3	Tap to reduce target attacking creature's power to 0 until end of turn.
Spitting Slug	Summon Slug	GG1	2/4	GG1: Spitting Slug may gain first strike until end of turn. If this ability is not activated, all creatures blocking or blocked by Spitting Slug gain first strike until end of turn.
Giant Spider	Summon Spider	G3	2/4	Is not flying but can block flying creatures.
Wooly Spider	Summon Spider	GG1	2/3	Can block flying creatures. Gains +0/+2 if blocking a flying creature.
Radjan Spirit	Summon Spirit	G3	3/2	Tap to remove flying from target creature until end of turn.
Floral Spuzzem	Summon Spuzzem	G3	2/2	If not blocked when it attacks, you may choose to have it not deal damage and destroy one artifact.
Shambling Strider	Summon Strider	GG4	5/5	RG: 1/-1 until end of turn.
Tarpan	Summon Tarpan	G	1/1	If goes to graveyard from play gain 1 life.
Chub Toad	Summon Toad	G2	1/1	Gets +2/+2 until end of turn when attacking or blocking.
Tracker	Summon Tracker	G2	2/2	Tap+(GG) Tracker does an amount of damage equal to its power to target creature. Target creature does an amount of damage equal to its power to Tracker.
Argothian Treefolk	Summon Treefolk	GG3	3/5	Ignores damage from artifact sources.
Ironroot Treefolk	Summon Treefolk	G4	3/5	

Card	Type	Cost	Power/ Toughness	Description
Wormwood Treefolk	Summon Treefolk	GG3	4/4	GG: Wormwood Treefolk gains forestwalk until end of turn and does 2 damage to you. BB: Wormwood Treefolk gains swampwalk until end of turn and does 2 damage to you.
Giant Turtle	Summon Turtle	GG1	2/4	Cannot attack if it did so last turn.
Marsh Viper	Summon Viper	G3	1/2	If Marsh Viper damages opponent, opponent gets 2 poison counters. If opponent ever has 10 or more poison counters, opponent loses game.
Carnivorous Plant	Summon Wall	G3	4/5	Wall.
Tinder Wall	Summon Wall	G	0/3	0: Sacrifice to add RR to your pool. R: Sacrifice to deal 2 damage to target creature it blocks.
Wall of Brambles	Summon Wall	G2	2/3	Wall. G: Regenerates
Wall of Ice	Summon Wall	G2	0/7	Wall.
Wall of Pine Needles	Summon Wall	G3	3/3	G: Regenerates.
Wall of Wood	Summon Wall	G	0/3	Wall.
Whippoorwill	Summon Whippoor-will	G	1/1	Tap+(GG) Until end of turn, target creature may not regenerate and damage done to target creature may not be prevented or redirected. If target creature goes to the graveyard, remove it from the game.
Wiitigo	Summon Wiitigo	GGG3	0/0	When comes into play put 6 +1/+1 counters on it. During your upkeep if it has blocked or been blocked since last upkeep put a +1/+1 counter on it; otherwise remove a +1/+1 counter. Ignore this effect if there are no counters left.
Dire Wolves	Summon Wolves	G2	2/2	Gains banding ability if you control any plains in play.
Timber Wolves	Summon Wolves	G	1/1	Banding.
Wolverine Pack	Summon Wolverine Pack	GG2	2/4	Rampage: 2

Card	Type	Cost	Power/ Toughness	Description
Wyluli Wolf	Summon Wolf	G1	1/1	Tap to give +1/+1 until end of turn to any creature.
Rabid Wombat	Summon Wombat	GG2	0/1	Does not tap when attacking. Gets +2/+2 for each enchantment on it.
Craw Wurm	Summon Wurm	GG4	6/4	
Johtull Wurm	Summon Wurm	G5	6/6	For each creature more than one that blocks it, it gets -2/-1 until end of turn.
Scaled Wurn	Summon Wurm	G7	7/6	

Gold

Enchantments

Card	Type	Cost	Power/ Toughness	Description
Enchant Creatures				
Chromatic Armor	Enchant Creature	WU1	--	When played, put a sleight counter on it and choose a color. Any damage dealt to target by sources of that color is reduced to 0. X: Put a sleight counter on Armor and change the color that it protects again. X is the number of sleight counters on it.
Spectral Shield	Enchant Creature	WU1	--	Target creature in play gets a +0/+2 bonus to its toughness. That creature cannot be the target of any other spells after Spectral Shield enchants it.
Wings of Aesthir	Enchant Creature	WU	--	Target creature gains flying, first strike, and gets +1/+0.
Independent Enchantments				
Dark Heart of the Woods	Enchantment	GB	--	While Dark Heart of the Woods is in play you may sacrifice a forest to gain 3 life. Counts as both black and green.
Earthlink	Enchantment	BRG3	--	During your upkeep pay 2 or bury. Whenever a creature is put into the graveyard from play its controller must sacrifice a land if possible.
Elemental Agury	Enchantment	UBR	--	3: Look at top 3 cards of target player's library and replace in any order.
Flooded Woodlands	Enchantment	UB2	--	No green creature can attack unless its controller sacrifices a land.
Ghostly Flame	Enchantment	BR	--	Both black and red permanents in play and spells cast are considered colorless sources of damage.
Glaciers	Enchantment	WU2	--	Controller must pay WU during upkeep or destroy Glaciers. Mountains become plains while it remains in play.
Monsoon	Enchantment	2RG	--	When an island is tapped, controller takes 1 damage at end of turn.
Reclamation	Enchantment	WG2	--	No black creature can attack unless its controller sacrifices a land.
Stormbind	Enchantment	RG1	--	2: Discard a card at random from your hand to deal 2 damage to target creature or player.

Instants

Card	Type	Cost	Power/ Toughness	Description
Essence Vortex	Instant	UB1	--	Bury target creature. That creature's controller may counter by paying the creature's toughness in life.
Fire Covenant	Instant	BR1	--	Deals X damage, divided in any way to any number of creatures, where X is the amount of life you pay. Damage cannot be prevented.

Sorcery

Card	Type	Cost	Power/ Toughness	Description
Altar of Bone	Sorcery	WG	--	Sacrifice a creature to look through your library and get a creature into you hand after showing it to all players.
Diabolic Vision	Sorcery	UB	--	Caster looks at the top 5 cards of his deck and puts 1 of them into his hand. The remaining 4 are placed on top of library in any order.
Fiery Justice	Sorcery	WRG	--	Deals 5 damage divided among any number of targets. Target opponent gains 5 life.
Fumarole	Sorcery	BR3	--	Pay 3 life to destroy target creature and target land. Damage cannot be prevented.
Hymn of Rebirth	Sorcery	WG3	--	Caster may take target creature from any graveyard and put it directly into play under their control. Treat it as if it were just summoned.

Summons

Card	Type	Cost	Power/ Toughness	Description
Centaur Archer	Summon Centaur	RG1	3/2	Tap to deal 1 damage to target flying creature.
Arcades Sabboth	Summon Elder Dragon Legend	UUGG WW2	7/7	Flying. (W):+0/+1. Your untapped and not attacking creatures gain +0/+2. Pay UGW during your upkeep or this card is buried.

Card	Type	Cost	Power/ Toughness	Description
Chromium	Summon Elder Dragon Legend	BBUU WW2	7/7	Flying. Rampage: 2. Pay BUW during your upkeep or this card is buried.
Nicol Bolas	Summon Elder Dragon Legend	BBUU RR2	7/7	Flying. If opponent is damaged by Nicol he or she must discard their entire hand. During upkeep pay BUR or this card is buried.
Palladia-Mors	Summon Elder Dragon Legend	GGRR WW2	7/7	Flying. Trample. Pay GRW during upkeep or card is buried.
Vaevictis Asmadi	Summon Elder Dragon Legend	BBGG RR2	7/7	Flying. (B or G or R): +1/+0. Pay BGR during upkeep or this card is buried.
Kjeldoran Frostbeast	Summon Frostbeast	WG3	2/4	At end of combat, destroy all creatures blocking/blocked by Frostbeast.
Marsh Goblins	Summon Goblins	BR	1/1	Swampwalk.
Scarwood Goblins	Summon Goblins	RG	2/2	
Adun Oakenshield	Summon Legend	BGR	1/2	Tap+(BGR) Bring creature from graveyard to hand.
Angus Mackenzie	Summon Legend	BGW	2/2	Tap+(UGW) No creatures deal damage in combat this turn.
Axelrod Gunnarson	Summon Legend	BB RR4	5/5	Trample. Gives you 1 life and does 1 damage to opponent when a creature goes to the graveyard on a turn in which Axelrod damages.
Ayesha Tanaka	Summon Legend	UU WW	2/2	Banding. Tap to counter effect of an artifact with an activation cost unless opponent pays W.
Barktooth Warbeard	Summon Legend	BRR4	6/5	
Bartel Runeaxe	Summon Legend	BGR3	6/5	Does not tap when attacking. Cannot be targeted by enchant creature spells.
Boris Devilboon	Summon Legend	BR3	2/2	
Dakkon Blackblade	Summon Legend	BUU W2	*/*	Where * is the number of lands you control.
Gabriel Angelfire	Summon Legend	GG WW3	4/4	Each upkeep can get flying, first strike, trample, or rampage: 3 until beginning of next upkeep.
Gosta Dirk	Summon Legend	UU WW3	4/4	First strike. Stops all use of islandwalk in play.

Card	Type	Cost	Power/ Toughness	Description
Gwendlyn Di Corci	Summon Legend	BBUR	3/5	Tap to force opponent to discard a card. Only be used during your turn.
Halfdane	Summon Legend	BUW1	*/*	Where /* is 3 at casting time and changes at each upkeep equal to the power of a creature in play. If there are no creatures in play * = 0.
Hazezon Tamar	Summon Legend	GRW4	2/4	On upkeep after Hazezon enters play you get a 1/1 white, green, and red Sandwarrior token creature for each land you control. The tokens leave play if Hazezon does.
Hunding Gjornersen	Summon Legend	UUW3	5/4	Rampage: 1.
Jacques Le Vert	Summon Legend	GRW1	3/2	All your green creatures get +0/+2.
Jasmine Boreal	Summon Legend	GW3	4/5	
Jedit Ojanen	Summon Legend	UWW4	5/5	
Jerrard of the Closed Fist	Summon Legend	GGR3	6/5	
Johan	Summon Legend	GRW3	5/4	If Johan does not attack and is not tapped then none of your creatures tap when attacking.
Kasmir the Lone Wolf	Summon Legend	UW4	5/3	
Kei Takahashi	Summon Legend	GW2	2/2	Tap to prevent up to 2 damage to a creature.
Lady Caleria	Summon Legend	GG WW3	3/6	Tap to do 3 damage to an attacker or blocker.
Lady Evangela	Summon Legend	BUW	1/2	Tap + (BW) Cause a creature not to deal damage during combat.
Lady of the Mountain	Summon Legend	GR4	5/5	
Lady Orca	Summon Legend	BR5	7/4	
Livonya Silone	Summon Legend	GG RR2	4/4	First strike. Legendary landwalk.
Lord Magnus	Summon Legend	GWW3	4/3	First strike. Stops all use of plainswalk and forestwalk in play.
Marhault Elsdragon	Summon Legend	GRR3	4/6	Rampage: 1

Card	Type	Cost	Power/ Toughness	Description
Merieke Ri Berit	Summon Legend	WUB	1/1	Does not untap during untap phase. Tap to gain control of target creature. Lose control of creature if you lose control of Merieke Ri Berit. Bury target if it becomes untapped or leaves play.
Nebuchadnezzar	Summon Legend	BU3	3/3	Tap+(X) Name a card and look at X cards from opponent's hand. If named card is present in revealed cards, it is discarded. Can only be used on your turn.
Pavel Maliki	Summon Legend	BR4	5/3	(BR): +1/+0
Princess Lucrezia	Summon Legend	BUU3	5/4	Tap to add U to your mana pool.
Ragnar	Summon Legend	UGW	2/2	Tap+(UGW) Regenerate a creature.
Ramirez DePietro	Summon Legend	BBU3	4/3	First strike.
Ramses Overdark	Summon Legend	BB UU2	4/3	Tap to destroy a creature with an enchantment on it.
Rasputin Dreamweaver	Summon Legend	UW4	4/1	Has 7 counters which can be used to prevent 1 damage to him or get 1 colorless mana. Add a counter during upkeep if untapped at the beginning of turn and has less than 7 counters.
Riven Turnbull	Summon Legend	BU5	5/7	Tap to add B to your mana pool.
Rohgahh of Kher Keep	Summon Legend	BB RR2	5/5	Your Kobolds of Kher Keep get +2/+2. Pay RRR during upkeep or taps and takes himself and Kobolds to opponent's control.
Rubinia Soulsinger	Summon Legend	UGW2	2/3	Tap to control a creature; may choose not to untap. Lose control of creature if Rubinia leaves play or becomes untapped.
Sir Shandlar of Eberyn	Summon Legend	GW4	4/7	
Sivitri Scarzam	Summon Legend	BU5	6/4	
Skeleton Ship	Summon Legend	UB3	0/3	If at any time the caster controls no islands this card must be burried. Tap to put -1/-1 counter on target creature.

Card	Type	Cost	Power/Toughness	Description
Sol 'kanar the Swamp King	Summon Legend	BUR2	5/5	Swampwalk. Gain 1 life each time a black spell is cast.
Stangg	Summon Legend	GR4	3/4	When Stangg comes into play also place a 3/4 red and green Stangg Twin token into play. If either Stangg or Twin leaves play the other does as well.
Sunastain Falconer	Summon Legend	GR3	4/4	Tap for 2 colorless mana.
Tetsuo Umezawa	Summon Legend	BUR	3/3	Tap+(BBUR) to destroy a tapped or blocking creature. Cannot be targeted by enchant creature spells.
Tobias Andrion	Summon Legend	UW3	4/4	
Tor Wauki	Summon Legend	BBR2	3/3	Tap to do 2 damage to an attacking or blocking creature.
Torsten Von Ursus	Summon Legend	GGW3	3/3	
Tuknir Deathlock	Summon Legend	GGRR	2/2	Flying. Tap+(GR) Give a creature +2/+2 until end of turn.
Ur-Drago	Summon Legend	BB UU3	4/4	First strike. Prevents swampwalk.
Xira Arien	Summon Legend	BGR	1/2	Flying. Tap+(BGR) Draw an extra card.
Giant Trap Door Spider	Summon Spider	GR1	2/3	Tap+(GR1): Remove target creature without flying that is attacking you from the game, along with Spider.
Storm Spirit	Summon Spirit	WUG3	3/3	Flying. Tap to deal 2 damage to target creature.
Mountain Titan	Summon Titan	BR2	2/2	RR1: For the rest of the turn, put a +1/+1 counter on Titan whenever you cast a black spell.

Index

Also available from Wordware Publishing, Inc.

Learn Magic™ Cards
by Larry W. Smith, Ph.D.
144 pages • 6 x 9
ISBN: 1-55622-460-5 $9.95

and

Mastering Magic™ Cards
by Larry W. Smith, Ph.D. and George H. Baxter
Foreword by Richard Garfield, Creator of Magic Cards
240 pages • 6 x 9
ISBN: 1-55622-457-5 $15.95

For more information or to order, contact:
Wordware Publishing, Inc.
1506 Capital Avenue
Plano, Texas 75074
(214) 423-0090